PURPOSE IN POLITICS

PURPOSE IN POLITICS

SELECTED SPEECHES BY

HAROLD WILSON

HOUGHTON MIFFLIN COMPANY BOSTON

The Riverside Press Cambridge

1964

First Printing C

Printed in the United States of America

FOREWORD

THE SPEECHES and articles in this book, spreading over a period of seven years, have been selected to give a summary of Labour's attitude to a wide range of contemporary problems, ranging from foreign affairs, and defence to monetary and tax policy, planning for expansion, transport, social security and, what I have long held is the key to Britain's future, the purposive application of modern science and technology to our industrial life.

Inevitably, they reflect the changing problems of Britain over the past few years, years in the main of a cosy stagnation fitfully broken only as the General Elections of 1959 and 1964 approached. Cyclical electoral policies inevitably produce a degree of cyclical repetition in analysis: the speeches appropriate to the restrictive policies of a Macmillan or a Thorneycroft in 1956-57 could have been used almost without amendment to deal with the effects of an Amory or a Selwyn Lloyd to batten down the hatches once again in 1960-61. The greetings given to the Government's sudden conversion to expansion in 1959 could well have applied as 1963 got under way.

But through all the speeches and articles on the home front run constant themes, the need to replace outmoded monetary controls by modern planning techniques: the need for a sense of purpose in British industry, reflected in both the personnel and the outlook of boards of directors, and in the leadership given by Government: the need for a merchant venturing spirit in overseas trade: the need for science, for automation: the impossibility of securing a sane and workable incomes policy except on the basis of a socially just budget: the need for Britain's social dividend to be shared more fairly among all her people.

In world affairs, too, the central thread is the need for an up-to-date re-appraisal of where Britain's strength and influence really lie – and the application of purpose in making that strength and influence a reality. Purpose abroad means purpose at home, in building our economic strength, it means developing the latent and so far untapped strength of our Commonwealth relationship, potent and vital in political no less than in economic questions. It means making a reality of our membership of UN. It means, too, a defence policy based on realism, in place of nostalgia and illusory prestige, so that Britain's contribution to our alliances can become real and purposive.

The subject matter of the speeches, if analysed chronologically, would appear to show a sharp break at the end of 1961 when I ceased to be Shadow Chancellor and became the Party's Foreign Affairs spokesman. But the break would be more formal than substantial. For one thing, many of the debates of 1961-63 were on the subject of Britain's attempt to join the European Common Market, a subject in which considerations of economics and foreign policy could never with any realism be disentangled.

But, in a wider sense, as I said in a speech which followed my 'translation', I did not regard the move as a complete break, since in the long run, as in the short, as Ernest Bevin so powerfully argued and demonstrated, foreign policy detached from its economic base becomes illusory and hollow.

What one learns in British politics, and in my case, this realisation has inevitably been more forcefully expressed since I was elected Leader of my Party, is the essential unity of the problems we are facing, the need for harmony and integration between domestic and overseas affairs. This is why I have more than once described the task of a party leader, be he Leader of the Opposition or Prime Minister, as essentially that of conducting a mighty orchestra. One false note, one badly scored part, can destroy the unity of the whole.

The interrelation and interdependence of defence and foreign policy, the dependence of both on economic strength, the relation of economic strength to overseas development, and to a strong Commonwealth policy, the relevance of racial policy to our standing in the United Nations, the bearing of economic strength on our provision for housing, for health, for pensions, the bearing of fairness in our health or pensions or housing policies on the incomes policy without which economic strength cannot be achieved; the bearing of education on production, and of economics on education: all these show the unity of approach, the unity of purpose that we need.

This is why I am a Socialist. We shall not achieve the Britain we seek to build except on the basis of a purposeful unity of our policies. This means planning. Just as the Government have, belatedly and unsurely begun to apply the techniques of appraisal, and quantitative analysis, even of statistical projection to the problem of economic expansion, so we have to approach all our other problems – colonial, foreign, defence, no less than town planning and transport, on clear and courageous assessments of objectives, resources and priorities. In this field, no less than in science and technology, we have to cease the affectation of amateurism and recognise that at every level, the trained mind, the professional, will be needed.

Socialism, as I understand it, means applying a sense of purpose to our national life: economic purpose, social purpose, moral purpose. Purpose means technical skill – be it the skill of a manager, a designer, a craftsman, an architect, an engineer, a nuclear physicist, or a doctor, a nurse, a social worker. But this is not to equate, as our opponents affect to do, Socialism with technocracy. The essential leavening which Socialism brings to the industrial revolution of our age, is the leavening of humanity, which was so clearly absent from Britain's first industrial revolution.

Politics is about people. So is Socialism. And most of us in the Labour Party owe our earliest lessons to our concern with ordinary families, our own families. Many of us were first moved by seeing the impact of depression and unemployment on, not only the living standard, but the dignity and pride of neighbours, friends and relatives. Housing, the care of the elderly, educational opportunity: these have a meaning for us which no Blue Book, or Ministerial pronouncement, no eloquence or oratory can impart.

Morgan Phillips once ascribed the inspiration of British Socialism to Methodism rather than to Marx. He was right, though the desire for alliteration involved injustice to the equal contribution of other religious denominations to the Socialist ideal. Socialism, my socialism, that of my colleagues in Parliament and in the Party throughout the country, is a Socialism which seeks to answer the question 'who is my neighbour?' For Socialism is not just about people, it is about the individual.

We reject the dead Marxian generalisations about the proletariat, as we reject aristocratic patronisings about 'the people'. Neighbours are not formless, anthropomorphic social groups: they are individuals, they are families, and as such they have rights. And in equal measure they have duties.

President Kennedy, in his inaugural address said, 'Fellow Americans, ask not what America can do for you. Ask rather what you can do for America'.

This is the key to the restoration of a sense of purpose in British public life. We are, we are told, an affluent society: there is room for argument. But there is no room for argument that we are to an intolerable extent, a frustrated society, that millions of our people are held back from the fullest realisation of their talents and abilities by the deficiencies of our economic system, its lack of adventure, its stereotyped lack of opportunity, its pre-occupation with social origins, its failure to provide real educational and vocational training.

So purpose in politics for Britain means above all the pursuit of measures which will release the energies of those who have their contribution to make, and who in making it, will produce the new Britain we all would like to see.

CONTENTS

INTRODUCTION
BRITAIN'S POLICY UNDER A LABOUR GOVERNMENT[1]

THE LABOUR PARTY'S approach to overseas affairs is conditioned by our loyalty to three groupings, the Western alliance, the Commonwealth, and the United Nations. I wish to deal here with the role we see for Britain in each of these environments, and then to draw conclusions both about East-West relations and about our conception of Britain's position in the postcolonial world.

Labour rejects a neutralist role for Britain. In common with all sane men all over the world, we look forward to a day when the rule of law in international affairs will have been so firmly established that the regional security pacts permitted under Article 55 of the United Nations Charter will no longer be required. But until the dangers deriving from the present division of the world are dissipated, we insist that the Western alliance be not merely maintained but substantially strengthened, both in Europe and in the wider areas where tension remains high.

It was a Labour Foreign Secretary, Ernest Bevin, who was one of the chief architects of NATO. Since that time we have stressed the need to make NATO a reality, particularly in the provision of adequate, and adequately equipped, conventional forces.

It is the Labour Party's view that the deployment of our limited defense expenditure and of our limited scientific resources on what has proved to be the vain task of providing an independent means of delivery of nuclear weapons has gravely weakened our contribution to NATO's conventional forces. We are not only below target, we are below the minimum safety level, both in the size of our contribution and, still more, in the equipment and mobility of the forces we have contributed. Short of an effective comprehensive disarmament agreement and a significant reduction of East-West tension, we are not

[1] This article was written for the *Atlantic Monthly* where it appeared under the title "Britain's Policy If Labour Wins" in October 1963.

hopeful of making any substantial reduction in the defense budget. What we do consider urgent is to alter the balance of our defense effort so as to provide more for our conventional contribution, in quantity and quality, both to NATO and to other areas essential for the interdependent Western defense effort.

Inadequate conventional forces in NATO are not only dangerous in their inability to withstand a purely conventional attack. They make it very much more probable that if a conventional attack does occur, there will be quick recourse to tactical nuclear weapons. And once tactical nuclear weapons are invoked, the danger of escalation to full-scale nuclear war is immeasurably increased.

It is our view that Britain can make its full contribution to NATO only if we come to terms with the facts of the nuclear age. To become an independent nuclear power in the modern world means to possess effective long-distance missiles, and in order to have these a nation must have the economic and scientific infrastructure capable of deployment on the research and development necessary not for one but for a dozen or more separate types. There are only two such superpowers in the world today. There are, however, great powers, among which Britain holds a unique position, which must play their full part in the Western alliance and in world affairs.

Britain staked its all on Blue Streak – and failed. After the V-bombers we shall no longer be an independent nuclear power; any effective nuclear weapons we then possess we shall have only by the grace and favor of a friendly ally.

But the Western alliance is not confined to NATO. It has an important role to play east of Suez, and here again the Labour Party feels strongly that Britain is dangerously ill-equipped to fulfill its part. Our exiguous strategic reserve is held, we are told, for the purpose both of reinforcing the British Army of the Rhine in case of a sudden crisis in Europe and of sending troops wherever they may be needed, from Brunei to British Guiana, from Kuwait to Hong Kong. A stage army capable, by rapid backstage mobility, of representing the whole of Caesar's legions may not be out of place in a touring theatrical company; it is dangerous to rely on it where the freedom of our way of life is involved. For crises, such as Suez and Hungary, Cuba and Ladakh, have a habit of coming not in a conveniently spaced series but simultaneously.

The total force we can deploy in the bushfire areas of Asia and

Africa is limited compared with that of the United States, but in many of these areas we have one advantage over our allies – we are there. Should trouble occur, it is far easier for Britain to expand its force in any given area than for the United States to enter an area previously evacuated by the West.

We fully recognize that Britain's overseas garrisons will shrink as year succeeds year, for the one fact we have learned, the hard way, since the war is that you cannot maintain an effective military base in a country which resents your continued presence. To that extent, the need for mobility is all the greater, and the resources required for mobility cannot be provided as long as Britain clings to its existing defense posture.

So far I have approached the problem in terms of the military effectiveness of the Western alliance. But there is a tremendous political problem, too, the question of the proliferation of nuclear weapons.

It is not necessary to stress the dangers of proliferation or the identity of the *n*th power. The United States has always been strongly against proliferation, and in his Ann Arbor speech of June, 1962, Secretary McNamara made no secret of his government's view that nuclear weapons should be confined to the two existing effective nuclear powers, the United States and the U.S.S.R., until a binding world agreement outlawed nuclear weapons altogether. This was equally the view of the Labour Party, as expressed in uncompromising terms by Hugh Gaitskell. Two world statesmen, and two only, expressed their disagreement – Mr. Macmillan and President de Gaulle. President de Gaulle was later reported as saying that he had been encouraged in his nuclear ambitions by Mr. Macmillan. The U.S. government, after the strongest pressure from London, reinterpreted Mr. McNamara's statement in such a way as not to prejudice Britain's nuclear claims. One cannot help feeling that a great opportunity was lost by Mr. Macmillan's desire to sweeten the French into dropping their objections to Britain's entry into the European Common Market; American enthusiasm for the same purpose was probably the cause of the retreat from the pure doctrine of Ann Arbor.

But once Britain was placed in an excepted category – quite apart from France – the problem of nuclear weapons for Germany could no longer be ignored.

The Labour Party has repeatedly made clear its opposition to any proposals which would lead to Germany's becoming, directly or indirectly, a nuclear power. This opposition is not based on any hangover from World Wars I and II. One of the most hopeful features of the post-war international scene has been the development of deep democratic roots in Germany, and no one who contemplates a Germany with Willy Brandt as Chancellor has any fears of revenge, irredentism, or a desire, through the ownership of nuclear weapons, to revive Germany's formidable Wehrmacht. Moreover, Herr Schroeder's rapid and warm acceptance of the Moscow test-ban agreement shows a readiness to accept a nonnuclear position for Germany.

Our opposition to a nuclear status for Germany is twofold. First, it would mark a point of no return in the spread of nuclear weapons. We would be on the road to the *n*th power. And, as Russian leaders made clear to me in Moscow, the rise of Germany as a nuclear power would make it infinitely harder for Moscow to deny China's nuclear claims. The Sino-Soviet rift owes a great deal to the flat Soviet refusal to help China with its nuclear ambitions.

The second reason why we oppose German nuclear arms is that they would end any hope of a real easement of East-West tension. The late President Kennedy and Dean Rusk are on record on this theme. Mr. Khrushchev expressed it in the strongest terms, and for good reasons. Russia's age-old respect for Germany's technical achievement, combined with its surviving memories of World War II, has created at all levels of Soviet society a positive obsession about Germany's military recovery. We may discount it, but the Russians do not.

In Moscow last June my colleagues and I tried to draw a distinction between direct nuclear status for Germany and the NATO multilateral force which the United States was at that time strongly pressing. We urged on Mr. Khrushchev the fact that the U.S. motive in proposing the MLF was not a desire to clothe Germany with nuclear weapons; on the contrary, it was a genuine, if in our view misdirected, attempt to avert the growth of nuclear ambitions in Germany. If we were convinced that MLF was the only way to achieve this, we would, reluctantly, feel that we had to support it. But we are certainly not convinced of this.

Labour's policy is to strengthen NATO, and we are prepared to examine any proposals for greater participation by both Britain and other NATO partners in nuclear policy, targeting, and agreement on what Mr. Finletter has called the "consensus" – the conditions in which the West, through NATO, would feel it had to have recourse to nuclear weapons. What we oppose is the creation of any machinery which could override the existing U.S. veto on the use of nuclear weapons. Equally we reject dangerous ideas that either France or Britain should have the right to start a catalytic war – the only logical reason which Britain and France have given for their national nuclear policies, for no one envisages either country using nuclear weapons against a non-nuclear nation or embarking on a go-it-alone nuclear war with the Soviet Union.

Turning from defense cooperation in Europe, what is Labour's policy on economic cooperation – in particularly, on Britain's entry into the Common Market?

Our position is clear. We have welcomed the creation of the European Economic Community. We began our policy statement on the Common Market issue, a statement agreed to by an overwhelming majority at the party conference in October, 1962, with these words:

> The Labour Party regards the European Community as a great and imaginative conception. It believes that the coming together of the six nations which have in the past so often been torn by war and economic rivalry is, in the context of Western Europe, a step of great significance.

On the question of Britain's entry, we have made clear that we are prepared to join if – but only if – we can secure acceptance of the five conditions we have laid down. President de Gaulle's intervention last January has made much of the controversy over the terms for Britain's entry academic, at any rate for the immediately foreseeable future. But our conditions remain. They were summarized by the party in these terms:

1. Strong and binding safeguards for the trade and other interests of our friends and partners in the Commonwealth.
2. Freedom, as at present, to pursue our own foreign policy.
3. Fulfillment of the government's pledge to our associates in the European Free Trade Area.
4. The right to plan our own economy.
5. Guarantees to safeguard the position of British agriculture.

At the time of the breakdown of the Brussels talks adequate assurances had been obtained on none of the five conditions. Provisionally agreed terms and the adoption of the severely restrictive, autarkic Common Market agricultural policy, with its penal import levy on imports from the outside world, threatened a collapse in British trade with the Commonwealth. On foreign policy, we were still not being frankly told whether membership in the Community would be a step toward an integrated Western European defense and foreign policy decided in Brussels by majority rule. There had been no guarantee of adequate associated status for our EFTA partners, particularly the three neutrals – Austria, Sweden, and Switzerland. There were still grave doubts about a British government's ability to take the measures necessary to protect full employment and our balance-of-payments position. (The measures taken by President Kennedy to strengthen the dollar, for example, would not have been open to Britain had we signed the Treaty of Rome.) Last, the position of British agriculture had still not been defined at the time of the breakdown.

The Labour Party believes that we should be prepared to reopen negotiations on these five conditions, but only on them.

At all times during the discussions, we had stressed the need to negotiate from strength. Britain's position had been immeasurably weakened by the fact that, having for years rejected the idea of entering Europe, the government decided to apply for entry at a moment of grave economic crisis. Europe was given the idea that there was no solution to Britain's problem except by entry into the Common Market, and inevitably the Six stiffened their terms. Moreover, Mr. Macmillan's need to sell the European idea to a party which, particularly at the grass roots, was still largely imperialist forced him and his ministers into a series of pronouncements on the theme that Britain was nothing without Europe. This, too, can only have made the Six more intransigent.

We, for our part, in addition to pressing for tough internal measures to strengthen our economic position, insisted that the government should have in reserve a viable alternative, both to strengthen our hand in the negotiations and to provide a tolerable fallback position if the negotiations failed. We stressed the alternative policy of an Atlantic economic partnership on the lines of the Clayton-Herter report to the Joint Committee of Congress, together with active measures to promote Commonwealth trade.

The breakdown of the negotiations left the government high and dry. It fell to us to propose a comprehensive series of foreign and economic policies – in the Commonwealth, in EFTA, in the Atlantic Community, in GATT, in the United Nations – and, through OEEC, to take all possible measures to prevent a further division of Europe.

This is still our policy, for we regard an Atlantic partnership – indeed, a wider-than-Atlantic grouping, covering the Commonwealth and Latin America – as the objective. We felt that membership in EEC would have been worthwhile as a stepping-stone to this wider free world unity. But we have become more and more worried about the development of autarkic policies in the Community, particularly in the sphere of agriculture, and it is now obvious that a growing number of U.S. leaders share our anxieties.

One of Labour's greatest anxieties about entry into Europe on the terms proposed was that it would have meant turning our backs on the Commonwealth. This fear was expressed last October in Hugh Gaitskell's memorable Common Market speech, in which he made clear that if we were faced with a choice between Europe and the Commonwealth, we would choose the Commonwealth. Britain has always had a window on the world through the Commonwealth, and we believe that not only Britain's interest but the cause of world peace would be immeasurably impoverished if we were corralled in Western Europe, forced to look at the world through European eyes.

For the postcolonial Commonwealth is the greatest multiracial association in the world, and Britain has a unique contribution to make through the Commonwealth in an age when race relations and the emergence to nationhood of the peoples of Asia and Africa are of central importance. It was the Labour government which began the process of decolonialization, with the creation of free and independent nations in India, Pakistan, Burma, and Ceylon. It was we who in Britain fought for sanity at the time of Suez hysteria – Britain's last attempt to re-create the days of gunboat diplomacy.

Had Britain shown, by entry into Europe on the wrong terms, that we were willing to destroy not only the economic cohesion but the political unity of the Commonwealth, we should have lost the unique influence which we still possess, and can possess in growing measure, in world affairs.

There are today two powerful defense blocs, headed by the United States and the U.S.S.R. But even the most powerful cannot rely on military strength alone. More and more it is becoming realized that a nation's influence depends increasingly on the extent to which it can make its attitudes and policies acceptable to the hundred-odd members of the United Nations, in which Asian and African countries, recently emancipated from their colonial status, are playing a growing part. This fact has been well recognized by the U.S. Administration; Britain's Conservatives, still driven by a nostalgia for a bygone age, are incapable of realizing it.

Hence, we have had ceaseless political battles at Westminster over Britain's role in Africa – over the imposition of an unwanted federation on the peoples of Nyasaland and Northern and Southern Rhodesia, on the question of white supremacy in Southern Rhodesia and, for many years, in Kenya. The same issue arose in the UN crisis over Katanga, where the Conservative government stood almost alone in its desire to placate Sir Roy Welensky and the shade of the long-dead Cecil Rhodes, against the vast majority of the UN members. It was the same issue which was at stake in our attack on Lord Home's backward-looking strictures on the United Nations during the Katanga crisis. It is the same issue which led to the sharp battle between Conservatives and Labour over the question of banning arms shipments to South Africa, an argument which has now been transferred to the United Nations.

The Labour Party's policy on world affairs, therefore, is based on working closely through the Commonwealth for economic and political cooperation in the United Nations and for much more positive measures to further the war against poverty and hunger in the Commonwealth and in the wider areas of the underdeveloped world.

For this, economic strength is essential, both in Britain and in the Western world of developed nations. Britain cannot put forth its full strength with a limping economy whose record in industrial production has for ten years past left it at the bottom of the league of advanced industrial nations. It is for this reason that in our domestic policies we have given priority to the measures needed to get Britain moving steadily forward, firing on all six cylinders, developing its basic industries, particularly those which can make a major contribution to our export drive.

But measures are also needed to strengthen the economic unity of the non-Soviet world. All of us wish to see urgent action taken on the lines of the Trade Expansion Act, to reduce and remove tariffs and other impediments to freer trade. But if we are successful in this, we shall only hasten the day when the whole economy of the free-trading world slows down through a shortage of monetary liquidity. In the past quarter century world trade has increased fourfold; monetary reserves have barely doubled. Thus, whenever Britain or the United States seeks to expand industrial production, one or the other – or both – runs into serious balance-of-payments problems. The internal expansion of credit by which British and American bankers financed the phenomenal increase in domestic production in our two countries in the nineteenth century has no counterpart in the international trading system of the twentieth century. We are still tied to gold.

This is why many of us, in both countries, have called for new machinery and new measures to ensure that international credit facilities increase *pari passu* with the growth of world trade. In a speech to the National Press Club in Washington in April, and in more detailed studies since, I have proposed that the International Monetary Fund be granted credit-creating powers to provide for the automatic expansion of monetary liquidity to meet the increased requirements of world trade. Tied to this, there should be a provision which enables the appropriate world development authority to certify to I.M.F. particular projects in underdeveloped countries, which could be financed by I.M.F. overdraft facilities, encashable in advanced countries where unemployment or undercapacity working is present. This would enable Brazil or India, for example, to build a steel mill or power station with equipment provided in the United States or United Kingdom with no adverse reactions on the overseas-payments position of either the undeveloped or developed countries concerned.

I now turn to relations between East and West, and Britain's role therein.

First, we stress that all initiatives for peace should be made within the context of the Western alliance. In many cases, Britain will be able to take initiatives, perhaps more than in the past, because of Britain's fruitful trading contacts with the Eastern world. But such initiatives would always be within the four corners of agreed Western policy.

Moving forward from the test ban – the main lines of which we had discussed with Mr. Khrushchev before the tripartite negotiations – a Labour government in Britain would press for further action to bridge the gap between the U.S. and Russian disarmament drafts, and for a worldwide antiproliferation agreement. It is our policy, too, to press for a measure of disengagement in areas of high tension, for the creation of nuclear-free zones in Africa, the Middle East, Latin America, and Central Europe. We would support discussions on the Rapacki Plan, as a basis for negotiations, as part of a wider agreement on measures to prevent surprise attack, but with the strict proviso that any agreement resulting would not disturb the existing balance of military strength in Central Europe.

There are, of course, issues where there is a clear difference of view between the Labour Party and the U.S. Administration. One is the question of recognition of Communist China and its admission to the United Nations. This problem will become more acute as the need to bring China within the scope of a test-ban and a general disarmament agreement becomes more pressing. Anglo-American discussions on this matter – and argument within the United Nations – are inevitable.

Another issue, and one on which both major parties in Britain are in agreement, is that of trade with the Soviet bloc. The American view is still based on a hope of containing Soviet economic growth by refusing to trade, especially in plant and equipment which incorporate Western know-how. The British view is that Soviet technological progress is continuing at a rapid rate, that refusal to supply equipment is followed by Soviet expansion of strategic industries, and that, provided there is no shipment of goods of direct military value, a reasonable flow of trade can help to improve contacts and reduce tension.

For the rest, however, the election of a Labour government in Britain should lead to a closer and more intimate contact with the United States through our insistence on all the measures necessary to make the Western alliance a reality, through our closer identity of view on nuclear policy and the prevention of proliferation, and through our common approach to colonialism and the problems of newly emerging countries and the Afro-Asian questions which will increasingly dominate exchanges at the United Nations.

It is this identity of view and interest that lies at the heart of the Anglo-American relationship.

SECTION I

Labour Faces the Future

This group of speeches and articles opens with the two keynote speeches delivered at the Party's Annual Conference at Scarborough in 1963, setting out Labour's view of Britain's place in the world, and of Britain's role in the scientific revolution. On the speech on science press reports, in almost every national newspaper, hailed it as a new statement of Labour's vision for the future:

> *Mr Harold Wilson today reached out to a new frontier in British politics. He gave the party conference here a vision of the new society Labour could create for the future by the proper use of our scientists, our technologists and our technicians.*
>
> – John Beavan, Political Editor, DAILY MIRROR

> *The Labour Party's attempt to marry socialism and science in full view of the electorate was given a superb start today by Mr Harold Wilson, who made the best platform speech of his career.*
>
> *The annual conference has not previously been a happy hunting ground for Mr Wilson, who prefers the intimacy of the Commons for his subtler shafts of scorn and wit. But the alchemy of leadership and a shrewd choice of subject today combined to produce a 50-minute speech which won him a long, standing ovation.*
>
> – John Cole, THE GUARDIAN

CHAPTER ONE

*

Eve of Conference speech on Foreign Affairs: Scarborough, 1963

WHAT YOU SEE tonight is a Labour Party united and confident; united in our attack on the Conservatives in Parliament and in the country: we are united equally in the constructive, relevant policy we put before the British people. And if there is one factor above all others which contributed to our unity it was the great speech[1] made a year ago at Brighton by Hugh Gaitskell.

We are united. Across the floor of the House of Commons we have the spectacle of a Party which is disunited, demoralised, leaderless: not only unable to agree on who their leader should be, but unable even to agree on the procedure by which he is to be selected.

The strategy of the Tory High Command is clear. Discredited, long before the impact of recent events, they now seek a sacrifice, a scapegoat, on whom all their ills can be blamed, and they have selected the man in whose shadow they climbed to and held on to power.

And if they succeed they plan a massive campaign of de-Stalinisation which will make the achievement of Mr Khrushchev at the 20th Congress look like the efforts of a well-intentioned amateur. What they did to Baldwin, to Chamberlain, to Eden, is nothing to what they have in store for the latest in the series of those who are deemed to have outlived their usefulness. We shall hear the pious condemnation of his appeal to selfish materialism which put them back in power four years ago, we shall hear the shocked tones in which they call the nation to a new spirit of service and sacrifice. We may even get the truth about Suez.

[1] Hugh Gaitskell's Common Market speech, Brighton, October 1962

This does not mean that I think the Prime Minister[1] should stay. He should go, not only because he has lost personal authority, but because his whole Administration has lost the authority to govern.

He should go, but not alone. I have every sympathy with the motorist who put on the back of his car, 'Why only Marples?'[2]

To judge from the Press, the only issue in British politics is the aftermath of the Denning Report[3]. I do not intend to spend much time on that subject tonight. Time and time again, I have said this summer that while we were right, indeed we were duty-bound, to probe to the very heart of the security question, the central issue in politics today goes much further back, and much deeper. The clear determination of the British people to have done with Conservatism and to turn to new measures and new men owes nothing to recent events. Before those events reached public consciousness last June, our lead in the Gallup Poll was 18½ points, the biggest lead any party has ever held in 25 years of public opinion polls in this country.

So all I will say about the Denning Report tonight is this. We welcome his repudiation of smears about the private life of public men. We regard his factual record of the laxity and ineptitude of Ministers in their responsibility for our security services as a complete validation of the criticisms we made last June, and as a validation, too, of the warnings I was giving the Prime Minister week after week, warnings which he made light of, not because the facts were not known, but because he was prepared to gamble with national security in the hope that the facts would never come out.

Of course, it's all a question of standards. I had the great privilege of serving under Clem Attlee[4], and it was my contrast between a Macmillan and an Attlee which helped the Prime Minister into taking the security question seriously. Clem would not have taken refuge in evasion, postponement, prevarication, nor would he have devolved his duties on other shoulders: he would have dealt with the situation with a few crisp sentences and equally crisp action. That's the difference.

And if he had set one security standard for civil servants or atomic scientists, he would have applied the same rigorous standard to his

[1] Rt Hon Harold Macmillan

[2] Minister of Transport

[3] Lord Denning's Report on the Profumo Affair.

[4] Rt Hon Earl Attlee, Labour Prime Minister, 1945–51

Ministers. And he would have known which Minister was responsible for security and seen that everyone else knew too.

These are questions for Parliament. Three months after we said this, Lord Denning has added his authority to the same conclusion. For however much Mr Macmillan and his colleagues have sought to devalue the House of Commons, Ministers in this country are still, under our Constitution, ultimately accountable to Parliament. And it is to Parliament they will account I hope – and I repeat this – at the earliest possible opportunity.

So we must now leave to Parliament this vital matter of the nation's security. It should be our resolve that we spend no further time at this Conference on the aftermath of Denning. For we have more important things to discuss about the future of Britain and the well-being of every family in our country – basic down-to-earth issues of economics, production, employment, industry, transport, agriculture, housing, rents, security of tenure, land prices, social policy, education, old age pensions, health. These are the issues which count and these are the issues we shall be debating in this Conference.

The press may find them dull – we cannot offer them the rewarding pabulum of conflict, disunity, the speculation about the snakes and ladders of Ministerial advancement, which I know they are looking forward to at Blackpool[1]. But the British people will not find them dull. What they will witness, in the press, on radio and television, is a great, human movement, preparing now for the responsibilities of Government, putting forward, constructively, urgently – and in unity, our policy for Britain.

For, as I said opening last year's Conference at Brighton[2], 'This Conference represents Britain, and it is our task this week to speak for Britain'.

That is what Hugh Gaitskell did[3]. This week more than ever it is our task. There is no one else. And I believe the world is listening because our friends abroad are deeply anxious to see Britain once again exerting her full strength, her full influence in world affairs.

A year ago, in September, 1962, Mr Macmillan went on television to persuade the British people that there was no salvation for Britain – except in Europe. He said:

[1] Conservative Party Annual Conference, Blackpool, 1963.

[2] As Chairman of the Labour Party at the Brighton Conference, 1962.

[3] At the 1962 Brighton Conference in his Common Market speech.

> If we were not in Europe, our influence would begin to decline, and with the decline of our influence in Europe we should lose our influence in the world outside . . . supposing we aren't in it? Supposing we stand outside. Of course we shall go on, but we shall be relatively weak and we shan't find the true strength that we have, and ought to have: we shan't be able to exercise it in a world of giants.

If we don't go into Europe, 'we shall lose our influence in the world outside'.

And now? We are not in Europe. If Mr Macmillan was right a year ago – and he based the whole complex of economic and overseas policies on the certainty that he was right – if he was correct, in his belief that we must turn our backs on the Commonwealth, in seeking entry into Europe regardless of the terms, regardless of the conditions; if all that were right, then our failure to get in would mean that we should be condemned to an inexorable decline, to second-class, ultimately to third-class nation status. For he has never repudiated that broadcast. Neither then, nor since the breakdown of the talks, has he or any of his Ministers put forward even the glimmering of an alternative policy.

Labour rejects this defeatism, this doctrine of humiliating impotence. And we reject the carping and jibing of those abroad, friends or enemies, who say that Britain has lost her way in the world, that our flame is burning low, that we have nothing to offer except the memories and nostalgia of a faded imperial grandeur.

The mistake they make is to confuse the image of the Britain we have presented under the Conservatives, with the Britain we really are, the Britain we are going to be.

We are not a flag-waving party. But we are a deeply patriotic party, because we truly represent the British people. And it is because of this that we are angered by the sight of this country lagging behind our industrial rivals as we do three years in every four, until the approach of the election brings on our accustomed quadrennial spasm.

To see smug and imperceptive articles written about us with such titles as 'The Sick Man of Europe', 'The English Sickness' – that angers more than the cartoons and comments about the events of this summer.

To see nations we have brought forth to nationhood – yes, and the credit is shared by both Parties – to see them bewildered as they watch this country take refuge in the use of the veto in the United Nations, a veto dictated by 10 years of misconceived and undemocratic, anti-democratic, policies in Central Africa.

To see, as vital issues of human freedom divide the United Nations, to see Britain who should be marching at the head of those who fight for freedom, driven into the squalor, the isolation of an alliance with Portugal, with South Africa, with the oppressors of human freedom.

To hear a British Foreign Secretary[1] attack UN with his sneers and thereby devalue not the UN but himself and his country, because he and the effete Establishment which represents the entire horizon of his life and thought cannot begin to come to terms with a world, and a world organisation, where the vast majority of nations are not even European, not even white, where many of them were until yesterday subject colonial peoples.

To see an entire Government reject the unique opportunity, the illimitable influence that is open to us, by turning their backs on the Commonwealth, the greatest multi-racial association mankind has known, in a world where race and race-relations and the race-explosion are coming to occupy a place even more central than the arms race.

When even the Top People who read *The Times*, not one in ten of whom have, I imagine, ever voted Labour in their lives, solemnly inform *The Times's* market researchers, by a majority of 61% to 8% that Britain's international prestige is declining, when this happens it really is time for a change.

And change there is going to be.

Like the Prime Minister, I read a great deal of history, like him I try to see our age as some historian will see it a century from now. And if the Prime Minister finds a measure of comparative relief in *Decline and Fall*[2], I believe we are on the eve of a new greatness for Britain, a greatness based not on military oppression or the ability to mount a colonial expedition, not on economic imperialism or colonialism, but on a contribution we have it in our unique power

[1] The Rt Hon Earl of Home, now Sir Alec Douglas-Home.
[2] Gibbon: *Decline and Fall of the Roman Empire.*

to make to the peace and happiness of mankind. A contribution based not on separatism, or nationalism, or on out-dated concepts of sovereignty, but on leadership in an interdependent world.

Because that is what a Socialist Britain can mean.

In Europe we are on the eve of a great social breakthrough.

Two years ago our American friends bade Mr Macmillan's Government play a bigger part in Europe through entry into the Common Market. But our future role in Europe is not going to depend on legal constitutions, on the nicely calculated less or more of tariff bargaining, of *ad valorem* duties and pig meat prices. It is going to depend on the new tide of change which is sweeping over Europe, a tide the Conservatives are incapable of seeing let alone harnessing. The tide of social democracy, of democratic socialism.

At Amsterdam[1] I illustrated it by reference to one country when I said that we are moving out of the age of Adenauer into the age of Willy Brandt, just as in this country we are preparing to cross the great chasm which separates the Macmillan age from the 1960s.

With Socialist governments spanning Scandinavia, with Socialist participation in governments in Austria, Belgium, soon we trust in Italy, with the SPD[2] victory we shall see in Germany, the European socialist movement is no concert of shadows. I say to our American friends, this is the new Europe, vigorous, determined, socialist, and you won't need the tired contrivances of mixed-manned forces and all the paraphernalia of the Adenauer age to come to terms with it, to speak to it and to listen to it. You have today the British Cabinet disastrously split on this mixed-manned force, with Ministry fighting Ministry in the public press with all the horrors of modern PRO warfare. A Government unable to take a decision because it has no authority, fearful to join because it will be destroyed by its backbenchers, equally fearful to say no, because they rely on the grace and favour of the US for their so-called British independent deterrent. So you have paralysis.

You see this is the point they refuse to admit. It is precisely because they claim to be a nuclear power, precisely because they have to go cap-in-hand to the US for the means of pretending to be a nuclear power, that when the crunch comes, they find they have lost their independence.

[1] Meeting, Socialist International, Amsterdam, 10th July, 1963.

[2] German Socialist Democratic Party.

I say this, too, to our American friends. We applaud the objectives which lie behind the multilateral force, for we are pledged to stop the spread of nuclear weapons, for we would regard, as America would regard, as the SPD would regard, the endowment of Germany with independent nuclear power as going beyond the point of no return.

But we do not believe Germany wants a nuclear potential, and with a British defence policy based on nuclear sanity and not nuclear illusions and nostalgic *folies de grandeur*, the whole situation will be changed.

And it is because the old familiar landmarks of Europe are changing, giving place to new, that we shall be able to face the new situation between East and West. We have welcomed the Moscow test-ban agreement. It is a step, no more than one step, on a very long road, but it is an important step in the direction of world peace.

If we are to move forward from that agreement we have to show a great deal more imagination and ability to respond to the new challenge. We stand by our alliance, but we regard western defence not as a sterile function in an irrevocably divided world, not as a system of trench warfare in an unending Cold War, but as a means of moving forward to real understanding, our guard never dropped, but our eyes ever open for the chance of a breakthrough to peace.

For one of the dangerous consequences of the Cold War was that it provided for statesmen well-worn grooves, or ruts, or channels of thought, chilling perhaps but providing the great comfort that you didn't have to use your imagination.

As a result of our talks in Moscow[1], I am convinced there is a chance of a breakthrough on two fronts: first, an agreement to stop the spread of nuclear weapons, second, agreement on areas of complete nuclear disarmament and progressive conventional disarmament. Why can we not agree now that the whole of Africa should become a nuclear-free zone. We must not pass on to new African states the vices of so-called advanced civilisations. And Latin America and the Middle East. Above all, in the high-tension area of Central Europe, we press again the urgent relevance of what has always been our policy: the creation of a nuclear-free zone, with effective inspection, a zone of controlled conventional disarmament.

[1] Labour Party delegation to Russia, June, 1963.

I believe that this proposal, providing no change in the balance of forces between East and West, could greatly lower tension in this area, could begin the process of détente between East and West and could begin to create the conditions leading to a unified democratic Germany.

I believe too, that as we have urged for 10 years, a dynamic and imaginative programme of East-West trade could be a powerful aid to peace.

I have talked about Europe, a Europe in which we can play our part without being corralled in Europe, without turning our backs, as Mr Macmillan would have had us do, on the Commonwealth, on the continents beyond Europe.

For here again, the world is on the move. And the Tory Government of Suez, of Hola[1], of the Devlin Report[2], of Katanga, of the UN veto is disqualified before the race begins. For on every major issue of freedom in Africa, the Government has sided with the Welenskys, and worse, with the Verwoerds and Salazars.

You now face the ultimate decision in Southern Rhodesia. We insist, as we have repeatedly insisted, that Britain cannot morally confer independence on a Southern Rhodesia which defies the most elemental claims of democracy, by denying the vote to 99% of the Africans who outnumber the Europeans by 15 to 1. We say, too, to the Government, your debts are too great, your moral reserves too low, the problem of Central Africa can no longer be dealt with on a unilateralist basis, it must now be referred to the arbitration and good offices of a Commonwealth Prime Ministers' Conference.

Equally, we must flatly resist Verwoerd's pressures on the High Commission territories[3]. They must be an example of progressive self-government; a shop window of racial equality; and a haven of refuge for those who are forced to flee from the oppression of apartheid.

The problem of Africa can now be dealt with only by a Government in this country whose hands are clean. Last March, in the name of this Party, I pledged the Government of this country to an embargo on the shipment of arms to South Africa. I had the united support of this movement and the united anger and abuse of the Conservative

[1] Hola Camp, Kenya.

[2] Justice Devlin's Report on Nyasaland Commission of Enquiry, 1958.

[3] High Commission territories of Swaziland, Bechuanaland, Basutoland.

Party and the Conservative press. We answered them: this was not a question of expediency or inexpediency, it was a question of right or wrong. When Mr Macleod[1], with a carefully prepared statement said in the House, 'We're all against apartheid, but the Opposition's policy is the wrong way of dealing with it', we told him, 'Yes, we're all against apartheid with our lips, the difference is between those who are accessories after the fact and those who are not'.

And what has happened? The United States has imposed an embargo. Socialist governments in Europe have applied an embargo. France has applied an embargo. And, now Her Majesty's Government are pretending that they, too, yes, they too, have really been following this policy all along.

Let us recognise this. There is in Africa now a deep and irreconcilable conflict on the race question, just as in America the conflict has reached a point where the future of a whole nation depends on the response which it will give to the courage of a President who has forced this issue into the open, regardless of short-term political advantage. And it is no more possible for us to ignore what is going on in Africa than it is for the Americans to ignore what is going on in Alabama.[2] There is no standing aside, no comforting refuge in abstentions or vetoes, we are either against oppression, or we condone it. In these issues, there can be no neutrals, no escape.

For in this shrinking world, while political isolationism invites danger, and economic isolationism invites bankruptcy, moral isolationism invites contempt. So this is the role for Britain, in Europe, in Africa, in the United Nations, in our reassertion of our abdicated leadership in the Commonwealth, not least in the role we must play in the challenging undeveloped areas of the Commonwealth and in the integration of Commonwealth trading relationships.

Tired men cannot put forth the energy that is needed. Neither can tired nations. When President Kennedy proclaimed the New Frontier he quoted Lloyd George – 'a tired nation is a Tory nation'. And the Tories cannot provide the dynamic we need, a dynamic which must of necessity go far beyond foreign policy.

There is no greater fallacy in human affairs than to think that you can divorce foreign affairs from economic policy at home. The image

[1] Leader of the House of Commons.

[2] Race riots in Alabama, USA.

you present abroad mirrors accurately the vigour and virility of your domestic strength, as surely as the image in your shaving mirror reflects the reality of your face. This was the great message of Nye's last speech[1] at the Blackpool Conference four years ago, that you can't talk about our obligations to Asia and Africa if we are not prepared to pursue a policy of purposive economic expansion at home, with all that means.

If Britain is to count in the world, as it should, we have to call into active endeavour the full energies of our people: all our people. We have reserves of skill, and craftsmanship, of science and technology, design and creative ability, of organisation and salesmanship, which, if given full scope, will make Britain what we should be, the pilot-plant, the tool-room of the world. What is wrong today, to use words I read this weekend, is the sharp distinction between the people who do the work and the power élite who make the decisions.

This country cannot put forth its true strength until it cuts out the dead wood at the top, in Cabinet room and board room alike, till it frees itself from the dead hands of the Establishment and the mesmerism of the old school tie, the nepotism and dynasticism which are as out of place in modern industry as they are in modern government.

It means a change in the motivation of British society, where service and national purpose will replace sectional selfishness and the pursuit of speculative gain which adds millions to private fortunes and nothing to our national welfare and well-being. It means a re-assertion of social purpose as the mainspring of government, social purpose in housing, in education, in providing for the under-privileged in our society. All these things we shall be debating, constructively, positively. We do not need to spend much time on the Tory record – our duty is to present Labour's alternative with all the responsibility that goes with the knowledge that we shall be fashioning the new Britain that is to be.

I want to conclude with some words of nobility addressed to a Labour Conference here in Scarborough in Labour's darkest hour, 1931, by one of the greatest of our leaders, Arthur Henderson, whose centenary we have celebrated this month:

[1] Speech by Rt Hon Aneurin Bevan, Labour Party Annual Conference, Blackpool, November, 1959.

> There comes to my mind certain words of one of our greatest pioneers, William Morris, which I think can express a lesson to this great conference: *Intelligence enough to conceive, courage enough to will, power enough to compel.* With these three things victory can be won.'

'Intelligence enough to conceive, courage enough to will, power enough to compel.'

That is the spirit we will carry with us in the challenging weeks that lie ahead.

CHAPTER TWO

*

Speech opening the Science Debate at the Party's Annual Conference, Scarborough, 1963

IT WAS HERE AT SCARBOROUGH, three years ago, that we began the hard climb back from the 1959 Election defeat with a debate, also on the Tuesday morning of that week, on Morgan Phillips's[1] document *Labour in the 'Sixties*; and anyone here then will, I think, always treasure the memory of that great speech of Ray Gunter[2], opening that debate. When I came to wind up that debate, I said then that we must harness Socialism to science, and science to Socialism. That, again, was one of the main themes of *Signposts for the 'Sixties* – the mobilisation of all the resources of science available to us in this new scientific revolution.

Now, this morning, we present this document to the nation, *Labour and the Scientific Revolution*, because the strength, the solvency, the influence of Britain, which some still think depends upon nostalgic illusions or upon nuclear posturings – these things are going to depend in the remainder of this century to a unique extent on the speed with which we come to terms with the world of change.

There is no more dangerous illusion than the comfortable doctrine that the world owes us a living. One of the dangers of the old-boy network approach to life is the thought that it is international, that whatever we do, whenever we run into trouble, we can always rely on a special relationship with someone or other to bail us out. From now on Britain will have just as much influence in the world as we

[1] General Secretary of the Party, 1944–1963.

[2] Member of the National Executive Committee of Labour Party and Parliamentary Committee.

can earn, as we can deserve. We have no accumulated reserves on which to live.

And if there is one theme running through this Conference this week – Fred Hayday[1] stressed it on Sunday night[2] in the first speech from this platform which set the keynote for all of us and Ray Gunter stressed it again yesterday – it is the theme of change, the overdue need for this country to adapt itself to different conditions. It is the theme and the challenge which faces the Labour Party, which faces every one of us.

It is, of course, a cliché that we are living at a time of such rapid scientific change that our children are accepting as part of their every-day life things which would have been dismissed as science fiction a few years ago. We are living perhaps in a more rapid revolution than some of us realise. The period of 15 years from the last time we were in Scarborough, in 1960, to the middle of the 1970s will embrace a period of technical change, particularly in industrial methods, greater than in the whole industrial revolution of the last 250 years. When you reckon, as it is calculated, that 97% of all the scientists who have ever lived in the history of the world since the days of Euclid, Pythagoras and Archimedes, are alive and at work today, you get some idea of the rate of progress we have to face.

It is only a few years since we first in this Conference debated automation, when almost every word uttered in that debate is already as out of date today as if we had been talking about the advent of the spinning jenny. Automation is beginning to make its impact felt in quarters of British industry, as many delegates here know – the engineers, the technicians, the chemical workers, the scientific workers, and, not least, the Post Office workers and the Post Office engineers, who have pioneered some of the major developments in automation and who, thanks to the combination of our trade union skill and of public ownership in the Post Office, lead the world in these developments.

Let us be frank about one thing. It is no good trying to comfort ourselves with the thought that automation need not happen here; that it is going to create so many problems that we should perhaps put our heads in the sand and let it pass us by. Because there is no

[1] Chairman of the TUC, 1962–1963.

[2] Speaking at Party Demonstration, Sunday, 29th September, 1963, Scarborough.

room for Luddites in the Socialist Party. If we try to abstract from the automative age, the only result will be that Britain will become a stagnant backwater, pitied and held in contempt by the rest of the world.

The danger, as things are, is that an unregulated private enterprise economy in this country will promote just enough automation to create serious unemployment but not enough to create a break-through in the production barrier. Let us look at what is happening in automation all over the world – and what I may say is elementary compared with the knowledge that some of our trade union delegates could present to you this morning.

Already in the engineering and automobile industries in the United States they have reached a point where a programme-controlled machine tool line can produce an entire motor car – and I mean an American motor car, with all the gimmicks on it – without the application of human skill or effort. They can do this without a single worker touching it. It is not commercially worth while yet, but it is technically possible.

Because we have to recognise that automation is not just one more process in the history of mechanisation, if by mechanisation we mean the application of technology to eliminate the need for human muscle. The essence of modern automation is that it replaces the hitherto unique human functions of memory and of judgment. And now the computers have reached the point where they command facilities of memory and of judgment far beyond the capacity of any human being or group of human beings who have ever lived.

A modern computer in a fraction of a second can make calculations and can make decisions of judgment which all the mathematicians in Britain and America combined could not make by ordinary methods in the space of a year. You have computers at work now controlling a planned productive system of machine tools which have an impulse cycle of three millionths of a second. They do their calculations and take their decisions in a period of three millionths of a second. Yet already those machines are out of date. New mass controllers are in production now with a speed 1,000 times as fast. It was not easy for me, at any rate, to be able to appreciate what three billionths of a second – one three-hundred millionth of a second – really means – perhaps some of you find it easier to visualise it – until it was explained to me that if you were to set out to walk right round the earth at the

Equator, assuming there was no water there, taking a step every three-hundred millionth of a second – that is, taking one step every time these machines actually do their thinking process – then you would circle the entire earth in one second. Now perhaps we have got it.

In America technological change is beginning to move now even more rapidly in the white collar professions than in engineering, because it is much easier to programme operations of costings, of wages sheets and tax schedules or of insurance premiums, than it is to programme an engineering job. And let us be clear that in America today and in Britain tomorrow we face massive redundancies in office work no less than in industry.

Already forward-looking labour leaders in the United States have calculated that at the present and prospective rate of technological change in that country, where at present there are about 70 million people at work, they are going to need to create 40 million new jobs by 1970 if they are to achieve and maintain full employment. Allowing for the fact that the automative revolution here will be later and slower, we have to be ready to create 10 million new jobs in Britain by, say, the mid-1970s.

Or listen to the problem in another way. We can now set a programme-controlled machine tool line so that, without the intervention of any human agency, it can produce a new set of machine tools in its own image. And when machine tools have acquired, as they now have, the faculty of unassisted reproduction, you have reached a point of no return where if man is not going to assert his control over machines, the machines are going to assert their control over man.

These facts, these inescapable facts, put the whole argument about industry and economics and Socialism in a new perspective. I am not going to waste much time this morning demonstrating that a Government of the kind we have in this country is incapable even of realising the implications of creating something like 10 million new jobs by the mid-1970s, considering that after twelve years in office they have succeeded in producing a situation in the whole of Scotland, for example, where there are fewer men in work than there were in 1951. Or considering the efforts they have been making, so we are told, to bring industry to the North-East which, since 1959, have added about 30,000 new jobs gross, making no allowance for redundancies in declining industries. When you present a Government such as the one we have in this country with a problem I have just been outlining, they are not living in the same dimensions.

The problem is this. Since technological progress left to the mechanism of private industry and private property can lead only to high profits for a few, a high rate of employment for a few, and to mass redundancies for the many, if there had never been a case for Socialism before, automation would have created it. Because only if technological progress becomes part of our national planning can that progress be directed to national ends.

So the choice is not between technological progress and the kind of easy-going world we are living in today. It is the choice between the blind imposition of technological advance, with all that means in terms of unemployment, and the conscious, planned, purposive use of scientific progress to provide undreamed of living standards and the possibility of leisure, ultimately on an unbelievable scale.

That is why we must, in the Labour Party, devote a lot more thought to providing facilities for the use of leisure, and this is why again, as this document suggests, we shall have to be a lot more imaginative about the provision for retraining the workers made redundant by the development of new skills and new techniques.

Now I come to what we must do, and it is a fourfold programme. First, we must produce more scientists. Secondly, having produced them we must be a great deal more successful in keeping them in this country. Thirdly, having trained them and kept them here, we must make more intelligent use of them when they are trained than we do with those we have got. Fourthly, we must organise British industry so that it applies the results of scientific research more purposively to our national production effort. These, then, are the four tasks: first, more scientists – we are simply not training anything like enough for the nation's needs. Russia is at the present time training ten to eleven times as many scientists and technologists. And the sooner we face up to that challenge the sooner we shall realise what kind of a world we are living in.

I know, of course, that a Government Committee has said that we shall have all the scientists we need by 1965. Of course we shall – if we do not use them. We shall have all the bull-fighters we need by 1965. But to train the scientists we are going to need will mean a revolution in our attitude to education, not only higher education but at every level.

I do not want to anticipate the debate on education, but it means that as a nation we cannot afford to force segregation on our children at the 11-plus stage. As Socialists, as democrats we oppose this system of educational apartheid, because we believe in equality of opportunity. But that is not all. We simply cannot as a nation afford to neglect the educational development of a single boy or girl. We cannot afford to cut off three-quarters or more of our children from virtually any chance of higher education. The Russians do not, the Germans do not, the Americans do not, and the Japanese do not, and we cannot afford to either. And if you want proof, only this month in part of my constituency we have a big new town where, thanks to the imagination of the Socialist authority there, every secondary school in that town is comprehensive. The children who live there have no conception of what it means to go along on a cold February morning to take an 11-plus examination or any other system of 11-plus selection either. There is a boy who, when his family lived in Liverpool, took the 11-plus examination and was not accepted for a grammar school place, but when he came to live in Kirkby he went to the comprehensive school, and this boy who, in the conventional jargon, failed his 11-plus, is starting this morning at Liverpool University with a State scholarship in physics. And how many more are there? But we cannot afford segregation at 11-plus nor can we afford segregation at 18-plus. There are students this year who are failing to secure entry to universities in State Colleges of Higher Education, who possess qualifications which a year ago would have got them in, because, to quote a phrase which I read in the paper this morning by the Director of the North-Western Council of Industry, Colonel Burford, they are facing an increasingly severe 'rat race' in the problem of entering universities.

Last year, 1962, a quarter of those who had the necessary qualifications at A level could not get in because there were not enough places, and this year a much higher proportion than that will have been excluded, despite the fact that they have got the necessary qualifications for entry. And as the number of boys and girls reaching university age rises, as a result of the birth rate of the 1940s – facts which were known to the Government a very long time ago – as a higher and higher proportion of those boys and girls stay at school – and we are glad they are doing it – we shall have a greater number of students every year failing to get in because the places are simply not there. The Government could have foreseen this, and they could have taken the steps necessary to see that the places were there. To give students today the same chances of getting a place in the late 1960s as they had even in the late 1950s, we are going to need between 180,000 and 200,000 places in our universities, and the Government's plan provides for only 150,000 – and that is only to get back to the same standards of entry as we had in the late 1950s; and in the late 1950s our rate was too small; we were near the bottom of the international league. This is why we in the Labour Party give such a high priority to plans for higher education.

I think the report of Lord Taylor's[1] working party has been one of the most important contributions to the study of the problem of higher education in this country. They recommend, and we accept, a crash programme, first, to make fuller use of existing universities and colleges of higher education. They propose, and every one of us must accept, a tremendous building programme of new universities, and in this programme let us try and see that more of them are sited in industrial areas where they can in some way reflect the pulsating throb of local industry, where they can work in partnership with the new industries we seek to create.

Not enough thought has been given, when we fight against the problem of declining areas and the migration of population away from some of our older areas, to the establishment of new universities who, by the very nature of their industrial research, can help to revitalise areas in which they are going to be sited. As Lord Taylor said in the report, our aim must be at the earliest possible moment to provide facilities for university education for at least 10% of our young people, instead of the 5% at which the Tories are tepidly aiming.

There is another thing we have got to do in the field of higher education, and this is to put an end to snobbery. Why should not the colleges of advanced technology award degrees? Why should not teachers' training colleges be given more and more their proper place in the educational system? You know, what is needed here is not going to happen by chance. We are going to need a Ministry of Higher Education. You can argue about whether you link it with the existing Ministry of Education, whether you link it with the new

[1] Labour Party Working Party on Higher Education.

Ministry of Science or, as may be right, constituting it as a Ministry in its own right under a Minister of Cabinet rank. You can all produce arguments. The important thing is that the Ministry of Higher Education must become the focal point of the planning of higher education in this country.

Relevant, also, to these problems are our plans for a university of the air. I repeat again that this is not a substitute for our plans for higher education, for our plans for new universities, and for our plans for extending technological education. It is not a substitute; it is a supplement to our plans. It is designed to provide an opportunity for those who, for one reason or another, have not been able to take advantage of higher education, now to do so with all that TV and radio and the State sponsored correspondence course, and the facilities of a university for setting and marking papers and conducting examinations, in awarding degrees, can provide. Nor, may I say, do we envisage this merely as a means of providing scientists and technologists. I believe a properly planned university of the air could make an immeasurable contribution to the cultural life of our country, to the enrichment of our standard of living.

Mr Chairman, because this morning we are talking about science I have been referring so far to plans for training scientists, but of course in the whole of our university and higher education expansion programme scientists will have their place but no more than their place in the development, because the development of higher education based purely on the training of scientists and technologists would, of course, fail to meet the full human requirements of our nation.

Secondly, we must hold our scientists in this country. The Royal Society has recently reported that 12% of new PhDs are now leaving this country every year to go abroad. We have heard recently of universities where practically the whole scientific department has emigrated en bloc. Only the other day I heard of one of our most famous scientific colleges where in one particular faculty nine PhDs have been awarded this year in a field which is as relevant to the future of Britain as any subject I could think of, and of those nine, seven have already left to go to the United States. Lord Hailsham tells us that this loss of scientists is due to the deficiencies of the American educational system. His Lordship is wrong. It is due not to the deficiencies of the American educational system; it is due to the deficiencies of the British industrial system, in that we do not put a proper valuation on our trained scientists; that they are not afforded the status and the prospects to which they are entitled.

I have talked in America to British scientists who have gone abroad. It is not so much a question of salary; it is the poor valuation put on their work by British industry and in some cases by impoverished British universities; the inadequate provision of adequate research facilities and equipment. It is because in so many cases in British industry today promotion for a scientist depends on waiting for dead men's shoes. Britain is not so rich in facilities for training scientists and technologists that we can let this brain drain continue. We are not even selling the seed corn; we are giving it away.

One message I hope this Conference can send out, not only to those who are wondering whether to emigrate or not, but to those who have already emigrated is this. We want you to stay here: we want those of you who have left Britain to think about coming back, because the Britain that is going to be is going to need you.

So the next point is that we must make a more intelligent use of our scientists when we have them. Until very recently over half our trained scientists were engaged in defence projects or so-called defence projects. Real defence, of course, is essential. But so many of our scientists were employed on purely prestige projects that never left the drawing board, and many more scientists are deployed, not on projects that are going to increase Britain's productive power, but on some new gimmick or additive to some consumer product which will enable the advertising managers to rush to the television screen to tell us all to buy a little more of something we did not even know we wanted in the first place. This is not strengthening Britain.

Scientific research in industry needs to be very purposively organised. This is one reason why we are going to establish a full Ministry of Science; not what we have today – an office of the Minister for Science, with no powers, no staff, no scientists, no clear direction of what he is about. The Labour Party has been saying for years, that we have got to get a proper organisation and a proper sponsorship of scientific research in this country, and we are glad now to have the support, the powerful if belated support, of the Federation of British Industries in their recent report to the British Government.

So now I come to the fourth point, the vital issue of applying the results of scientific research in industry, because – let us be clear –

unless we can harness science to our economic planning, we are not going to get the expansion that we need. Of course, the Labour Party welcomes the Government's conversion to the idea of economic planning. We have been pressing for it for years. We welcomed the signs of conversion, of repentance, two years ago, when they told us about this. But we must warn the Government that planning based on paper targets alone, planning which requires for its enforcement monetary regulation and manipulation of the tax system, is not going to produce the changes in British industry which we shall require if we are to expand the production year by year, without running into an export/import crisis. The 'stop-go' economy of the last 12 years failed because the expansionary phases have not created the growth of those industries which can provide the permanent break-through in our export trade or can provide a lasting saving in imports, and the margin between continual repetitive crisis, on the one hand, and economic solvency on the other, is a narrow one. Monetary planning is not enough. What is needed is structural changes in British industry, and we are not going to achieve those structural changes on the basis of pre-election spurts every four years in our industry, or in the hope of just selling the overspill of the affluent society in the highly developed markets of Western Europe. What we need is new industries and it will be the job of the next Government to see that we get them. This means mobilising scientific research in this country in producing a new technological break-through. We have spent thousands of millions in the past few years on misdirected research and development contracts in the field of defence. If we were now to use the technique of R and D contracts in civil industry I believe we could within a measurable period of time establish new industries which would make us once again one of the foremost industrial nations of the world.

We know this can be done. The National Research Development Council set up by the Labour Government, with total funds of only £5 million, has already produced new industries based on State sponsored research. What we now need to do and what we are committed to doing is, first, carefully to expand the scope of this research development and, secondly, to ensure that where new industries are established on the basis of State sponsored research the State will control the industries which result.

There are today groups of scientists in our universities, in our national research laboratories, in NRDC and in public and private industry who are frustrated because they are not being used. Harwell and Capenhurst are running down and hundreds of trained technicians will be redundant. The cancellation of missile contracts is freeing for productive work scientists and technologists who are both highly qualified and used to working in research teams. So why should we not give to these scientists, or, if you like, to groups of young scientists fresh from universities, the chance of producing a feasibility project study leading to full-scale Government research and development contracts. There are delegates here with experience over a wide range of British industry, who know that if we could mobilise these scientists on research projects of this kind, we could within a very short period produce a major break-through in a whole number of fields: perhaps some new break-through in marine propulsion, in aircraft guidance, in transport, in electronics, in agricultural or textile machinery. Some of these projects may fail, but many will succeed and in succeeding will provide Britain with new industries with which to conquer markets all over the world.

Yesterday we were talking about modernisation in transport. I remember seeing in a national newspaper two or three weeks ago the details of an imaginative new scientific approach to the problems of the railways. I do not know whether that is a winner or not. All I know is that it is not going on, through lack of money, and I know if somebody had produced something equally imaginative, perhaps equally fanciful, in the field of defence they would have had the money years ago to push on with it. While we are not doctrinaire, while we are prepared to see the fruits of this sponsored research developed by public and private industry alike, and while we are prepared to establish productive partnerships between the public and private industries to exploit these research successes, we hold it as a basic principle that the profits which result from State sponsored research should accrue in good measure to the community that created them.

These policies I think will provide the answer to the problem of Britain's declining industries and Britain's declining areas. We reject the Conservatives' solution of mass depopulation of Britain's traditional industrial areas. Remember this: when we set up new industries based on science there need be no argument about location, no costly bribes to private enterprise to go here rather than there: we shall provide the enterprise and we shall decide where it goes. Some of our declining industries will be revitalised, not on a basis – and I want to make this plain, because this is not our policy – of uneconomic protection or subsidies, but revitalised by mobilising these industries for new tasks.

Let me give an example. Anyone who has discussed trade prospects with Soviet leaders, as many of us have, or with some of our great Commonwealth countries, knows that there is a great demand for new chemical industries based on British research. We have the best chemists in the world, but we have never mobilised to the full the possible resources of chemical engineering to enable us to ship complete factories to these areas on a scale commensurate with their needs or our capacities. For some reason in so many of our universities, while the chemist is exalted the chemical engineer is told to go and sit somewhere below the salt. For some reason we have not developed the chemical engineering industry of this country on an adequate scale.

The Russians have talked to me of orders amounting to hundreds of millions over the next few years. A Labour Government would initiate a State sponsored chemical engineering consortium to meet the needs, not only of Eastern Europe, but far more important, of developing Commonwealth countries. We would train and we would mobilise chemical engineers to design the plants that the world needs, plants which are at present being supplied far too often by Germany or by America on the basis of British know-how and research. And in the fabrication of this plant which the new chemical engineering industry would call into being we could bring new orders to our depressed marine and heavy engineering shops in shipbuilding and other areas.

Here again lies the answer to the economic problems that we are going to face when, as we all hope, the arms race ends in a comprehensive disarmament agreement. The economic consequences of disarmament cannot be dealt with except on a basis of socialist planning. Advanced capitalist countries are maintaining full employment today only by virtue of vast arms orders and panic would be the order of the day in Wall Street and other Stock Markets, the day peace breaks out. We have announced that the Labour Government will include a Minister for Disarmament, and among his duties will be to prepare for the economic problems that will follow hard on the heels of massive disarmament, because Conservative economic policies, thermostatic monetary controls, cannot deal with the problems of physical adjustment of the moving of real resources that we shall have to face.

You know this is the answer to another great problem that besets this country, the problem of employment for our young people. Last month the Ministry of Labour told us that 38,000 boys and girls, who left school in July, had not found work. This figure, as we all know, excluded many who, unable to find work, had returned to schools unfitted and ill-equipped to take them back. It excludes, too, the many who found temporary employment in blind-alley jobs. That this country should not be able to provide employment for boys and girls leaving school and going out into the world for the first time is an intolerable reflection on our so-called civilisation. Galbraith warned the world a few years ago that social imbalance is the inevitable consequence of the unplanned affluent society[1], and we are finding this imbalance in the growing number of young people and of old people who cannot find employment. That is why we need the new industries, the revitalisation of declining industries and declining areas, to provide new hope for the nation's youth.

Again we must relate our scientific planning to the problems of the war on world poverty. In a system of society beset by the delirium of advertising and the ceaseless drive to produce new and different variants of existing consumer goods and services, there is no thought being given to the research that is needed to find the means of increasing food production for those millions in Asia and Africa who are living on the poverty line and below the poverty line.

It is very nice that we should be putting so much research into colour television, it is very nice that we should be putting all our energies into producing bigger and better washing machines to sell in Düsseldorf. What we should be doing is to be developing the means of mass producing simple tractors and ploughs to increase food production. In an advanced world which has long by-passed the steam engine in favour of oil and electricity as a means of propulsion we ought to be giving more thought to developing the research of this country for producing little simple one- or two-horsepower steam engines, because that is what the world needs, able to use local fuels,

[1] J. K. Galbraith: *The Affluent Society.*

and capable of lifting water from *that* ditch to *those* fields a few hundred yards away. Swift saw the answer and the problem in *Gulliver's Travels* 250 years ago when he said: 'Whoever could make two ears of corn or two blades of grass to grow upon a spot of ground where only one grew before, would deserve better of mankind and do more essential service to his country than the whole race of politicians put together'.

Again, I should like to see the scientific departments of the new universities that we have been talking about mobilised to direct their scientific research to the special problems of underdeveloped countries, the needs of biological research to provide new break-throughs in plant breeding, in the use of fertilisers, and in animal husbandry; in all the things that are needed to increase crops and to increase food.

Then again, what is the sense of closing down railway workshops that could provide the transport equipment that would make all the difference between poverty and solvency in newly developing countries?

Labour means business about world development. We are going to establish a full-scale Ministry of Overseas Development, with a Minister of Cabinet rank, to join with the Ministry of Science in mobilising Britain's scientific wealth for the task of creating, not the means of human destruction, but the munitions of peace.

Let me conclude with what I think the message of all this is for this Conference, because in this Conference, in all our plans for the future, we are re-defining and we are re-stating our Socialism in terms of the scientific revolution. But that revolution cannot become a reality unless we are prepared to make far-reaching changes in economic and social attitudes which permeate our whole system of society.

The Britain that is going to be forged in the white heat of this revolution will be no place for restrictive practices or for outdated methods on either side of industry. We shall need a totally new attitude to the problems of apprenticeship, of training and re-training for skill. If there is one thing where the traditional philosophy of capitalism breaks down it is in training for apprenticeship, because quite frankly it does not pay any individual firm, unless it is very altruistic or quixotic or farsighted, to train apprentices if it knows at the end of the period of training they will be snapped up by some unscrupulous firm that makes no contribution to apprenticeship training. That is what economists mean when they talk about the difference between marginal private cost and net social cost.

So we are going to need a new attitude. In some industries we shall have to get right away from the idea of apprenticeship to a single firm. There will have to be apprenticeship with the industry as a whole, and the industry will have to take responsibility for it. Indeed, if we are going to end demarcation and snobbery in our training for skill and for science why should not these apprenticeship contracts be signed with the State itself? Then again, in the Cabinet room and the board room alike those charged with the control of our affairs must be ready to think and to speak in the language of our scientific age.

For the commanding heights of British industry to be controlled today by men whose only claim is their aristocratic connections or the power of inherited wealth or speculative finance is as irrelevant to the twentieth century as would be the continued purchase of commissions in the armed forces by lordly amateurs. At the very time that even the MCC has abolished the distinction between amateurs and professionals, in science and industry we are content to remain a nation of Gentlemen in a world of Players.

For those of us who have studied the formidable Soviet challenge in the education of scientists and technologists, and above all, in the ruthless application of scientific techniques in Soviet industry, know that our future lies not in military strength alone but in the efforts, the sacrifices, and above all the energies which a free people can mobilise for the future greatness of our country. Because we are democrats, we reject the methods which communist countries are deploying in applying the results of scientific research to industrial life. But because we care deeply about the future of Britain, we must use all the resources of democratic planning, all the latent and under-developed energies and skills of our people, to ensure Britain's standing in the world. That is the message which I believe will go out from this Conference to the people of Britain and to the people of the world.

SECTION II

Economic Policy

The speeches in this section were all made in the House of Commons when I was financial spokesman (Shadow Chancellor) for the Opposition. The 1956 Budget Debate took place on Mr Macmillan's first and only Budget. He had become Chancellor the previous December, succeeding Mr R. A. Butler. The background to the Budget had been the election budget of April, 1955, when Mr Butler had reduced income tax, followed by the autumn budget when taxation had been increased again mainly through higher rates of purchase tax – including the extension of tax to a wide range of household articles previously free of tax.

The financial crisis nevertheless continued, and early in February, Mr Macmillan made a crisis statement, raising the Bank Rate to 5½%, abolishing the investment allowance (a tax subsidy to capital investment) and imposing a wide range of cuts.

In his April Budget Mr Macmillan introduced a number of tax measures designed to encourage personal saving, including the controversial Premium Bonds scheme. But the theme of his economic policy was the appeal for wage restraint and price stability. Mr Macmillan said:

> *I think we have learned this lesson from the events of the past year. We cannot afford to run our economy flat out.*

The brakes were on in the Tories' stop-go cycle.

After the disastrous Suez expedition in October, 1956, the Opposition called the Tory Government to account for the financial costs involved. Speaking on behalf of the Party, as Shadow Chancellor, I made Harold Macmillan, then Chancellor and First Lord of the Treasury, the main target for attack as Macmillan was the custodian of the nation's finances and economic wellbeing. For that reason, I felt he should have argued in Cabinet against the operation on financial grounds. Macmillan, as I contended later, had been 'first in, first out' of Suez – a fierce advocate of the action until its failure became obvious.

By the following Budget, Mr Macmillan had become Prime Minister, and Mr Thorneycroft had succeeded him as Chancellor. His Budget concentrated on remissions to surtax payers and to overseas subsidiaries of British firms. The brakes were still on – it was still two years and more before the election – and he rejected our plea for plans to revive capital investment.

In September, 1957 came the crash, with panic measures including a 7% Bank Rate (the highest for a generation) and cuts in social expenditure. These measures created a deflationary situation which in due course produced a serious growth in unemployment. As the election drew nearer Mr Amory (who had succeeded Mr Thorneycroft as Chancellor on the latter's resignation) decided that he was, after all, an expansionist and introduced the biggest give-away election budget in Britain's fiscal history.

This helped to win the election, but by 1960 the brakes were on yet again.

By 1961 Mr Selwyn Lloyd was Chancellor. There was great concern about the stagnation in production. In the debate of 6th–7th February, I put forward the idea of a four-year plan for Britain and later elaborated it in an article, Four-Year Plan for Britain, *published by the* New Statesman *in March. The figures set out in that article closely anticipated the NEDC targets, published 18 months later. In 1963 I said that if the Four-Year Plan had been put into effect in 1961, the Gross National Product by 1963 would have been £3,000 millions higher, and the Chancellor's tax revenue would have been up by £1,000 millions a year, without any change in tax rates. His budget made large tax concessions to the surtax payers, and these coming on top of – indeed being made possible by – swingeing increases in health charges and health insurance stamps announced early in February, led to great political controversy. I forecast in the 1961 Budget debate that we were facing an imminent economic crisis. In July two major debates were held, one preceding, the other following Selwyn Lloyd's crisis measures, which included, of course, the 7% Bank Rate, social service cuts – and substantial overseas borrowing. Deflation – and unemployment – were the result.*

In the autumn of 1961 I ceased to be financial spokesman and became the Party's foreign affairs spokesman.

CHAPTER THREE

*

Extract from 1956 Budget speech, 18th April, 1956

THE NATION YESTERDAY was awaiting a clear statesmanlike call from the Chancellor[1] of the efforts and, if necessary, the sacrifices that are needed to lift the country out of the perpetual series of crises and near crises that have dogged us ever since the war. That was what we were led to believe would happen.

What did we get? We had a shambling, fumbling, largely irrelevant and, at one point, degrading speech. The Chancellor told us that the Budget was prepared under the piercing eye of Mr Gladstone[2]. There was one passage that was quite obviously written under a portrait of Horatio Bottomley[3].

With few exceptions, the Chancellor's proposals were imprecise, not fully worked out, and half-baked. They were the sort of thing we might have expected him to jot on the back of an envelope the day after he arrived at the Treasury. There were vague references to an Economic General Staff. We would like to know a little more about that some time. There was a promise, too, of a £100 million cut in Government expenditure – we have heard that one before, as the Lord Privy Seal knows[4] – but, again, there were no specific proposals.

For this Committee, the starting point of the debate is the Economic Survey which is a brutally frank report. The Chancellor still takes an impish delight in revealing to the nation the economic consequences of the Lord Privy Seal.

[1] Harold Macmillan.
[2] The Chancellor of the Exchequer's room at the Treasury.
[3] Reference to Mr Macmillan's 'state lottery', a proposal associated a generation earlier with Horatio Bottomley who ended up in gaol.
[4] The Rt Hon R. A. Butler.

The very first sentence in the Survey tells us that

> In 1955 world economic conditions were highly favourable.

What was the record of this nation under Toryism in the face of these 'highly favourable' conditions? In production, we had an increase smaller than that of every other major industrial country in Europe – the Survey says so. While every other country is still increasing its production, ours is now falling. I would like the Chancellor to tell us what are the prospects for production. Yesterday he refused to assess them, and after the gross miscalculations of his predecessor in every sphere I can understand his shyness.

The nation, however, has a right at least to know this. Is the Chancellor aiming at an increase or a fall in production this year? In his speech he used these words:

> I think we have learned this lesson from the events of the past year. We cannot afford to run our economy flat out ...

Does that mean that the Chancellor wants to see production – and employment, too – less this year than it was last year, when we were flat out? The nation has a right to know. Are the Government trying to cut production below the present level, or do they want it to expand?

Turning to the trade figures, there is a 16% increase in world trade in manufactured goods. Ours is up by 4 or 5%. The Survey tells us that conditions were favourable for rising gold and dollar reserves. The whole of the non-dollar world outside the Soviet bloc saw its gold and dollar reserves rising, according to the Survey, by 1,600 million dollars. Ours fell by £642 million.

I turn to investment, about which the Chancellor made the most perfunctory reference in his speech yesterday. It is, at any rate, the brightest feature in the Economic Survey, though the Government do not seem to agree with that. At long last, in 1955, the long hoped for improvement in capital investment in the private sector began to take place. Year after year we on this side have drawn attention to the fact that while investment in public industry was expanding at a highly satisfactory rate private industry was stagnating.

Year after year the Lord Privy Seal stood at that Box wringing his hands and wondering what he should do about it. I will say this for him. He gave industry every incentive known to his philosophy.

Thinking that the problem might be lack of funds, he gave industry large tax concessions, though the fall in raw material prices after 1952 gave them large liquid surpluses. In 1954, he introduced the investment allowances and went off to the Tory conference in the autumn of that year to exhort everyone to 'Invest in Success'.

Then, in 1955, when industry finally and belatedly responds, the Government panic and run away. Their reactions to this remind me of the old story of the Scottish country preacher who was praying for rain and found his prayers suddenly answered with a cloud burst. It burst with a deafening noise over the tin roof of his little church, and he exclaimed, 'Lord, I was praying for rain, but this is becoming ridiculous'. That, very largely, was the Government's attitude to the increase in investment. They prayed for it for many years. That was all they could do, having no control. When they found their prayers answered, they said, 'This is becoming ridiculous, and it must stop'. Their panic and efforts to restrain investment we regard as a short-sighted, retrograde step, as we have said not only in this debate but over the past few months.

I am not saying how much of the increased investment is essential. How much of it is frivolous the Government have been coy in revealing. We know the volume of new office building has been trebled in the last year. We know that the Government allowed the motor car manufacturing industry to embark on a £250 million expansion programme, and that in the middle of it the Government decided that the industry was becoming too big and must be forced into a depression. The Economic Survey says:

> It became clear that a considerable upsurge in the capital expenditure of industry was being superimposed on the buoyant level of consumers' expenditure.

Whose fault was it that expenditure was so buoyant? How great is the responsibility of a Chancellor who, a year ago, gave away £150 million in tax concessions on the eve of the election, a Chancellor whose policy of deliberately increasing the cost of living and of relaxing the restraints on luxury expenditure was a provocative inducement to higher wage claims?

Because consumption was buoyant the Government decided investment had to be cut, so we have had the long, weary tale of cuts in public industry and in the capital programmes of local authorities;

and the credit squeeze which hits the small industrialists while leaving the giants largely untouched. We find the shadow of short-time working spreading in one industry after another, while the little man, who responded to the Lord Privy Seal's appeal to invest in success, finds himself facing the prospect of bankruptcy. I believe that this panic in the face of increasing industrial investment is the worst indictment in the economic as distinct from the social and fiscal record of the Government.

We are a low investment industrial nation and we ought to be a high one. The Economic Commission for Europe has recently published figures showing the record of each country in investment. The figures relate to 1954, before this increase began, and they show net fixed investment as a percentage of net national production. These are the percentages: Norway, 22; Finland, 21; Austria, 15; Western Germany, 15; Switzerland, 14; the Netherlands, 13; Denmark, 13; Italy, 12; Sweden, 11; Greece, 10; Turkey, 9; France, 8; Belgium and the United Kingdom, 6.

That was the position from which the increased investment of last year began, and I am sure that the Committee[1] will agree that it is no exaggeration to say that the whole future of this nation rests on its becoming a high investment Power. I referred in February[2] to the pace of industrial development in the Soviet Union and in the United States. As soon as it began to quicken here the Government ran away from it. Over the past four years the increase in production, with the windfall gained in the terms of trade, gave this country a large dividend in terms of real resources. I have no hesitation whatsoever in saying – and I do not care what political unpopularity is involved in saying this – that far too high a proportion of those resources which became available were spent on consumption and far too little on investment and exports.

While referring to investment, perhaps I might mention here the Chancellor's comments on borrowing by publicly owned industries. Some hon Gentlemen opposite will perhaps not like the direct assumption by the Treasury of responsibility for meeting those needs. We on this side do not object, though we see no reason for the limitation to two years. When hon Gentlemen opposite complain about

[1] The House of Commons sitting in Committee of Ways and Means as this was a debate on a Budget and therefore a money proposal.

[2] Speech in the House on 21st February, 1956.

the volume of borrowing by nationalised industries, we must remind them that a great deal of this, in the case of coal and railways, for example, is necessary to make good the deficiencies of a generation of private ownership, whereas in the gas and electricity industries it is needed to meet the demands of an expanding economy for which far too little provision was made in pre-war days.

The Chancellor seemed pleased at the degree of control that he will now be able to exercise over the capital investment programmes of public industry. We thought that he had cut them to the bone already. But even if he abuses this control, as we fear he may, it will serve to recall to us on this side how often we reminded hon Gentlemen opposite that the public sector can be planned by the Government in a sense that the private sector cannot be planned. It is possible for a Government to distinguish between the essential and the inessential proposals of public boards. The Government have certainly no such control over the oil companies, for example: while he is cutting down essential investment by public boards, at the very same time he is allowing a great deal of inessential and frivolous expenditure by the oil companies.

Turning to the problem of inflation, all of us are only too well aware of both the symptoms and the main consequences of inflation. I come now to the measures which the Government have proposed for dealing with it. First, of course, the Chancellor, slavishly following his predecessor, as he was instructed to do, relies – and, as we say, over-relies – on the monetary weapon. We have debated this in the past. We have talked about the effect on the National Debt charge, the increased payment of £150 million on overseas interest payments. We have outlined the increased cost of loan charges for housing, the increases on mortgages.

It is right at this point to draw attention also to the effect on invisible earnings, to which the Chancellor referred yesterday. For example, our acceptance business is more and more being driven abroad, especially to Amsterdam, New York and Zürich. One of the most serious factors is the extent to which the sterling area is being driven to borrow in areas other than London. I doubt whether the sterling area, as we know it as an economic unit, can long survive these high interest rates, because more and more Commonwealth countries are being driven to America and elsewhere for their borrowing. I will say no more about that at the moment. Perhaps there will be another opportunity on the Finance Bill to follow this up. I hope that the Chancellor will then say a little more about the debate on interest rates which has recently come to a head in certain of the financial journals. He contributed less than nothing to that debate by his intervention yesterday.

One serious development is that it would appear to be the case that the classical effects of the Bank Rate are not now working; conditions have changed. It would look as though there is reason to think that the real effect of an increased Bank Rate is an impact effect, a temporary effect, due to a sudden disparity between the Treasury bill rate and the deposit rate at the bank; and that that wears off in time. If that is so, the Chancellor's reliance on the monetary weapon must mean that he may be forced year by year to keep on increasing the Bank Rate once a year or at more frequent intervals, depending upon how often there is a Budget or a crisis speech, and we shall see these interest rates rising to the most disastrous level.

Of the three incentives introduced by the Chancellor, the Premium Bond Scheme is the one thing in this Budget which has hit the headlines. I do not want this debate to be too much distracted from the really serious and important issue of our economic policy by this proposal of the right hon Gentleman, but I am bound to say: what a commentary it is on the financial stewardship of the party opposite when the Chancellor of the Exchequer has to have recourse to such measures. In 1951, they promised us a 'Britain Strong and Free'[1]. Now Britain's strength, freedom and solvency apparently depend on the proceeds of a squalid raffle. The Tory Party used to have the slogan, 'Land of Hope and Glory'. We can recall the right hon Member for Woodford (Sir W. Churchill) enthusing about it. They will be fighting the next Election on 'Honest Charlie always pays'.

. . . I now turn to another of the weapons of the Chancellor in his attack on inflation, namely, the Government's newly started campaign for wage and dividend restraint. Recently, the Government launched an attack on wages, and indeed, dividends. This is a great change from a year ago. A year ago, during the election, when we pointed out how wantonly the Government had broken their 1951 pledges of the cost of living, their reply was, 'Yes, prices have gone

[1] The 1951 Tory Party Election Manifesto.

up. We admit that, but wages have gone up more, so everything is all right'.

The Government said that it did not matter about prices rising if wages went up still more, so when the cost of living continued to rise after the election, it was natural that wages went up as well, as people all over the country took the Government at their word. For four and a half years, both in their propaganda and in their actions, the Government have been expounding the doctrine of a free for all, grab all you can, let prices find their own level. Indeed, in recent months, they have been making a virtue of saying that prices should always rise to the economic level. This is happening now in the case of potatoes, apparently.

I ask the Government what would happen if we had the economic price for labour in this country in conditions of a sellers' market? There has been a sellers' market for labour ever since the war. The remarkable thing is that with all this Tory propaganda the unions have not responded to the Tory philosophy. The miracle is not that wages have risen, but that they have not risen a great deal more. But higher wages, which, a year ago, were a means of increased votes to the party opposite, have suddenly become the villain of the piece. We have the White Paper on the Economic Implications of Full Employment, and we have the 6d coloured version[1]. We do not object, indeed we welcome the use of media of communication of this kind, though we would like them to be a little more honest and a little more objective.

In page eight there is a picture of the 10s note – the 10s increase in prices. Only one-sixth of that 10s, states this document, is due to the changes in indirect taxes and subsidies. Subsidy cuts – I quote –

> have had some direct effect on prices but only a small one. They explain only about one-seventh of the rise.

Have the Government still not recognised how much of the wage-price spiral increases of the last few years have been due to the push they gave it in 1952? It was a year of falling world prices in which we were presented with a great opportunity to get domestic prices on to a stable basis. But the former Chancellor of the Exchequer, so eager was he to break his election promises, had the Budget a month earlier, and the main thing he did in that Budget was to slash the food sub-

[1] A Central Office of Information popular coloured version of the White Paper.

sidies. Later in the year, of course, the right hon Gentleman admitted that the price rise was the result of deliberate action in his Budget.

When there is such a wage-price relationship as we have had in a sellers' market, one push may be decisive, even if, to quote the Government's words, 'it was only a little one'. So it is no use the Government coming along and saying that the cut in the food subsidies accounted for only one-seventh of the price increase. This argument is about as convincing as the defence of a man who gives his wife a gentle push over the cliff and then says that her death was to be explained as to one-seventh push and six-sevenths gravity.

As far as I can see, the Government today are in a state of complete schizophrenia about the wage-price problem. First, we have the flat earth school, obviously working towards an attempt to persuade prices to remain stationary for long enough to enable the Prime Minister[1] to appeal to the unions for wage stabilisation. The Prime Minister started on these lines until rebuked recently by the Chancellor of the Exchequer. Now, of course, we have the Minister of Transport saying that fares and charges must be pegged despite a rise in costs. That is one school.

Then we have the intellectuals. There is the Postmaster-General[2], who just cannot wait, on hearing of a wage award, before he rushes to put up his prices. Also, we have the Economic Secretary[3], the Rasputin of the Treasury, a mystic of little power but enormous influence, sufficient to persuade two Chancellors of the Exchequer of widely different views, even if he could not persuade anybody else, that the way to lower the cost of living is to raise prices so as to mop up some of the increased wages.

The Government would be wise to drop this argument. We are as keen as anyone to see the wage-price spiral stopped, so that wages can rise with productivity. But do not let the Government slide out of their responsibility for the increased cost of living – the subsidies, the Purchase Tax, decontrol, wider margins in distributed profits.

Our attack on the Government is not merely on their ways and means or devices – it is on their whole approach to the economic and social problems of the land. What we had yesterday was cynical opportunism in place of leadership, an appeal to cupidity rather than

[1] The Rt Hon Sir Anthony Eden.
[2] Dr the Rt Hon Charles Hill.
[3] Sir Edward Boyle.

to the moral purpose of the nation. The Government offered a scramble and free-for-all in place of a common effort.

In recent weeks we have seen a welcome tendency – even on the part of Ministers – to praise Sir Stafford Cripps and to recall the appeal that he was able to make to the whole nation eight or nine years ago. This is a wonderful change. In the words of the poet[1],

> The hooting mob of yesterday in silent awe return,
> And glean up the scattered ashes into history's golden urn.

Those who wish to have the appeal of a Cripps must have his sense of purpose and sense of moral justice.

Nearly nine years ago this nation faced economic crisis – the crisis of a community devastated by war. We lacked food, shelter and tools. There were those who called on us to consume the seed grain, to sacrifice the future to the present greed of a few. Sir Stafford Cripps stood firm. He insisted that we abstained and invested in the future.

Now, nine years later, after four years of easier living, in easier conditions, after four years' squandering of the harvest that those measures made possible we are back again – 11 years after the war – facing the same crisis. So, nine years afterwards, the words that Sir Stafford Cripps used in winding up that memorable debate in August, 1947, are still as apposite today. They were:

> The quality of effort that is needed in the next few years is not such that it can be evoked by mere material considerations or by the intensification of self-interest or competitive self-seeking . . . It has been truly said that by our faith we can move mountains . . . it is by our faith in the deep spiritual values that we acknowledge, in our Christian faith, that we shall be enabled and inspired to move the present mountains of our difficulties, and so emerge into that new and fertile plain of prosperity which we shall travel in happiness only as the result of our own efforts and our own vision.

It is, in our view, only by such an appeal that this nation can win through. The tragedy is that this Government, by their policies, their cynicism, and their sacrifice of social justice to self-interest, have forfeited the right to make it.

[1] James Russell Lowell: *The Present Crisis.*

EXTRACTS FROM THE 'COST OF SUEZ' SPEECH, 12TH NOVEMBER, 1956

MR HAROLD WILSON (HUYTON): I beg to move, at the end of the Question, to add:

> but humbly regret, in view of the serious economic problems facing the country, which have been aggravated by the effects of the Government's policy in the Middle East, that your Majesty's Gracious Speech gives no indication that your Ministers intend to pursue policies adequate to deal with the situation.

For the past fortnight the House has debated the cost in political and moral terms of the Government's action in Suez. Today, we have to count the reckoning in economic terms as well. When I say 'economic terms' I do not mean merely the cost in terms of Government expenditure. We are no longer in the days of the nineteenth century colonial wars, when the cost of these ventures could be reckoned in terms of another 2d on the Income Tax or another 1d on tea, and while I hope that the Chancellor[1] will be frank in telling the House what the events of the past two weeks mean in terms of national expenditure, I think that the whole House will be much more concerned to assess their wider economic effects on the balance of payments, on the gold reserves, on the strength and position of sterling, on exports, on production, on employment, and on our ability to aid Commonwealth development – if hon Members opposite can be persuaded any longer to take an interest in the Commonwealth.

Before we come to the cost of Suez, what we all have to realise is that this is an additional economic burden, the strain of which the Chancellor himself has said, is: 'a strain which is more than we can bear'.

Those were his words a few days ago. This burden has to be borne by a country which was already, as a result of five years of Tory financial stewardship, facing a desperate economic crisis. I doubt whether there is an hon Gentleman opposite who, even before this latest action of the Government, in his private thoughts and private conversation, was not fearing a further economic crisis, not excluding the possibility of devaluation, in 1957.

[1] Harold Macmillan.

Is there a single hon Gentleman who could say he was not fearing such a crisis even before the Government's action in Suez? Certainly, international financial opinion had written sterling down as something which it was unsafe to hold before the Suez invasion. So I think that we can better appreciate the additional and crippling burdens which the country has to bear as a result of what history will no doubt call 'Eden's war' if we spend a little time surveying the position we had already reached, say, in September or October, after five years of Conservative Government.

The right hon Gentleman gave no sign that he realised, even before our aggression in Suez, that this country would be facing in 1957 a desperate struggle for economic survival. That was the position at the end of October.

Now on top of this, piling Pelion upon Ossa, came the Government's ultimatum and all that followed it. I hope that the Chancellor or the Minister of Supply[1] will tell the House frankly today what, in the view of their advisers, will be the economic consequences of this military action. After all, it was long prepared. What estimates did the Government make of its cost and its economic consequences? What estimate do they make now? In his Budget speech the Chancellor of the Exchequer referred to Mr Gladstone. I must remind him today of the words of Gladstone during the Crimean War. In his 1854 Budget speech, Mr Gladstone had this to say:

> The expenses of a war are a moral check which it has pleased the Almighty to impose upon the ambition and lust of conquest that are inherent in so many nations . . . The necessity of meeting from year to year the expenditure which it entails is a salutary and wholesome check, making them measure the cost of the benefit upon which they may calculate.

Whatever the benefit on which the Chancellor and his colleagues may have calculated in going in for this operation, the right hon Gentleman certainly has a duty to the House to give us his estimates of the cost.

I must say this to the Chancellor. It would be some consolation to the country, when it considers the Bill for the Government's actions, to feel that he, at any rate, was so conscious of his responsi-

[1] The Rt Hon Aubrey Jones, MP

bilities to the nation that he urged restraint on the Prime Minister[1]. It has been traditionally the role of the Chancellor to resist expenditure on military preparations. Gladstone restrained Palmerston in the 1860s and Lord Randolph Churchill resigned over the cost of a battleship.

If that is the Chancellor's duty on military preparations, how much more is it his duty to use all his powers to restrain military action? Will the Chancellor tell us that he tried but was overborne by his colleagues? I fear that the truth is otherwise. I fear the truth is what the country believes, that the Chancellor, so far from being a restraining influence, was in the van of those who since July have been calling for war. I say to the right hon Gentleman in all sincerity that the Chancellor's first responsibility is not only to ensure the economic survival of this country, but to act in the Cabinet as trustee for the peoples of the entire sterling area. That should have been his mission in these critical months, not to act as the spokesman of the Suez group in the Cabinet.

We have complained, in our amendment, that the Government have offered no indication of any solution to these economic problems. We have Premium Savings Bonds, of course[2]. We hear a lot about them from the Chancellor. What a wonderful sense of relevance and timing the right hon Gentleman has. On the day the bombs started dropping on Egypt there was the Chancellor, like a broken-down showman, peddling his bonds in Trafalgar Square.

What authority does the Chancellor think he has now to speak to the industries of this country, on whom mainly rest our hope of avoiding economic catastrophe? I say that he has not that authority. The Government have not only lost the right to govern, but I believe that they have forfeited the power to govern. If the Chancellor and his colleagues have any longer that sense of responsibility to the national interest, and especially to our hopes of economic survival, that I believe they once had, there is only one patriotic and honourable course left to them – to get out and to make way for those who can deal with these problems.

[1] Anthony Eden.

[2] Premium Bonds Scheme, introduced by Harold Macmillan in his Budget of 1956.

CHAPTER FOUR

*

Extract from debate, 11th July, 1960

MR HAROLD WILSON (HUYTON): The situation which we are debating today is painfully familiar. Once again, within a few months of a General Election which was fought on prosperity, the magic has gone and we have to face economic realities. Hon Members opposite toasted themselves in champagne only a few months ago, and now we have the morning after.

I will not embarrass hon Members by quoting the extravagant claims which they made last October on the hustings, but typical of them were the boasts of the Prime Minister, whose regard for objective truth in these matters has always been somewhat elliptical, not least on the hustings. This is what he said:

> ... today, the British economy is sounder than at any time since the First World War. Sterling has been re-established as a sound and respected currency. Our balance of payments is strong.

The right hon Gentleman also said:

> I do not remember any time in my life when the economy has been so sound and the prosperity of our people at home so widely spread.

Within nine months of the election we have had in quick succession a tough Budget, hire-purchase restrictions, the reintroduction of the credit squeeze, an announcement about cuts in Government expenditure and now a crisis level Bank Rate of 6%. I notice that hon Members opposite are much more silent now.

This is 1955 all over again, because within nine months of the 1955 election we had the present Home Secretary's autumn Budget[1]. He

[1] R. A. Butler.

need not be so shy; I am glad to see him here. Within the same nine-month period, and as the first fruits of the reign of 'Super-Mac' at the Treasury, we had the credit squeeze, a 5½% Bank Rate, the clamp-down on production and the scrapping of the investment allowances. What is going on now is all so sickeningly familiar.

It has happened simply because we increased production. After three years with no increase at all, the boom which they engineered for the election has proved too much for us. One thing is very clear. After eight and a half years of stewardship by right hon Gentlemen opposite, the economy is so weak, so vulnerable, so narrowly based, that we cannot stand even a single short-lived spurt in industrial production. Production, even in 1959, was only 22% above the figure for 1951, and it was still the worst record in Europe.

During the years of the great stagnation I more than once gave the House the comparative figures for Europe. Hon Gentlemen opposite should have the figures today after a year's boom, because they are still as bad. West Germany has shown an increase of 91% since 1951; Italy, 82%; Austria, 63%; France, 61%; the Netherlands, 51%; Finland, 40%; Norway, 38%; Denmark, 35%; Britain, 22%, with only Sweden at 21%, Luxembourg at 17%, and Belgium at 12% lower. I ask hon Gentlemen to contrast those figures with those for 1945 to 1951, when year by year Britain proudly led Europe.

For a brief few months, we tried to join the European race, but our muscles and wind are in such poor shape that the effort was too much for us. We have had to retire from the race. We are back once again to restriction, to the Prime Minister's 1956 policy of clamping down, and, worse still, of mortgaging the future by holding down investment.

The truth is that our economy is too weak to stand a sustained expansion of production, simply because Ministers squandered the great opportunities of the 1950s and squandered the chance held out to us by the most favourable world economic conditions we had since before 1914.

... Let us look, then, at the economic position today, nine months after the election, 18 months after the beginning of the election boom. First, we find the Government hag-ridden by the fear of renewed inflation. There are some of the old familiar signs – a depressed gilt-edged market; war loan has reached its lowest-ever figure, lower even than it was under the right hon Member for Monmouth (Mr Thorneycroft[1]); and Consols are at almost the lowest level for 40 years. So much for the Tory concern for the small investor and for the Home Secretary's call to 'Invest in Success'[2].

It was the labour position which caused the panic. The Bank Rate went up to 6% on the very day when, for the first time for nearly three years, the number of unfilled jobs equalled the number unemployed. Under this Government, whenever we have reached a position when there was no longer a surplus of men running after every job, we have had a foreign exchange crisis. Here we are, 15 years after the war, and we are still so vulnerable that we cannot achieve full employment without lurching into crisis.

Faced with this situation, what have the Government got? The Chancellor[3], like a tired and discredited witch doctor, has given us his usual ritual incantation, ending with a 6% Bank Rate which is the last refuge of every Tory Chancellor. We all know that this is the Chancellor's last economic debate, and I want to say on behalf of my right hon and hon Friends that however much it has been our duty to criticise his policies, on personal grounds we regret his retirement from the office that he holds. Whatever our differences – and they are, and have been, fundamental – we have nothing but the highest praise for the courtesy and consideration that the right hon Gentleman has shown to us and to the whole House at all times. In every personal sense, we wish him well.

Our feelings about the right hon Gentleman's retirement, of course, are not eased by rumours about his successor – [An Hon Member: 'Which one?'] There are quite a number of aspirants. Some people say that the Foreign Secretary[4] will get a Department of his own at last. Others, with a grotesquely misplaced sense of humour, say that we shall get the Minister of Education[5].

The Member for Shipley (Mr Hirst) – whom I see is in his place – after making a personal attack on the Chancellor in a recent statement, in terms that I personally would deplore, goes one worse. He wants to bring the Prime Minister back out of the misty stratosphere

[1] Thorneycroft had resigned from the Treasury and Government in January, 1958, on the question of the level of Government expenditure.

[2] R. A. Butler, then Chancellor of the Exchequer, in October, 1954.

[3] Rt Hon Heathcoat Amory.

[4] Rt Hon Selwyn Lloyd.

[5] Sir David (later Lord) Eccles.

– in which, of late, he has been disporting himself, with singularly little result – and get him to put his oar in here. May I say, and this cry comes from the heart, 'For heaven's sake, spare us from that'.

The Prime Minister's year at the Treasury was, without exception, the most disastrous in our financial history. Even the present Home Secretary[1] – nay, even the right hon Gentleman the Member for Monmouth[2] – appeared in shining raiment by comparison. The economic problem is too serious for there to be put forward such frivolous suggestions as that made by the hon Member for Shipley. The hon Member knows, as, indeed, every hon Member knows, that for four years the Prime Minister's stock in trade has been an elegant improvisation and always to seek to solve this year's problem with last year's gimmicks. It is very plain to us all that the problems facing us are not capable of solution by any gimmick, so I hope that the hon Member for Shipley will not press that.

We have just had the Blue Streak farce[3], and the failure of the Government's recruitment policy, with the likelihood of additional expenditure being involved there. I do not think that half the Ministers have their hearts in the job, not when there are votes in their minds.

The Prime Minister pledged his reputation on this undertaking to hold Government expenditure down to the then current level four years ago, and since that time Government expenditure has gone up by £1,000 million a year. Indeed, it has gone up by £600 million since the right hon Member for Monmouth[4] resigned on this issue two and a half years ago. I have as little confidence in the Government carrying out the Chancellor's announcement on this matter as the hon Member for Shipley has, and I have every reason for saying that.

There is something warped in the minds of hon Members opposite when they come to look at economic and social problems. Anything in the private sector is good; it is productive. In the public sector it is waste; it is parasitic and leads to inflation. I remember years ago, in a previous crisis – I think that it was the Home Secretary's[5] crisis,

[1] R. A. Butler.

[2] Peter Thorneycroft.

[3] Failure of the Blue Streak project debated in the House on 27th April, 1960, see page 167.

[4] Peter Thorneycroft, Chancellor, 1957–58.

[5] R. A. Butler.

but I am not sure – when I said, referring to investment, that the test should not be 'Is it public or private?' but 'How essential is it?' Because the Government reject controls, they reject this test.

If one builds a vast block of offices for property speculators, or advertising agents or company promoters, this is a desirable addition to our national wealth. If one builds a hospital our economy is endangered. One can build a pub, or a bowling alley; that is sacrosanct. But one more school – that is inflation. One can spend £120 million a year, with tax relief from the Chancellor and an initial allowance, on private cars for business firms; but another million or two on investment in the public sector – that is uneconomic and unproductive, and the hon Member for Kidderminster (Mr Nabarro) keeps us up half the night. One can spend £60 million on television advertising, to try to stimulate demand for goods to a point which even the Chancellor now regards as excessive. Yet one cannot find a million or two more for mental health.

A financial speculator can clear £1 million overnight on a property deal, buying and selling a block of flats with someone else's money. That is smart business. But if we pay a decent wage to an engine driver, with the lives of hundreds of people in his hands, that is raging inflation. The banks can lend tens of millions of pounds more, as they have, to Stock Exchange speculators; that is in the national interest. But local authorities trying to cope with their heritage of slums or with chronic overcrowding are forced into costly borrowing operations at penal rates of interest.

The Chancellor can knock £5 million off the tax on port, but he cannot find an equal sum for removing the individual prescription charge for chronic sick people. Private enterprise can use able-bodied men in their thousands to go touting round, putting coupons or advertising literature through letter boxes, or inflating the cost of the Health Service by pressing new branded drugs on hard-worked doctors. Yet we cannot afford a few more factory inspectors. We can titillate the consumer with striped toothpaste, or all the other lunacies of an Americanised society, but our beaches and rivers are a disgrace. This is the society that we are creating under the right hon Gentleman.

Aneurin Bevan once said, 'The language of priorities is the religion of Socialism'. It is more than that. It is the means to creating out of great potential wealth a civilised society. Under the present Government our priorities are all wrong. We call for a new order of priorities, first, as between private and public expenditure, and the test must be not private profit or the lightening of the burdens on those best fitted to bear tax burdens, but national survival and social interest.

Secondly, we call for a new order of priorities between private consumption and national investment. We are falling behind Europe in our provision of the instruments of production. Before long we have to make, as a matter of urgency, our decision about Europe. Let me say to the Government, including the Prime Minister, that this is a decision that cannot be side-stepped by some new evasion, or gimmick. There is no gimmick in this. Whatever our decision in Western Europe or out of it, we can only compete and live if we devote a much higher share of our current production to strengthening the means of further production so that we can maintain a steady and purposive rate of economic growth.

This debate is not just concerned with the analysis of the present economic situation, nor the lurchings of the economy, nor the devious and outmoded devices by which Ministers seek to prod the financial and industrial system in one direction or another. We are concerned today with fundamental differences of view about the degree of responsibility which Parliament should assert over our economic life. By and large, Conservatives and Liberals accept the existing economic structure of the country. Their argument is about the division, and the method of division, of the national product.

We on this side of the Committee[1], deeply concerned though we are about the distribution of the national dividend, are equally concerned about the control and ownership of the instruments by which that dividend is produced. We cannot be neutral about the accountability of the strategic sectors of industry and finance to the nation as a whole. For the Conservatives the commanding heights of the economy are and should be in private hands, working for the consolidation of the existing order, and with profit as the sole criterion.

For them, too, the role of the State is confined to guiding, influencing and holding the ring – doing no more than prescribing the conditions in which that profit is made, always with the minimum disturbance to the existing order. For hon Members on this side of the Committee the commanding heights of the economy should be in

[1] House of Commons sitting in Committee of Ways and Means.

the strategic sectors of industry, owned by and answerable to the community, and working in its interests.

Hon Members opposite are blind to the world in which we are living. At a time when the biggest challenge to our way of life comes from countries which plan their economic life in a purposive and rational manner – however much we may detest their political framework – hon Members opposite scoff at Socialism as something which belongs to the politics of a bygone age, its case destroyed – if they are ready to concede there ever was a case – by the 'Ten Hours' Act[1] or, at the latest, by the acceptance by all parties, even their own, of full employment as a necessary objective of economic policy.

By these attitudes they show it is they who are living in the past – because our demand for Socialist economic policies relates not to the conditions of the 'twenties and 'thirties, unanswerable though they were, to the problems of the mines and transport, the squalor and inequality of mass unemployment. We do not base our case on any assumptions, even about the recurrence of mass unemployment. We base it on the much more compelling demands of the world into which we are moving in the future. It is a world characterised more and more by a scientific revolution beyond the dreams of only a generation ago. The potential release of energy – in the widest sense of the word – of productive power, of facilities for material development and for leisure alike, defies the measuring rod of the market place or counting house, or any system dedicated to private profit and speculative gain.

Hon Members opposite believe that the fulfilment of this release of energy can be left to a system which, in its essentials and institutions, and, above all, in its motivation, has changed little since the Forsytes[2]. Our merchant bankers, our discount houses, our bank parlours, our daily more powerful insurance companies all have a job to do, and an important job, but they exceed their function if they claim to be the regulators and the directors of our economy. Our economic development will be safeguarded only when the Government party in this House accepts that, however vital, finance is the handmaiden and not the controller of our economic development.

Under the present system, those things – and only those things – will be developed which yield, on a narrow but highly personalised

[1] Ten Hours Act – limiting the hours of work of children employed in factories.
[2] Galsworthy's *Forsyte Saga.*

basis, a private profit, irrespective of the relevance they bear to the nation's real interest, and the wider needs of a rapidly changing world. Ministers keep repeating – and I have no doubt that they will repeat again today – that 18 months ago they were able to escape from a recession in the private enterprise part of the economy – which they had done much to create – only by priming the pump with a particular type of consumer boom. They could stimulate a languishing rate of capital investment not by creating new instruments of production, but only by touching off a consumer boom based on mass advertising.

This, in turn, primed the pump for an investment boom. But the investment boom which resulted was inevitably based on the production of the consumer goods they had called into being. If the boom is in soft drinks and television sets the capital goods called into being are plant and machinery for making and distributing soft drinks and television sets, and not the types of investment – public and private – which are most related to the needs of Britain and the world.

I would put this to them: faced with this recession, which they have done so much to create, why should they not have started the process of stimulating investment by building, in an area of high unemployment, a State-owned machine tool plant, producing the latest type of product which is so greatly in demand here and in the export markets all over the world? Now that a world boom has begun, the development of our machine tool industry is inadequate to take advantage of the orders available.

Similarly with trade. We are relying more and more for our exports, to the dollar area and Europe – to take two very important parts of our export market – on the overspill of our consumer goods production. That is the main reason why I fear an economic integration with a European market, which would mean gearing our production and our exports to a consumer goods economy not very different from our own. We must not only transform our industrial system by making it more purposively directed to expansion and to the nation's needs; we must extrovert it by relating our products to the needs of a largely hungry world, whose wants are not for consumer luxuries but for the primary basis of life itself – basic, elemental goods and the means of producing them.

These are the main issues underlying the debate today. These are the real issues to which the Chancellor, even in his forthcoming retirement, should be addressing himself. Hon Members opposite no doubt scoff at the arguments that have gone on in the Labour Party[1] in the past few months. I do not apologise for those arguments. I should feel it right to apologise if we were not having arguments, because this is a debate about the future of the nation in a changing world economy. Let hon Members opposite realise: we are arguing about the future: they seek only to consolidate the past.

EXTRACT FROM DEBATE, 18TH JULY, 1961

MR HAROLD WILSON (HUYTON): This has been a remarkable debate. I do not think that in the 16 years that I have been in this House I have ever heard a more one-sided debate. The right hon Gentlemen opposite have been right up against the ropes the whole day. It might have been a little more dignified if they had thrown in the towel round about half-past four.

Taking the home situation, we have the fact that production has been virtually at a standstill for 15 months. Today we have the figure for the latest month – still no change. Here we are, with what we all welcome, a big increase in industrial investment, and with a shortage of labour – we keep hearing from the Minister[2] that our labour resources are strained to the utmost – yet production remains stagnant. Does it not strike the Government as something very strange that in a time when we have all this new investment and additional employment, production is stagnant and productivity is actually falling?

But this, of course, was deliberate policy. Last year, the Government used every weapon at their command to hold down production, so what do they expect? They believe that if we hold production down, wages and prices will remain stable, but the events of the last three years have proved the exact opposite. As we have told them in

[1] Argument over the abolition of Clause IV in the Party's Constitution relating to public ownership of industry.

[2] Rt. Hon Iain Macleod: Minister of Labour.

debate after debate, it is when production is held down and productivity is battened down that costs and prices rise. In 1959, when production and productivity were rising, costs and prices were kept steady. If the Chancellor wants to stop this present, sudden, sharp increase in costs and prices – 5% increase in the last 10 months – and if he wants to hold it, the way is not by restricting production but by expanding it.

Surely the Government have learned by now that when one restricts production, whether by hire-purchase restrictions, interest rate policy or any of the other techniques which they have used over the years, the result is not a fall in prices but an increase in unit costs – and that means higher prices. Surely they have learned that lesson by now. Yet here we have a sharp rise in the cost of living. Prices, costs, fear of the wage spiral, all at a time when, by common consent – and hon Members have agreed with this – export markets are becoming more competitive every day.

I am not going to weary the Committee by quoting all the warnings that we have issued year after year in economic and Budget debates. They are all on the record and I challenge hon Members to look them up. If they do, they will find that we would have to withdraw precious few of the warnings that we have uttered. Compare that with the complacent outpourings of right hon Gentlemen at the Dispatch Box year after year.

Basically their fault is three-fold. First, in their mad rush for freedom to make profits, freedom to speculate and make more out of capital gains and more out of rents, the country has lost its dynamic, its sense of purpose – its economic, social and moral purpose. It has rejected the planning measures needed to strengthen the foundations of our economic base.

Secondly, when the call has been for expansion, more production, more investment and more exports, the Government have met every crisis with panic measures and restrictions which hold down production and hold back investment, so that when the next crisis came the nation's economic base was too narrow and thin to sustain the burdens and strains which were put on it. The main measure which one can take in a crisis is to build up the basic industries and, above all, the export industries so that when the next crisis comes we can meet it. Right hon Gentlemen opposite have panicked into further restrictions.

Thirdly, when the need of the country has been for sacrifice, discipline and leadership so as to build up investment in export industries, they have gone in for the lush and easy profits of the home market. Above all, when the call to the hustings has come they have twice, in 1955 and 1959, sacrificed the prerequisites of our economic survival to a vote-winning consumption boom for which we are still paying the price. This crisis is, at the same time, the pay-off for 10 wasted years and for their 'never had it so good' election boom.

Some of my hon Friends have been calling for a four-year plan. We should make no mistake – right hon Gentlemen opposite have got a four-year plan. They have been working to it. They have followed it religiously in two Parliaments. The plan is this: in the first year – that is, in 1955 and 1959 – they win an election on a home market boom. In the next year – in 1956 and 1960 – one cannot get tough too quickly, so they have a standstill Budget and restrictions on production. In the next year – in 1957 and 1961 – they begin on a vast handout to their friends the Surtax payers, financed in 1957 and 1961 by increases in insurance contributions. The pattern is very regular.

Then in the summer we get a major crisis. We get a high Bank Rate, emergency measures bringing expansion to a stop and deflationary measures directed to producing that necessary little margin of unemployment that we keep being told about. All this time our production is failing to increase. It is falling below that of other countries. Then we come to 1958 and 1962 – another 'standstill, wait for it' Budget. They know that memories are rather short, so they do not want to give it away too long before the election. Then, while production and investment are still languishing, with unemployment growing, we are all ready for election year when we have to take up slack in the economy, with a magnificent tax handout for everybody. There is more for the rich even so, but something for everybody, plus 2d off beer. That is a special dodge of the Prime Minister's. So it really is a libel on right hon Gentlemen opposite to say that they have no plan. They have a plan, but it is not directed towards our national economic strength. It is directed to keeping the Conservatives in power.

Tonight, again, the Prime Minister is not with us. It is really becoming a scandal that the First Lord of the Treasury is not here to answer. I suppose he has some sense of shame. We do not mind that. He should take it a little further and get out altogether. But, so long as he is Prime Minister, he ought to be here.

Now, we read in the Conservative Press the ominous news that the Prime Minister has decided to intervene in the economic crisis. This is no idle threat. No one bears more responsibility than he for our economic crises. He was the first to propound the doctrine that the right way to fight inflation was to hold production down. On becoming Chancellor, he was panicked into abolishing the investment allowance, and this caused a stagnation in our industrial investment which lasted for three vital years. As we all know, the Prime Minister is more responsible than anyone else for the smug complacency which has pervaded the nation as a result of successive speeches he has made. While his own Chancellor has been telling us how serious the economic situation has been, the right hon Gentleman has been travelling the country saying that we have never been so well off, and all the rest. [An Hon Member: 'He said it today'.] He said it again today in the House.

One of the most serious features of the Prime Minister's leadership – if that is the right word to use in speaking of the right hon Gentleman – is that he has been speaking all over the country, degrading, debasing and debauching our national life by preaching the gospel of the free-for-all, the gospel of grabbing all one can. His is the gospel of the self-regarding affluent society where, as I heard a distinguished churchman[1] say the other day, the verb 'to have' means so much more than the verb 'to be'. That is the affluent society which hon Members opposite have preached, and many of them are here now only because of their success in preaching that doctrine at the last General Election.

Now, safely in mid-term, counting on the short memories which throughout history have always been the Conservative Party's greatest asset, right hon Gentlemen opposite tell us that we must stress the moral aspects of our national life. The Home Secretary[2] is another notable absentee tonight. I do not blame him.

What did the Home Secretary say?:

Nations gain their right to rise,
By service and by sacrifice.

[1] The Archbishop of York, Dr Coggan.
[2] R. A. Butler.

I commend this thought to the Home Secretary:

> Nations gain their right to rise,
> By service and by sacrifice.
> So Britain aims to reach the top.
> With capital gains and the betting shop!

I ask the right hon Gentleman: what service and sacrifice does he see in a situation in which industries, like the shipyard industry on Clydeside, cannot offer security to their workers who are emigrating to Hamburg where things are better?

Last week, the Home Secretary said, after he got from poetry back to prose:

> Out of our economic difficulties good may come, especially if our party gives a lead to the country in calling for moral values to emerge instead of materialist appetites.

That was after materialist appetites were sated to the tune of £83 million last April for the Surtax payers only. Is it the argument of the Government that their friends can gorge themselves to the full while they themselves now preach the virtues of fasting and restraint to the rest of the community, with one-fifth of the manual workers getting less than £11 a week? It is they who have to exercise restraint.

The condemnation of 10 years' rule by Members opposite is that they have left this country in a position of desperate economic weakness when the decision on whether or not to enter the Common Market has to be taken. It is not much use posturing about whether one is to go into the Market or not when one has been driven to one's knees by the Government's economic policy.

Unless we take the steps necessary to refashion our economic policy and recapture our lost dynamic drive then, as we say in our policy statement, whether we enter the Common Market or stay out will only settle the question of whether we are to be a backwater inside Europe or outside it.

EXTRACT FROM DEBATE, 26TH JULY, 1961

LAST WEEK, I APPEALED to the Chancellor not to deal with the short-term problem of the run on sterling by measures which would make our long-term position worse through harming production and investment. The right hon and learned Gentleman has ignored that warning. We face an immediate run on sterling. The economy is so weak that last year we avoided a disaster only through borrowing hundreds of millions of 'hot' money which was attracted here by high and costly interest rates. This year that money is moving out again.

To deal with this the Chancellor borrows hundreds of millions of pounds from the International Monetary Fund. Of course, the immediate effects of doing this were predictable. Once the Chancellor made clear to the speculators that sterling would not be devalued, once he buttressed his scanty reserves by massive borrowing, it was obvious that the 'bears' would run to cover and the immediate crisis would be resolved for a time.

But, of course, like every one of his immediate predecessors – we see the Minister of Aviation[1] sitting opposite – he had to satisfy the international banking community by masochistic and irrelevant cuts in our standard of living, harmful restrictions on our production and needless increases in our costs and price structure, because he believes that international speculators are impressed only by actions which in the long term harm the economy.

The right hon and learned Gentleman obviously believes that these financiers are dictated not so much by economic considerations as by a rather twisted, morbid psychology. In fact, if international financiers do reason in this irrational way it is a grave reflection on Conservative economic management in the past 10 years that we are now so much in their power.

So we say to the Chancellor, 'Borrow – go ahead'. The Government's policies are so bankrupt that all we can do, 16 years after the war, is to go for international aid and to buttress the economy with costly, unnecessary short-term borrowing at 7% which is a magnet for 'hot' money from all over the world to come here once again.

[1] Peter Thorneycroft.

This is a hard thing to say, but it is not imagination. One of the leading German periodicals has an article in this week's issue headed, 'The Sick Man of Europe'. Fundamentally, as the whole House knows, our latent virility, vigour, skill, ingenuity and inventiveness are such that instead of presenting this image of sickness we could present an image to the world of bounding energy and enterprise. All that is lacking is the leadership and inspiration, the call for service and sacrifice which this Administration is unable to give.

We welcome the fact that the Prime Minister is to speak in this debate. It is right that he should be called to account in a debate such as this, because no man bears a heavier responsibility either for misdirected policies or for the inculcation of this climate of national complacency. I do not want to address too many words to him. I suppose that it must seem to him years since he strutted on to the platform of that 1958 Conservative conference as the mighty Wurlitzer organ throbbed to the strains of 'Mr Wonderful, that's you', and then called his troops to the forthcoming election battle with a speech which was an orgy of self-satisfaction and boasts that our economy was in such fine shape.

The right hon Gentleman, who pledged himself, on television, on becoming Prime Minister, to 'make Great Britain great' has so imperilled and squandered our economic security that we are in danger of earning for ourselves the gibe which the Czar Nicholas addressed to the dying Ottoman Empire, 'The Sick Man of Europe'. That is his contribution.

All of us know, and the world knows, that a further devaluation would not be like the last one – a readjustment forced on us four years after the war by the consequences of the war and a hungry post-war world. A second devaluation would be regarded all over the world as an acknowledgement of defeat, a recognition that we were not on a springboard, but a slide. I myself have always deprecated – perhaps rightly, perhaps wrongly – in crisis after crisis, appeals to the Dunkirk spirit as an answer to our problem, because what is required in our economic situation is not a brief period of inspired improvisation, work and sacrifice, such as we had under the leadership of the right hon Member for Woodford (Sir W. Churchill), but a very long, hard, prolonged period of reorganisation and rededication. It is the long haul, not the inspired spurt, that we need.

But perhaps in the crisis we face today – this continuing crisis – we do need the realisation which the right hon Member for Woodford inspired in the nation 21 years ago in the memorable speeches he made – the realisation that in a very special sense today, as then, we stand alone, that we can look to no one to provide an easy way out, that no one owes us a living, that on our own efforts, our own sense of purpose and our unity in overcoming these problems – that in these things alone lies our hope of success. In that sense, if in that sense only, we do need the spirit of Dunkirk.

We shall not create that spirit by appeals to materialism, or selfish acquisitiveness, or competitive social emulation – keeping up with the Joneses – by either snobbery or its no less ugly partner, inverted snobbery. We shall not realise it by sinking back into the syrupy, demoralising persuasion which pours into our homes night after night via the commercial channel. Only when this country loses its soft centre, its candy-floss philosophy, and is allowed to aspire to more astringent policies can we succeed.

In that spirit, I want briefly to put the headings – no more – of the sort of policy which we feel could unite our people and strengthen our economy. It may not command the support of all hon Members opposite. I do not expect it to, but I accept that we have a duty to put forward an alternative in this debate. We also have a right, because the country has tried the Tory way and it has failed.

First, I repeat our proposal for a plan – a four-year plan, a five-year plan, if necessary – for steady and sustained economic expansion, setting the national targets, and especially the targets which need to be achieved in the industries which can make the most contribution in the markets of the world. It should be a plan worked out in consultation with management and workers, giving a real priority to the investment we need, and not, as the Chancellor proposes, a mere coordination of planners and consultation systems. It should be an effective, purposive plan, to which private profit and sectional interests would be subordinated.

What the Chancellor proposes is a paper plan. No Conservative will give it the backing it needs in terms of controls and an extension of public ownership in the key centres of the economy. But such a plan we need, a plan, above all, to raise our investment in the industries where it is most needed, a plan to apply more purposefully the results of scientific discovery in our industrial machine.

My second point is on exports. The Government must now take

positive action to help our exporters. We need in this country to alter our sense of values so that the man who exports and takes risks in world markets is regarded as a man worthy of the nation's respect, a man to honour, not a sucker. It should be recognised that it is he, not the advertising agent or the sharepusher, who is top of the scale.

Therefore, the Government should make the job of the exporter easier. Eighteen months ago we suggested fundamental improvements in our export credit system. This was in the debate on the Radcliffe Report[1], on 26th November, 1959. We suggested improvements in export credits so that we can offer the same terms as our ruthlessly efficient competitors on the Continent. The Government have limped along very slowly since that time, but what about our proposal for a British export-import bank? Has that ever been seriously considered by the Cabinet?

Again, where there are controls or instruments available to the Government – there are not many – the Government should use them blatantly and unashamedly in the interests of the exporter. Non-discrimination is a fine liberal principle, but too often it is the last refuge of a tired or complacent administration. After all, the apotheosis of non-discrimination is death. We want to see something done, but too often because of non-discrimination nothing has been done to help the exporter.

I know all the difficulties of discriminatory taxation. I looked into it when I was in the office held by the Right Hon Gentleman[2], but I think that there are a number of things we can do. I would have an open mind – this needs to be looked at – on the question whether we should supplement the Purchase Tax by some kind of industrial turnover tax, with total exemption for exports, such as they have in Germany. I ask the Prime Minister to study this suggestion very carefully before tomorrow night. I want him to take it seriously. The Government should have an open mind on it. They should study the proposal. It should apply in industry, but not to the things covered by Purchase Tax. The yield from it might enable us to remove Purchase Tax from some essential goods where it has been placed by the Right Hon Gentleman the Home Secretary[3]. Right Hon Gentlemen will know perfectly well, if they have studied the trade situation,

[1] See page 71.
[2] President of the Board of Trade, 1947-51.
[3] R. A. Butler.

that anybody who goes to Germany is told there that this is the biggest single instrument in the success of the German export drive.

I have many reservations, doubts and anxieties about the proposal, but I hope that the Government will examine it and see whether it is a feasible one. I am not talking about a general sales tax. We have been over that argument year after year. I am talking of an industrial turnover tax, with blatant discrimination in favour of exports. I hope that the Prime Minister will have my suggestion carefully examined.

I suggest, also, that the Chancellor of the Exchequer tackles the business expenses problem – the entertainment problem – by providing that only half business entertainment expenditure should rank for tax exemption, except where it is shown to be directly related to exports. I should make no bones about that kind of discrimination. The same might be considered in connection with expenditure on advertising.

Lastly, I turn to costs. I think that the whole House will agree that we need a spirit on both sides of industry which can produce the efforts and sacrifices which will be necessary. We need two things. We need a more sustained increase in production, and a greater determination to control rising costs. It is, I think, a truism to say that we cannot afford, year by year, an increase in economic rewards – whether profits or salaries, or rents, or wages – greater than the increase in productivity which provides the means to all rewards.

The nation, and I make this clear, cannot, over a period, afford wage increases – I say this quite frankly – greater than our national rise in productivity. That, of course, is an argument in favour of giving much higher priority to increased productivity instead of these repeated lurches into economic restrictionism. It is no good the Chancellor complaining that wages and other payments have outrun productivity when it has been Government policy to hold production down, so that, over the past year, productivity actually fell.

It is well within the capacity of the nation, and nobody will be defeatist enough to deny it, to achieve an increase, year by year, of 4% or 5% in productivity and of 4% or 5% in wages – and if this means an increase of 4% or 5% in profits and dividends, no one will lose sleep. What we cannot afford are the predatory dividend increases of the kind quoted by the President of the Board of Trade,[1] or

[1] Reginald Maudling.

uncovenanted capital gains cornering for a few favoured shareholders a disproportionate share of our increased national assets.

We need a national attack on the spirit of lethargy which pervades too great a part of our industry. That is why I advocate the ending of restrictive practices wherever they occur – on either side of industry – which hold back our natural national inventiveness and skill. That is why we on this side condemn equally those who shirk their task, whatever their role in industry – the fomenters of unofficial strikes and those who too easily follow them – and the businessmen who cling to out-of-date methods and out-of-date machinery because it yields them a profit, who turn their backs on export orders, and who devote their ingenuity, not to increasing production or lowering taxation, but to tax avoidance. To say this is not idealism, or puritanism; it is plain common sense for the nation.

Neither in power nor in opposition has this party or the trade union movement shirked the task of calling for wage restraint when it was needed in the national interest. We do not shirk it now. But we cannot ask for that sacrifice from one part of the nation only – and that the least well paid. We cannot make that appeal to men earning £8 or £9 or £10 a week when the Government have just issued a statutory promissory note on next year's Budget to people who are immeasurably better off.

If, therefore, we are to tackle the job of controlling our national costs it must be a national endeavour, and the Government, whether Conservative or Labour, must give the lead, because it is the Government which create the climate of opinion that can make this possible. There is no sacrifice harder to make than the sacrifice of dearly-held doctrine and ideology. That is why, though it is hard for the Government to concede, my Right Hon Friend[1] was right in asking for the repeal – the postponement, if Hon Members like – of the Surtax concession in the Budget until the national economy permits of a fundamental reconstruction of our tax system.

The Government cannot ask for a national endeavour in production and restraint in incomes when they refuse to deal with capital gains, or when they refuse to institute measures that really get at the root of the problem of coping with land speculation and property deals, or when they refuse to restore the tax on dividends.

[1] Hugh Gaitskell.

If the Chancellor would restore the tax on dividends today – yes, another tax; the Prime Minister can make a note of it – the yields from it would enable us to recast our whole system of industrial taxation. To encourage investment, we could enable expansion-minded industrialists to write off a great deal of their capital expenditure much more quickly than they can under the obsolete rules that we have at present; writing off, perhaps, the whole amount in a single year, as they did under the Swedish proposals. That would be financed out of the tax on dissipated dividends. What we need, as I am sure the House will agree, is a system of industrial taxation that does far more to reward enterprise in expanding firms and, at the same time, penalises the slothful firms, and those which refuse to play their part in the national economy.

We cannot make the national appeal we need in an economic society dominated by the take-over bidder. We cannot appeal for restraint in productive industry when the Stock Exchange behaves like a casino. I do not apologise for saying that because, as the Prime Minister knows, it is taken from a famous book of his written before the war, and if it was true then it is no less true today. The Chancellor knows this. Let him, then, put duties on all Stock Exchange transactions in industrial securities, including all those speculative deals within the account which at present escape taxation altogether.

The Right Hon and learned Gentleman yesterday referred to the banks.[1] I hope that he really will stop the banks, by direction, if necessary, lending for speculative deals; and it is worthy of consideration whether the interest on borrowed bank money – at any rate, the bank money borrowed not for the purposes of trade – should no longer rank as a charge against taxation.

These are a number of things which I hope the Government will consider, because the statement that we had yesterday contained no proposals related either to production or exports. I know that these proposals – and I could suggest many more – may be controversial, but at least they are relevant. They would provide the political and economic and social background of purposive planning, of mobilisation of the nation's resources for national needs, of social justice not only done but manifestly seen to be done, because, without these

[1] Selwyn Lloyd: Chancellor of the Exchequer.

things, no Government can conscientiously appeal for the efforts and sacrifices that are needed.

The Government, by their drift, by their complacency, by their perpetuation – indeed, increase – of injustice, have lost the moral right to make that appeal. They have themselves become an irrelevance, a tedious, boring, ineffective irrelevance, and that is why, in our amendment, we call not only for new measures but for new men, who can lead the nation to its rightful place in the world.

SECTION III

Monetary Policy and Taxation

The speeches and articles in this section are on specialised aspects of monetary and fiscal policy.

The debate on monetary policy on 25th November, 1959, took place on the Report of the Committee, presided over by Lord Radcliffe, on Monetary Policy and Institutions. This Committee had been established by Mr Macmillan, when Chancellor in 1956, and its highly technical and authoritative report was widely regarded as having confirmed the arguments put by Labour spokesmen in the 1950s. In particular, the Committee attacked the 'automaticity' of a system of monetary regulation – 'this is no gentle hand on the steering wheel' – the system of local authority financing, the policy of high interest rates, and the theory enunciated principally by Mr Thorneycroft that the economy could be kept in balance by a tight control on 'the quantity of money'.

The Committee's Report was so unacceptable to the Government that the motion moved by Mr Heathcoat Amory, the then Chancellor, merely 'took note' of it; the Labour amendment I moved 'welcomed' it, thanked the Committee and went on to specify the particular recommendations which the Opposition particularly welcomed.

The speech on world liquidity made before the American Chamber of Commerce, on 15th May, 1963, was an elaboration of a theme which I had developed in a speech to the National Press Club of Washington the previous month. (See Section V chapter ten.) In the Washington speech, I surveyed the international scene, with particular reference to Anglo-American relations and called for a new and dynamic approach to problems of liquidity.

The two articles on taxation were written for The Financial Times *and appeared in each case on Budget Day, ie before the Chancellor's Budget Speech. The article of 1960, written on the theme 'The Budget I would like', turned out to anticipate, to a surprising extent, the Chancellor's actual proposals, particularly in the field of anti-avoidance measures.* The Financial Times *leader the next day commented wrily that this article was by far the most accurate of all the forecasts, but pointed out that it had been written not as a forecast, but as the proposal of a Socialist Shadow Chancellor.*

CHAPTER FIVE

*

Radcliffe debate, House of Commons
25th November, 1959

MR HAROLD WILSON (HUYTON): I beg to move,[1] to leave out from 'House' to the end of the Question and to add instead thereof:

> Welcomes the Report of the Radcliffe Committee, thanks the Committee for its thorough and authoritative survey, and calls on Her Majesty's Government to implement, in particular, those recommendations of the Committee which relate to the supremacy of the Chancellor of the Exchequer in financial policy, the relations between the Treasury and the Bank of England, local authority borrowing, capital needs of publicly owned industries, and the position of part-time directors of the Bank of England.

The Chancellor's[2] speech was profoundly disappointing. Although he did make some perfunctory remarks of gratitude to the Radcliffe Committee, it was quite clear that he has virtually rejected every recommendation in the Report. Apart from one or two slightly fussy alterations in the mechanism by which changes in the Bank Rate will be announced, and a general promise to look at the statistical position, he has not accepted any of the fundamental recommendations of the Committee. It was quite clear from the right hon Gentleman's speech that the Report is to gather dust in the Government's already overcrowded pigeon-holes.

The Chancellor came to bury Radcliffe, not praise him. It is yet another case of the Government appointing a high-level committee

[1] The Government had moved merely to take note of the Report.
[2] Mr Heathcoat Amory.

to look into these questions, to spend quite a long time, in this case two-and-a-half years, saying, 'No, we cannot talk about monetary policy because we have this Committee', and then, when the Committee produces its report, the Government say a few well-chosen words about it, reject its main conclusions and go on as before. There have been even more spectacular illustrations of that in the course of this year's history.

Our approach is that this is a most valuable Report. We are certainly not committed to all its details or lines of reasoning. Why should we be? Is there any reason? We do not agree with every detail or all its lines of reasoning, but it must be regarded as an important and abiding study of the working of our monetary system and institutions. No one would regard the Committee as composed of revolutionaries. All its members are men of the highest distinction. Most of them would have been regarded as safe and orthodox, men who might be expected, wherever possible, to endorse the existing system.

What has happened? They have produced a unanimous Report. There are different kinds of unanimous reports, but this one is not based on the lowest common multiple of committee harmony. It is a Report which is positive and stringent. While the Committee treated established doctrines and institutions with due courtesy and respect, it has been effective and at times devastating in tearing away the veils of obscurantism and mystique with which so much of our monetary system is surrounded.

The Committee has been equally frank in exposing the arguments which have sometimes masqueraded as sound economic theory, arguments with which we have become familiar week by week in the financial journals, arguments which we have heard so often from right hon and hon Members opposite when they have sought to rationalise or to provide some kind of rationalisation for policies that were proving so costly to this country and its place in the world.

Above all, I would characterise the Radcliffe Report as belonging not to 1914 or to 1939, but to 1959 and the 1960s, and being animated by neither mystique nor intellectual dishonesty, but by plain and informed commonsense. It is inevitable that comparison will be made with the Report of the Macmillan Committee,[1] which, with

[1] Presided over by Lord Macmillan (a Law Lord) and including Mr (later Lord) Keynes and Mr Ernest Bevin.

all its faults, remained for so many years the classical analysis of the City in the early thirties. If that comparison is to be made, Lord Radcliffe and his colleagues need not fear it.

We all recognise that in this debate we are dealing with part of a much wider subject: the conduct of the economic policy of the country and of the responsibilities that we bear in a much wider sense, both in relation to the sterling area and as a nation which has a decisive part to play in world trade and finance.

In this House, we differ greatly about methods, techniques and ideologies in these questions about economic and social priorities, but there can be no disagreement on either side about the fundamental objectives of our economic policy. We have to play our part in expanding world trade and in creating a system dedicated to economic growth, and particularly to the advancement of the underdeveloped countries. At home, we have to secure full employment without causing the social distortions and hardships that are inseparable from inflation and rising prices. At the same time, and by all the means open to us, we have to secure a degree of economic growth which both quantitatively and qualitatively measures up to the needs of our position in the world. We have to do all this while securing equally for all our people a fair and equitable share in the fruits of our national production. These are our aims and there would be no disagreement on either side of the House about them. To achieve them, we need – and I hope that we are all agreed about this – not one policy, but an armoury of policies, budgetary, monetary and social, as well as more direct controls influencing both public and private industry.

I am sure that Lord Radcliffe and his colleagues would agree that their Report can be studied only as part of a much wider setting in which all these instruments play their full part. They would agree that their Report discusses only one aspect of the kind of policy – an informed and positive policy – carried out by Ministers, whatever their political views, impelled by a sense of purpose. Without that, the Report does not make sense.

If the Report does one thing, it is to discredit the notion of monetary policy as a single panacea which is adequate in itself to deal with the problem. Although we shall, naturally, devote most of this debate to monetary matters, it will be meaningful only if we regard monetary policy, important though it is, as having a strictly limited rôle to play in attaining the economic objectives that we have set ourselves.

I do not intend to spend much time on the Committee's useful analysis of the big changes which have occurred since the time of the Macmillan Report. We should all agree that the Radcliffe Committee is right in emphasising such things as the acceptance of the need for full employment, the structural changes in British industry which have taken place, especially in our export trade, the tendency here and abroad to persistently rising prices, the steady and virtually insatiable pressure from overseas demand, particularly for capital goods, and the striving for economic advancement, and the resulting world-wide shortage of capital from which the country, in terms of both economic and social capital, has not been immune.

In listing all these changes, the Committee is right in drawing attention to the vast technological developments, particularly since the war, requiring a high capital ratio in investment and, particularly in this country, also the growth of hire purchase, the development of new financial institutions, the problems presented for monetary management by high taxation and the growth of the National Debt and the new problem presented by the nationalised industries and the size of the national Budget, not to mention the problem of the local authorities.

The Committee is right, too, in emphasising, as the Chancellor has said, the importance of external considerations, the problem of reserves and external indebtedness. All of these present revolutionary changes from the days when monetary techniques were first originated and developed in this country.

It is not possible for anyone today to do justice to all the descriptive sections of the Report – for example, Chapter III, 'The financing of the public sector', and Chapter IV, the authoritative description of the financial institutions in the private sector. I would, however, draw attention on Chapter IV to the virtual omission of any description, almost of any reference, to the Stock Exchange. It may be that hon Members think that it defies description or analysis of the kind that the Radcliffe Committee has applied to other sections of our financial institutions, but since it is always held out as an essential mechanism in providing funds for investment, it is difficult to justify its exclusion from this survey.

I hope that the Chancellor will consider this matter and will consider whether we do not need in the modern world, at present, an independent inquiry into the Stock Exchange parallel to that which the Radcliffe Committee has done with great thoroughness and even ruthlessness into other financial institutions such as the joint stock banks, the acceptance houses, the discount houses, and all the rest. I put it to the Chancellor that he should consider this.

Looking at all of these descriptive chapters, including, for example, the one on the Bank of England, we can only regard this as an interim debate. We shall all be much more fully informed on both the descriptive and the analytical sections of the Report when we have the volumes of the written and oral evidence before us. That will show us in great detail not only what is happening, but, no less revealing, what those who are at the centre of things think is happening, which is just as much a fact as what is actually happening.

Undoubtedly, the central chapter of the Report is Chapter VI, called 'The influence of monetary measures', which provides a fresh and, some would say, devastating analysis of the use of monetary measures in the eight years since they were revived with such a flourish of trumpets from 1951 onwards. This chapter also gives us the Committee's view about the scope and relevance of such measures in the years immediately ahead of us.

The classical picture of monetary techniques with which we have been so often presented is that of a beautifully sensitive instrument, delicately calibrated and adjusted, capable of bringing into play powerful forces at the mere touch of a lever here or the application of pressure there, all this working in a way that is somehow supposed to be neutral – that is, innocent of all the distortions of production and trade which are said to be inherent in physical controls or even budgetary policies.

I shall not weary the House with quotations of all the moving speeches that we have had on this theme from four successive Chancellors of the Exchequer, not to mention such apostles of the classical thesis as Sir Oscar Hobson, Lord Robbins, Sir Roy Harrod, and others on whom these Chancellors have relied so greatly for publicly or privately-expressed views.

We were given to understand that this delicate instrument – the rate of interest – supported with all the other monetary levers, would bring savings into equilibrium with investment, and, in particular, would regulate in the national interest capital investment in stocks of materials and in work in progress, and, ultimately, through the supply of money, the rate of interest would control the total volume of demand in the country, not to mention its powerful effect on foreign exchanges, both by altering the interest differential between countries and also by creating confidence in financial centres abroad.

We were also told that, with all these monetary techniques, we should be able to see an advancement and not a retardation of industrial progress and capital growth. This theory, I do not think the Chancellor will disagree, has been the central inspiration of the entire economic policy of the Government for eight years, and the effect of the Radcliffe Committee's commentary on it, after a full investigation of the history of those eight years, is utterly to destroy this theory.

First, let us look at the Committee's analysis of the effect on capital investment in plant, machinery and stocks. We all remember the classical exposition of this thesis in the imperishable words of the present Viscount Chandos, speaking from this Box on 2nd November, 1950[1]:

> If the industrialist thinks that a 5% interest rate for borrowing his money will still leave him with a profit, the plants will be built, but the marginal capital investments will be discarded. – (OFFICIAL REPORT, 2nd November, 1950; Vol. 480, c. 332.)

With all respect to the noble Lord, everything he said on that occasion has been proved by the Radcliffe Committee to be nonsense. The Chancellor will be surprised, and perhaps even flattered, to know that I study his speeches with more care than perhaps he does himself. We know how modest he is. Only two or three weeks ago, I quoted one of his Budget speeches, with which he immediately disagreed, not realising the source from which I was quoting. I can assure him that his speeches are my favourite bedtime reading, and that is why I never get enough sleep. I also assure him that I was not misrepresenting the view which he put across. I do not say that he has ever said that this monetary policy alone would solve all problems. Of course, I have not said that, but what the Chancellor has done, though in not quite so picturesque a fashion as his predecessor, is to suggest that

[1] Then Mr Oliver Lyttelton, Conservative 'Shadow Chancellor'.

the rate of interest and control over the supply of money were at the root of this problem. I will give some quotations to bear this out. First, perhaps the right hon Gentleman will not mind this somewhat long quotation from paragraph 451 of the Radcliffe Committee's Report:

> When we confined our questions strictly to the direct effect of interest rate changes in making business men alter their decisions to buy or sell goods and services, we were met by general scepticism. The insignificance of interest changes in relation to other costs and to the risks involved was emphasised to us again and again, in relation not only to fixed investment but also to stocks of commodities. We were told also how taxation in effect halves the interest cost; this belief has evidently bitten so deeply into business consciousness that it may well weaken the force of interest rate changes even when it is not strictly applicable. We heard from the executive heads or financial directors of several great industrial firms which are themselves responsible for about one-eighth of the gross fixed investment within manufacturing industry in the United Kingdom that in their plans for capital development they assume a more or less steady interest charge and would not alter their existing plans even if they thought somewhat higher rates had come to stay.

The Committee went on to say that, even when they took evidence about smaller firms, and from experienced bank managers about the position of smaller firms,

> Here also we were met with general scepticism.

What was true of interest rates was true also of the credit squeeze policy of making money hard to obtain. Here I think the Radcliffe Committee, echoing what has frequently been said from this Box, fairly emphasised that the credit squeeze had borne more hardly on the smaller firms than the large firms. The Government's financial policy has been based on a wider claim than the effectiveness of rates of interest. They have claimed that high interest rates and the credit squeeze were a powerful influence via the supply of money on total internal demand in this country.

Here, again, I could quote from all the four Chancellors of the past five years, but I will spare the House that. I will, however, quote one or two passages from the speeches of the right hon Member for

Monmouth (Mr Thorneycroft), the arch-apostle of this school. On 19th September, 1957 – the day of the 7% Bank Rate – referring to his financial measures, he said:

> Their object is to ensure that the supply of money and the consequent pressure of demand do not exceed the manpower and resources which are in fact available.

Five days later, in Washington, he said:

> The purpose of the measures which I announced before leaving London has been to go to what I concede to be the root of any inflation – namely, the supply of money . . .

Again, a few sentences later:

> Our purpose then is to limit the money supply.

Again, at the annual Bankers' Dinner at the Mansion House on 9th October, he said:

> There is, however, no doubt about one thing, and that is what enables inflation to go on. What enables it to go on is the supply of money, whether it be new money, or existing money travelling rather faster. Our policy is to halt the increase in the supply of money.

On the next day, at the Conservative Party Conference, he said:

> We are not prepared to finance inflation. We do not intend to provide the cash for an upward spiral of costs and prices. We have planned to put a limit on the supply of money. Our policy goes to the root of the problem. It tackles the main source of inflation which is the supply of money.

And much more in the same vein, though I will not weary the House with any more of these quotations.

We remember – and this is the more serious point – that this crude theory that we could limit the total volume of internal demand by attacking the supply of money was pushed to the point where right hon Gentlemen opposite were prepared to see unemployment develop in this attempt to hold down the supply of money. Indeed, the unemployment which did develop last year was a direct result of these policies, and that unemployment would have risen further this year but for the fact that a windfall gain in import prices enabled the Government to reverse these policies.

The point of the right hon Gentleman's policy was that it made deliberate cuts in the capital investment programmes of Britsh Industry. They created the unemployment, and indeed, as one of my hon Friends reminds me, capital investment in this boom period has not picked up. We have now reached a point where the Governor of the Bank of England is beginning to warn about the boom getting out of hand, yet we are still in the position that capital investment has barely begun to pick up.

Let us see what the Committee had to say, after taking evidence from all who could help them on this question of the supply of money, including the right hon Gentleman the Member for Monmouth, the Governor[1] and Lord Robbins. In the first place, the Committee rightly pointed out, as we have done once or twice, that the supply of money was not so rigidly controlled as the Government intended. Hire-purchase finance and the independent finance houses, including mushroom banking companies, fill a very large part of the gap. The Committee points out, too, the grave harm done to the economy by the harsh and unilateral cuts in the investment programmes of the nationalised industries. The Committee calls them the residuary legatees of Government financial policy. It points to the effect of these cuts in investment programmes on certain important sectors of the engineering industry.

The Committee concludes with these words:

> It does not seem that changes in interest rates or interference with sources of funds for hire purchase companies have had much ultimate effect on the total pressure of demand for goods.

Again, says the Committee,

> Our broad conclusions on the effects of these measures during the 1950s are that (1) the obstructions to particular channels of finance have had no effect on the pressure of total demand, but have made for much inefficiency in financial organisation; (2) that the controls of hire purchase terms have had sizeable impact, of a once-for-all kind, on each major change; and (3) that these sizeable effects on total demand have implied major directional effects which, though

[1] Of the Bank of England, Mr (now Lord) Cobbold.

> sometimes deliberately sought, have in general been detrimental to industrial efficiency.

So, according to the Committee, monetary measures were ineffective, detrimental, and they were not even neutral for they had 'major directional effects' harmful to industrial efficiency.

Indeed, the Committee goes on to say that if a Government is seeking to limit total demand, as every Government must at some time, the manipulation of interest rates is not to be compared, for its total impact on demand, with either hire purchase restrictions or, of course, with the possibilities of Budget policy. Then comes 'the most unkindest cut of all' in the Committee's final judgment on monetary policy in the 1950s:

> It is far removed from the smooth and widespread adjustment sometimes claimed as the virtue of monetary action; this is no gentle hand on the steering wheel that keeps a well-driven car in its right place on the road.

The only concession the Committee makes is that, in an emergency, a sharp rise in interest rates combined with other measures, in what the Committee calls a 'package deal', can have an effect both at home and abroad. We all agree about that. But this, again, is not 'the gentle hand on the steering wheel'. It is a shuddering and screeching of brakes, a scorching of tyres, deliberately intended to produce shock and abrasions. But the whole classical theory of monetary management tells us that the purpose of monetary policy is to avoid such emergencies and disasters.

The Committee clearly feels that hire purchase controls, not to mention such direct controls as building licences, have their part to play, especially in critical conditions. 'But,' says the Committee – and here I quote from paragraph 514 –

> When all has been said on the possibility of monetary action and of its likely efficacy, our conclusion is that monetary measures cannot alone be relied upon to keep in nice balance an economy subject to major strains from both without and within. Monetary measures can help, but that is all.

So the emperor had no clothes after all. As in the Hans Andersen story, the Establishment was wrong and the less sophisticated onlooker was right.

I turn now from that rather central chapter of the Report to the analysis of the monetary institutions, especially the joint stock banks and the discount market. Here, I think – I believe the Chancellor will agree – the Committee is clearly right in showing how ineffective control based on the old 8% cash ratio concept has become, and the Committee rightly stresses the greater importance of the liquidity ratio. But, as we are all aware, control of this ratio in modern conditions is very far from being automatic, and the Committee once again stresses the ineffectiveness even of interest rate changes for this purpose.

We all know that higher interest rates can force losses on the banks if they are forced to sell some of their short bonds before maturity, although, even there, as a result of higher interest rates, the banks are, of course, able to charge higher rates on their advances and so compensate themselves, in whole or in part, for any loss they make on realising their bonds. It is for this reason – the relative ineffectiveness either of cash ratio or liquidity ratio control – that other methods have been advocated, from compulsory liquidity ratios to special deposits from Treasury deposit receipts to a compulsory advances-deposits ratio. I am sorry that the Chancellor did not deal with any of these questions this afternoon.

On many occasions, we have pressed the Government to adopt a system of mandatory liquidity ratios, with power to vary the percentage as circumstances change. It is interesting to note that this view has been supported by the Radcliffe Committee. It supports the principle of mandatory liquidity ratios. We would support, also, its proposal for a mandatory ratio between advances and deposits, again, leaving room for flexibility on the percentage, with power also – I think that this will be necessary – to extend control to competing financial institutions. Certainly, in periods of potential danger, this kind of control would be effective in preventing the banks from strengthening or reinforcing their liquid assets through sales to the discount market of longer term securities in exchange for Treasury Bills or other short-term assets and thus getting round or circumventing the liquidity ratio control.

The Chancellor, eighteen months ago, when he announced the end of the credit squeeze, went so far as to institute a system of special deposits, a system designed to freeze or sterilise a proportion of the banks' liquid resources. I am sure that the right hon Gentleman will not mind if I remind him that we had proposed such a system as long ago as the 9th May, 1956,[1] as an alternative to the credit squeeze which we then opposed. I am glad that, in the end, he came to accept this proposal. He will recall that, when we first proposed it, we based it not so much on the Treasury deposit receipts system but on the Australian model which, I am sure, was very much in his mind when he made his announcement eighteen months ago.

Although this is actually beyond the ambit of the Radcliffe Report itself, Mr Deputy-Speaker, I should like, once again, to press on the Government the suggestion we made that special deposits or a revived system of Treasury deposit receipts, if one likes, could be used, just as Budget surpluses could be used, to enable the Government to operate the system we have advocated for two-tier interest rates – one rate, the higher rate, for the general purpose of the market and the lower of the two interest rates for such essential purposes as local authority housing, colonial development, and farm credit. I am sorry that the Committee did not consider this proposal together with its recommendation about local authority borrowing through the Public Works Loan Board to which the Chancellor referred and to which I shall turn in a few minutes.

I have not time to comment on the Committee's examination of most of the other financial institutions to which it referred. I think that we shall be debating some of them quite soon. I want, however, to say a word about the discount market. Here again, I was surprised that the Chancellor had so little to say. There are many people who have questioned whether the discount market has any real function to perform in the modern world, whether it is anything more than just a survival from the age of the Forsytes.

Certainly, the Committee, in its examination of the problem, has stripped the subject of much of its mystique. The discount houses are not needed to ensure that the Treasury bill tender is fully taken up, and no one, incidentally, has ever satisfactorily explained to me why the joint stock banks should not tender direct for Treasury bills. Perhaps the Chancellor will tell us at some time. Again – I know that this has caused concern in high places – the Committee, on balance, condemns the discount markets' syndicate or cartel system in bidding for bills. I think that the Committee is probably right in saying that

[1] On the Second Reading of the Finance Bill of that year.

this syndicate system inhibits lending by other concerns. Indeed, the Committee says that the discount houses have deliberately manipulated their bids up and down in order to discourage outside tenderers. To this extent, the practice is putting up the cost to the Treasury and is causing instability in short-term money rates.

Thus, the justification for the continued existence of the discount houses lies not on their alleged indispensibility to the Treasury in covering the bill tender but in the much humbler rôle of providing a useful market for short-term Government securities. I think that no one will disagree with that.

Sir Henry d'Avigdor Goldsmid (Walsall, South): The right hon Gentleman is always fair-minded. I should like to bring to his attention that there are five particular virtues or qualities of the discount market which are mentioned in the Report, of which the most important, I suggest, is the last, that the discount houses are doing work at a trifling cost in labour and real resources, and the work they are doing is saving the banking system the inconveniences which would arise from fluctuations in their liquidity, apart also from producing the market in bills and bonds to which I think the right hon Gentleman has referred.

Moreover, it is not, I think, correct for the right hon Gentleman to say that the discount market makes profits from manipulation of the rates because, as is also pointed out in the Report, the banks are very quick indeed to adjust their buying rate for bills to that established at the last tender.

Mr Wilson: I hope that the hon Gentleman will have the opportunity of developing this point at greater length. I would just say that I stressed the importance of the discount market in relation to providing a market for the short-term assets.

The last point which he mentioned was in relation to their inability to exploit their monopoly profit. In fact, I was just coming to that when the hon Gentleman interrupted me, because I think one ought to draw attention to a significant paragraph in the Report, paragraph 168, where it states that the safeguard against the discount market exploiting its quasi-monopoly position by increasing its profit margin on bills is the fact that the joint stock banks can always, in turn, squeeze the discount houses by altering the terms on which they lend money to the market, so that the monopoly profit is merged into the total profit position of the clearing banks.

Unfortunately, the Committee says that this is a subject into which it has made no inquiry. One wonders why not. One accepts the position of the discount market, but surely there should have been an inquiry into what the banks do with the profit. Surely the taxpayer is entitled to know how much the whole operation is costing the country, and I hope that matter will be investigated.

The amendment which I have moved calls upon the Government to implement, in particular, certain recommendations of the Report. First, there are the statistical improvements, to which the Chancellor referred. We all remember that the Prime Minister, when he was Chancellor, promised us three years ago a fundamental improvement in monetary statistics. We remember his elegant remarks about looking up trains in last year's Bradshaw. The Report shows that we are still doing it: indeed, for some trains, the statistics are three years old and for others there are no statistics at all. Worse than that, the Committee confirms the impression which many of us get from reading the evidence given to the Parker Tribunal[1] that so many of the major decisions on monetary and economic policy in recent years have been taken in the most amateurish fashion, on the basis of hunches, guesswork and contacts from the 'old boy' network. We have never known until years afterwards – which is a criticism of the Labour Government equally as of the present Government – whether a fall in the gold reserves, as happened in 1951, was not associated primarily with changes in stocks. We did not know the facts about that for many years afterwards. Even last year's much vaunted balance of payments surplus of £450 million turned out to be overestimated by over £100 million when the Chancellor came to do his figures again this autumn.

Again, referring to the central problem of debt management, the Committee says:

> The authorities themselves, in assessing the demand for debts, rely mainly on their personal contacts in financial and commercial circles.

In its demand for what the Committee called 'cleaner statistics' – and

[1] The Tribunal of 1957–8 into allegations of a leakage of the Government's intention to raise the Bank Rate on 18th September, 1957.

there is no immorality in the use of this word; we know what it means – and for figures on such things as the holding of bonds of different maturities, in particular, I hope the authorities and the Chancellor will really implement the Report in full and not be put off with any obscurantism on the part of any of these financial institutions, however powerful.

Equally important is the recommendation about publication of more information by the Bank of England which it already possesses but has not made public. I think in this respect we lag behind almost every other reputable central bank in the world. Only the Gosbank tells us less than the Bank of England about the monetary state of the country.

The second recommendation to which I turn deals with relations between the Chancellor and the Bank of England, to which the right hon Gentleman referred. I do not think there should be any need to stress the primacy of position which the Chancellor should occupy in this matter and no one will suggest, after reading the Report, that to stress it will mean that the Bank will lose in either authority or influence as an institution. But we really cannot have vital economic decisions, such as, for example, the biggest Bank Rate increase for forty years, discussed with part-time directors nearly three weeks before the Chancellor hears about them.

I think I can claim that in this section the Radcliffe Report closely follows the line which we took in the Bank Rate debate in 1958. On that occasion, we advised against the proposal that the Bank of England should become a Government Department, but we stressed that

> the initiative and control should lie in the Treasury, and any doubt about where the power of decision lies should be removed.

We also stressed the idea of a joint committee very similar to that proposed by Lord Radcliffe and his colleagues and the need for a more systematic exchange of staffs at all levels between the Bank and the Treasury. The two institutions are only three miles apart, but sometimes they could appear to be 3,000 miles apart.

I suspect that the Bank and the Treasury have adopted more intimate association in discussing how they could best put the Radcliffe Report into cold storage than on any other major issue in the past five years. I think that the Joint Committee of both institutions has been functioning over the last five months. Perhaps, over-simplifying, one can say that Bank officials have great expertise without much political insight or responsibility, while Treasury officials, responsible as they are to a political head, have a sense of political responsibility but inevitably less expertise. I want more of both qualities and I think that an exchange of staff would help to promote that.

On the question of part-time directors, too, the Report underlines the warning which we gave in February, 1958. We advised against confining the board to full-time directors. I think, here again, that both sides are in complete agreement. We do not want to see a full-time executive board on the lines of the Federal Reserve Board in the United States, for example. We supported, and this may surprise some hon Members, the system of part-time directors of standing and experience, but suggested two things: first, that they should be drawn from a more representative circle; and, secondly, we also said that there was no need at all for part-time directors to be involved in major and secret policy decisions.

Referring to the crisis of September, 1957 – and the circumstances of that time are rather special – the Radcliffe Committee has expressed itself with great frankness and realism. I ask the House to consider the implications of the following paragraph. I apologise for so many quotations, but I think that it is important. It states:

> In such a case the embarrassment to which a director can be subjected is a reality. If he is actively participating in the conduct of any such business as that of a merchant bank or issuing house which operates in the City's markets for money or capital he may be called upon to discuss or decide upon questions to which his knowledge of the authorities' impending action is very relevant. He cannot, of course, take advantage of that knowledge: on the other hand it is not always easy for him to adopt an attitude of silence or neutrality without giving just that warning of some action to come which it is his whole concern to avoid.

That very frank and fair comment by the Committee is exactly what we said was the danger in the debate of 1957.

I hope that one result of the Report will be that the Government will accept the views that we have more than once stated, that the joint stock banks should be more fully represented in the counsels of the Bank of England. I once referred to the merchant bankers going in by the gentlemen's gate to the pavilion and the joint stock bankers going in by the players' gate. But we cannot afford any of these Edwardian notions in the modern world.

In this connection, I welcome the innovation by one of the Chancellor's predecessors when he himself met the joint stock banks' directors. I think that until that time strict protocol demanded that all contacts between the Chancellor and the joint stock banks had to be made through the Governor. I hope that the Chancellor will tell us that he will make a regular practice of such meetings as that started by one of his predecessors.

I now turn to the last two points highlighted in the amendment – borrowing by local authorities and publicly-owned industries. The Chancellor, very fairly, described the history of these particular problems. The House will remember how right hon Gentlemen ended the system of direct borrowing through the PWLB[1] and drove local authorities to make their terms with the market. When that happened and ever since we bitterly condemned their action. It has been costly, and I would go further than the Committee and say that it has put up house rents and has discriminated between larger and smaller local authorities.

In this matter, local authorities and the citizens they serve – ratepayers, tenants and consumers of local authority services – have been notably sacrificed to private gain. The Committee drew attention to the problem of monetary managment, saying:

> For all these reasons we recommend that the Exchequer should stand ready to provide long-term capital through the Public Works Loan Board, at the current gilt-edged rate (at time of borrowing) for the relevant maturity, to any local authority that is not able, or does not want, to raise the money it requires in the market on its own credit at a comparable rate.

As the House knows, we would go further and propose a two-tier interest rate system to benefit local authorities.

Similarly, we have the problem of financing the nationalised industries. Again, the Chancellor gave us the history. The present Prime Minister, then Chancellor of the Exchequer, took powers in

[1] Public Works Loan Board.

the 1956 Finance Bill, in the interests of monetary management, to arrange for all the investment needs of publicly-owned industries to be supplied direct from the Treasury. These powers were limited in time, and the present Chancellor, not showing great courage, has twice renewed those powers for one year only. We can understand the difficulties of the Chancellor and of successive Tory Chancellors on this question. They have to deal with a number of active back benchers whose support for the Government's maintenance of public ownership in these industries falls somewhat short of enthusiasm.

Only this summer we moved an amendment to the Finance Bill to make this system permanent. We pressed the amendment to a division. The Chancellor and his supporters voted against it. Once again, the Radcliffe Committee has endorsed our line and I hope that this time the Chancellor will take his courage in both hands – he knows that this is right both for the publicly-owned industries and for the Treasury – and will legislate on a more permanent basis.

There are one or two things with which I should like to deal briefly. I hope that the Chancellor will study again the part of the Report dealing with the Post Office Giro system, which is only lightly, but encouragingly, touched on. I suggest that the Chancellor joins with the Postmaster-General in setting up an objective and factual committee of inquiry to see whether such a system could be introduced. We know that it is in great vogue on the Continent and is very useful. I hope to suggest that the Chancellor should have this matter considered technically by a separate committee. I have a perfectly open mind on it.

Obviously, when dealing with a Report of this length and complexity, we can only pick out certain things. I have picked out the points which I thought were of fundamental importance, in view of our past debates.

I should have liked time to deal with some other important issues, including farm credit, but I must say a word about the key subject of export finance. Both sides of the House would be ready to pay great tribute to the Export Credits Guarantee Department, a publicly-owned body which has been highly successful in a sphere where private insurance could not have been expected to tread. I am not making a party point, but the Report confirms what many exporters know, namely, that present facilities are inadequate. The ECGD, probably rightly, maintains its limit at five years, and through the Berne Club it is instrumental in stopping an international rivalry in Government credit terms.

I do not think that we want an international competition to see how long we can offer credit to particular exporters, but, especially for capital goods with a long life and exports to under-developed areas, better terms are needed than those it is possible to obtain through the ECGD. Perhaps private enterprise, with the help of the insurance companies and the banking system, can co-operate to provide this help as they do, for example, in tanker finance.

If this is not possible I seriously put to the Chancellor the proposition that he should consider the establishment for this country of something on the lines of an export-import bank. I would not want him to follow all the precedents set by the Export-Import Bank in the United States, but this point is worth considering. In the era of keen competition which we must expect in world markets, most of all in heavy capital goods, we must not allow our industries to be handicapped by deficiencies in the financial system.

As the Report makes clear, as we look ahead to the future of world trade and payments, one thing stands out clearly – the shortage of world liquidity and the danger this represents not only to the stability of individual currencies but to the future of world trade itself. During the past twenty years, the value of world trade has increased about fourfold, whereas the volume of the currency reserves of the world has increased by only 50%. Even the recent measures to expand the resources of the International Monetary Fund, which we all welcome, will make only a small contribution to the problem. I should, therefore, like the Chancellor to consider this matter. I have given him notice of it only today, but I hope that we shall hear from him on a later occasion.

There have been times under both Governments when the £ has been weak, our reserves consistently inadequate and the future of trade in danger. Today, for as long as it lasts and for reasons which we all understand, the dollar is in a relatively weak position. All of us realise, I think, what would happen if the US were to feel itself driven into protection or, for that matter, deflation, which might have just as serious an effect.

Now is the time, I suggest, when the £ is not under attack by financial gossip-mongers, for this country to take the initiative in proposing a world monetary conference to examine the whole problem of world liquidity and, whatever we may or may not succeed in achieving about the international price of gold – we know the difficulties there – to suggest that at the very least the lending powers of the International Monetary Fund be expanded, for instance, by increasing the first *tranche* of lending to 40% of the quota, and to propose – this is a more fundamental suggestion which I should like the Chancellor to consider at his leisure – that member countries should legislate to provide that deposits with the International Monetary Fund should be regarded as equivalent to gold. I hope that the right hon Gentleman will consider this matter and will put it forward on an international basis.

In the nineteenth century, private banks began to regard their fundamental reserves as being not only their gold, but any money that they were holding at the Bank of England and they could settle debts by cheques drawn on the reserves they had at the Bank of England. Why should not we do this on an international scale? Why should we be tied to gold reserves as the only acceptable international currency? Why should not our quotas with the International Monetary Fund be added to the gold reserves, to increase fundamentally the volume of world liquidity? I would hope to see the IMF in time, with suitable safeguards and changes, transformed into something more approaching an international central bank to deal with problems of world deflation, not excluding the use of open market operations. I hope that the Government will look at this proposal with an open mind and will take the initiative now, when we are relatively strong – the initiative for which, I believe in this respect, the whole world is waiting.

To sum up, we on this side regard the Report as very useful. It sets in proper perspective the rôle of monetary policy and shows how limited that rôle must essentially be. It does not set out to solve the central problem of our age – how to expand production and promote lasting economic growth without sliding into inflation. It is interesting to note that even the Cohen Council[1] which is not usually quoted with approval from this side of the House, states in its third Report that we have not solved the problem that all the monetary squeezes of the past few years have involved – a very heavy cost, in terms of figures, to expand and invest enough. When we get the Cohen Council

[1] The short-lived Committee on Prices and Incomes set up by Mr Peter Thorneycroft in 1957 and known as The Three Wise Men.

saying that – taking the line that we have taken so often ourselves – there is obviously need for some new thinking on the subject.

The solutions of that problem – whether by measures of public or private investment or by radical changes in taxation affecting investment, and so on – all lie outside the field of this debate. What is relevant is how we are to prevent the expansion we need – which, for the moment, we are getting – leading to inflation; and here, especially in relation to a cost-push inflation and rising incomes and costs, the Committee has little to contribute.

We have certainly never had a clear statement from the Government on this from the days when the right hon Gentleman the Member for Monmouth was Chancellor of the Exchequer, because the Government have always thought that all problems of inflation, wherever they come from, can be dealt with by attacking total demand.

That is why, throughout the past few years, we on this side have always emphasised that this problem cannot be solved in a democratic society without a purposive policy involving budgetary needs, monetary policy and physical controls, and, above all, the creation of a social climate which will enable a Government of whatever party to appeal for, and to deserve, co-operation from every section of the community.

SECTION IV

Common Market

The Common Market controversy was at the centre of British politics from the summer of 1961 to the abrupt breakdown of the negotiations in January, 1963. On 31st July, 1961, Mr Macmillan announced the decision of the Government to apply for membership. A two-day debate took place in the Commons on 2nd–3rd August. The Prime Minister and Mr Gaitskell spoke on the 2nd and I opened the debate on the second day.

Formal negotiations began in October and from that time onwards there were regular reports to the House by the Lord Privy Seal, Mr Heath, who was in charge of the negotiations, with debates from time to time.

In the summer and autumn of 1962 the pace quickened. The Commonwealth Prime Ministers' Conference showed the great perturbation felt by most Commonwealth countries about the likely terms of Britain's entry. Mr Gaitskell presided over a Conference of Commonwealth Labour leaders and this hardened his attitude against entry on anything like the terms then being discussed.

The two Party Conferences, Labour's in Brighton and the Conservatives' in Llandudno, were dominated by the issue, the main event at Brighton being the historic speech delivered by Hugh Gaitskell when introducing the Party's policy statement.

The first opportunity for a debate came on 7th–8th November, and I wound up on the second day. Further developments in the Brussels negotiations led to a further debate on 13th December.

As a result of the breakdown of the negotiations in January there was a major debate on 11th February, 1963 which I opened on behalf of the Opposition (three days before my election as Party Leader).

CHAPTER SIX

*

Debate, House of Commons, 3rd August, 1961

MR HAROLD WILSON (HUYTON): Not one speaker in this debate so far, I think, has failed to realise the momentous nature of the issue which we are discussing and deciding in this two-day debate. Even though we sometimes find him lacking in certain of the qualities which we consider essential to statesmanship, the Prime Minister does possess in a large degree one quality which is essential, and that is a deep sense of history. I do not think that he will have missed the parallel between this decision which has now to be taken and that which faced Sir Robert Peel 115 years ago[1], though I think that, for some of the reasons which the right hon Gentleman and my right hon Friend the Member for Leeds, South (Mr Gaitskell) stated, in the sphere of world politics the importance of this issue transcends even that of the Free Trade issue of 1846.

Our position has been stated by my right hon Friend[2] yesterday in his speech. We do not oppose the decision of the Government to embark on negotiations to ascertain the conditions on which Britain can join the European Economic Community, but we do utterly reserve our position on the decision which must be taken when the Government return to this House from the negotiations. We set out in our Amendment some of the conditions we regard as fundamental. Frankly, until we know what terms we can get, anyone who can claim to see this issue in simple black and white terms, in or out, is either a charlatan or a simpleton.

[1] Repeal of the Corn Laws, 1846, which brought to a head the Free Trade issue and split the Tory Party.

[2] Hugh Gaitskell.

I regard it as my duty this afternoon to set out some of our anxieties particularly, but not exclusively, in the field of economics and trade, anxieties which, in our view, must be resolved if the final outcome is to be regarded as acceptable. Our Amendment refers without qualification and without apology to the fact that we shall be negotiating from a position of grave economic weakness. It is no good burking this fact. It will profoundly affect the negotiations. Equally, without going over all the ground of the debates we have had in the last few weeks, the clear responsibility for this weakness lies with the Government who, in unprecedentedly favourable economic conditions, have created weakness out of great potential strength. To be on one's knees through the crippling blows which our economy has sustained and is sustaining is not the right posture for negotiations which can decide our entire future.

The Prime Minister referred to the historical fact that over the centuries Britain has intervened in Europe at times of great crisis, and I think that that is true. He no doubt had in mind, in reviewing the centuries of the past, as other speakers have said, the actions of this country in the reign of Elizabeth I against Philip of Spain and the actions of Chatham and the younger Pitt, two centuries later, but his sense of history sometimes leads him astray. In the reign of Elizabeth I our invisible exports were powerfully aided by the proceeds of piracy – State-supported piracy at that. Today, the pirates are satisfied to batten on the home market, again with State support. The older and the younger Pitt organised the great European coalitions with vast subventions from our national Treasury, but today we have to go cap in hand to the bankers of Europe for loans. So there is a difference this time.

In the economic debate, I warned the Government not to regard their decision about Europe as an exercise in economic escapism. We shall survive – inside or outside Europe – only as a result of our own efforts, our own ability to increase food and exports and to restrain costs. There is no escape and certainly no justification for escapism, but what a difference there would be if we were taking the decision not from weakness, but from the strength which should have been ours to command.

There has been great argument about the economic consequences of going into Europe or staying out – because the decision to stay out would have economic consequences no less profound than the decision to go in. I shall give my views. We already feel some of the effects. As I said in the Common Market debate a year ago, so far we feel them more in terms of a diversion of investment than in a diversion of trade. From the long-term point of view, I think that there is a strong case for saying that in terms of our own industry and our trade in Europe we may gain from being in Europe.

When British industry, which is, perhaps, a little more versatile and adaptable than sometimes appears, has made the changes necessary, we may, and I think that, on balance, we should, gain. But precisely because of our present weakness, I hope that the House will bear with me if I do not spend so much time on the long-term economic position, but spend a little time on the short-term position which would result from a decision to go in now.

Yesterday, the Government announced a loss of £114 million from our gold reserves in July, almost the worst month ever recorded. It was more than 10% of our total reserves gone in a single month despite the special help we are getting from the European central banks. We also read the news of the humiliating necessity of having to borrow – we have not been told officially yet – £700 million from the International Monetary Fund. If that figure is correct it is only £200 million less than we had to borrow in 1946, a year after the war, when our export trade had not been rebuilt and we were still suffering from the shortages caused by the war. Now, 16 years afterwards, if these figures are right, we are borrowing a sum only a little less than what we borrowed just after the war and which has provided a field of propaganda for hon Members opposite for the last 15 years.

The reason why I mention this and the amount of 'hot' money which is pouring in because of the excessive Bank Rate is its relevance to whether we should go into the Common Market or not. I wonder what calculations the Government have made about the short-term effects on sterling if we go in. We can only guess. My view is that the short-term increase in exports will not be as great as the short-term increase in imports to this country. I hope that I am wrong.

In the economic debate, I said that British industry, at any rate in the short-term, is not very responsive to the cold draught of import competition which we hear so much about. If we look at the figures for 1958 to 1960, following the liberalisation of a great deal of our import trade, we find that our imports of manufactured goods from the Common Market countries have risen from a monthly average of

£23½ million to £34·9 million, an increase of 49%, while exports of the same kind of goods, Class D manufactures, rose from £27½ million to £34½ million, an increase of 25%. This may be the pattern if we go in.

What of capital movements? Can anyone challenge the view that if British investments and speculators were free to invest in Europe there would be in the short term a massive withdrawal of funds from this country? As long as there is this grave weakness and this imminent fear of devaluation there will always be those, perhaps in high places, who may say that it is anti-British or derogatory to sterling but it makes sense to them.

The premium on the soft dollar, the only legal route into Europe in recent months, is one measure of the danger. Even if there were no possibility of devaluation, the initial freedom to get into Belgian, French and German securities would mean a fairly big net outflow unbalanced by an equal inflow. Most of these countries have had considerable freedom to bank funds here.

But I do not think that anyone would maintain that there is freedom of capital movement into Europe as there would be under the Treaty of Rome. Of course there is not. If there is, the Government had better look to its economic defences. On balance, I should judge – and I should like to know whether the Government agree – that there would be an immediate and dangerous outflow on current capital account which could quickly exhaust our £700 million loan.

Recently, in the economic debate the President of the Board of Trade[1] stressed the special vulnerability of sterling because of our position as an international banker. He was right, of course. I wonder how the Government view the position of Britain as banker for the sterling area if we went into Europe. Could we still remain as banker for the sterling area? This is an important question, but we have had no guidance at all from the Government about it. The sterling area depends on sentiment as well as on hard cash. It could hardly survive otherwise.

If this sentiment is impaired, and countries such as Ghana or Malaya saw us turning to Europe, and felt that it would be from Europe, not from Britain, that they would get more and more developmental capital, if they felt that the currencies of the countries

[1] Reginald Maudling.

which would be supplying them with capital equipment – such as Germany – offered better long-term security than sterling, would there be not a rush to convert their sterling balances at present held in this country, at any rate sufficiently to break Britain's position as banker of the sterling area?

This is a very serious problem and I know that the House will take it seriously. I hope that we shall have a serious reply from the Government today. There we have the possible combined effects of a worsening trade balance for a year or two, an outflow of capital from Britain and the breaking up of our position as sterling area bankers – all this happening in the first year or two; it is a formidable prospect.

We are told that our capital problems are understood in Europe, that they are willing to waive or defer the operation of greater freedom of capital movement and that they would not be as quick as might be thought to rush into applying that part of the Treaty. I profoundly hope that there is this view in Europe and that it will be made a sticking point by the Government in the negotiations, otherwise none of us can be answerable for the consequences. So much for the short term.

I have referred to the long term. I believe that we could gain, but not on the basis of the degree of lethargy and sloth which is still characteristic of so much of British industry today. There is no more dangerous illusion than that laissez-faire and the cold east wind will do the trick. Positive, purposive, economic planning will be needed, as we have frequently and recently stated. If I may adopt a phrase from our policy statement, 'Signposts for the Sixties'[1], if there is no fundamental change in our internal economic policies, what we are debating today is whether we shall be a backwater in Europe or a backwater outside Europe, and both are an equally dangerous position to occupy.

We see evidence that a number of the more progressive businessmen in the country want to go in. I think that that is true, especially some who are efficient and confident that once they are presented with a very big market they will be able to earn a great deal more foreign exchange and to sell more goods. But they are not representative of the entire community, and I do not think that hon Members can deny for one minute that there are some who are anxious to get

[1] Labour Party policy statement on economic and domestic policy published 1961.

in with one reason only – to have a wages showdown which they have not been able to have in the last four years.

It is five years since the Prime Minister, when Chancellor, announced his restrictive policy and in collusion, I think, with the then Chairman of the Engineering Employers' Federation, had a showdown on engineering wages. That was in 1956. That, of course, failed and ever since attempts to have a wage freeze and a wage showdown have not succeeded. There are some people, I do not say on the Conservative benches, who resent that. One hears murmurings from time to time that we had better get into Europe so that we can have this showdown once and for all.

I do not want to identify myself with any particular industrial view on this, but I must, in fairness to the Government, right away give a pledge. While hon Members on both sides of the House have their constituency responsibilities, I want to give a pledge which we gave over four years ago, when we first debated the original Free Trade Area proposals. We give a pledge that as a party, whatever decision we might take on the broad essential principles to go in or not to go in, we do not intend, whether we decide to go in the Common Market or not, to make common cause with protectionist industrial interests in this country. We will not make mischief about whatever decision is taken by allying ourselves with individual protectionist interests. I gave that pledge four years ago and I repeat it.

I have referred to the need for planning. I ask the Government: how far, under the Treaty of Rome as it is, could we undertake the degree of centralised economic management that we on this side of the House feel is needed? Hon Members will form their own view. I say frankly to the House that as I read the Treaty of Rome, and the intentions of those who at present operate it, the measures necessary to fulfil the policies set out, for example, in 'Signposts for the Sixties' cannot be implemented without substantial amendments to the relevant articles to the Treaty. That is my own personal view. This may not worry the Prime Minister very much. I think that that was shown by the levity with which he answered questions put to him by my hon Friend the Member for Nuneaton (Mr Bowles) on Monday.

But if this is his attitude, do not let him talk, as he did on Monday, of this being an all-party operation. In these negotiations he is acting on behalf of the whole nation, including the 12 million who voted

Labour and who voted for planning and purposive economic policies. Even the Prime Minister can claim to be Prime Minister for the whole nation and not just for the Conservative Party, or he would be representing a very small minority of the electorate at the present time. He is negotiating on behalf of those 12 million and millions more who would be voting for these policies if they had a chance of electoral expression today.

I hope that the Prime Minister accepts this responsibility. If he is negotiating simply the terms on which a Conservative laissez-faire Administration can enter the Common Market, if that is all he is doing, he will understand if we reserve our right here and now, clearly and unequivocally, to judge the final outcome of the negotiations on that criterion as well as on the other criteria which my right hon Friend mentioned yesterday.

I hope that the Prime Minister will be careful to see how far even the minimal amount of planning which the Government do would be permitted under the Treaty of Rome – exchange controls, control over capital movements and the import controls which may one day have to be introduced, although we all hope not. Even Bank Rate, on which the Government rely, would be susceptible to challenge in the Commission or in the Council of Ministers under the Treaty of Rome.

I hope that the Prime Minister will not think me too hag-ridden by references to 1931 if I conjure up the possibility of a situation in which, perhaps, our exports do not increase as much as it is hoped and we go to Europe in a weak condition, needing economic assistance, and in which the central bankers of Europe tell us that we must change our financial, economic and perhaps social policies before they give the assistance. The bankers' ramp of 1931 might become a central bankers' ramp now. I do not think that this is entirely imaginary. It is a possibility – just as much under a Conservative Government as under a Labour Government, and I hope that the Government are taking it seriously.

I intend to say little about agriculture. As far as I can judge – although I am not qualified to judge at all – though big changes would be inevitable, though some sectors such as horticulture and the production of individual commodities such as potatoes might suffer great grave damage; in general, as far as it is legitimate for me to express an opinion, I feel that the problem of agriculture is not insoluble – though I recognise that some of my hon Friends with far greater knowledge of, and interest in, agriculture take a different view.

Our present system of support prices and deficiency payments, at least on a national basis, would have to go. But I feel like my right hon Friend, who said yesterday that when the obvious adjustments have been made it will be the housewife rather than the farmer and the farm worker who will be feeling the draught. I think that that is probably fair. The fundamental issue in the question of imports of food and agricultural products relates not to the British farmer, but to the Commonwealth, and to this subject, which is the central theme of our amendment, I now turn.

During the debate some hon Members on both sides of the House have accepted rather too easily the decline in recent years of our trade with the Commonwealth, as though it were something inevitable. Last night, the President of the Board of Trade[1] took a slightly different view and was more hopeful, but he went so far as to explain the decline in recent years as being due to what he called historical reasons. He is flattering himself and his two predecessors when he uses that phrase 'historical reasons'. The cause, in the main, is the Government's ineptitude and their doctrinaire approach to certain problems which I shall describe.

Under the Labour Government trade with the Commonwealth as a percentage of our total trade was an all-time high, higher than ever before and certainly higher than it has been since. Right hon Gentlemen opposite, scrapping bulk buying and long-term agreements and bilateral arrangements, destroying, as they have, the sterling area as a trading entity – that is what they have done – bear the first responsibility for the decline of Commonwealth trade over the past 10 years.

The second reason is the lack of enterprise and drive on the part of many of our manufacturers. Repeatedly in these debates I have given the figures of the imports of Commonwealth countries into the sterling area, showing how much of the increase which has taken place has been scooped by Japan, Germany and the United States, while our exports to those areas, through sheer lack of enterprise, have been falling.

It is no good Ministers standing at the Dispatch Box and complaining about the decline in Commonwealth trade and shrugging their shoulders, because they are very largely responsible for it. It is

[1] Reginald Maudling.

utterly defeatist to accept as inevitable the recent decline in Commonwealth trade. With the right priorities and drive, it could be sharply reversed. I make no apology for saying that in present circumstances the three Ministers who recently toured the Commonwealth[1] should have been authorised – as Ernest Bevin, Stafford Cripps and I were authorised 14 years ago – to propose a free trade area to the Commonwealth first, before taking the final decision about Europe. The offer might have been refused, as it was refused 14 years ago, but at any rate it should have been tried. It has been suggested from these benches a number of times in the past few years.

Let us examine this problem of the Commonwealth and Europe. I would like to say how much I welcome the statements by prominent European statesmen that they recognise our obligation to the Commonwealth. M Spaak said in the Belgian Assembly on 14th June, 1961 – I have the text in French and this will be a somewhat limping translation:

> If the Commonwealth is one of the essential facts of our time, I understand this perfectly clearly and no one would wish to face Great Britain with a choice between the Commonwealth and Europe. That is why it is necessary to find a technical solution which will enable us to make effective the maintenance of the Commonwealth and the adhesion of Great Britain to the Common Market.

It may not be a very good translation, but the idea is there. I very much welcome a statement of that kind from M Spaak.

Now let us see what needs to be done to make those phrases a reality. The whole House will agree that there is not one Commonwealth problem, but at least three. First, I take it as inconceivable that Europe could fail to offer, or that the Government could fail to insist on getting, a protocol guaranteeing our dependencies and former dependencies, in Africa for example, the same terms as the former French territories are granted. That would be automatic. Kenya coffee and Ghana cocoa should not be prejudiced as compared with the products of Belgian or French territories, or former territories.

Secondly, there is the major problem of the products of temperate

[1] To 'sell' to the Commonwealth the idea that Britain should enter the Common Market.

zone countries. This is very difficult. New Zealand, Australian and Canadian products face the likelihood of a 20 to 24% tariff compared with duty-free entry today.

That is the essence of the problem, but it is not the whole of the problem, because anyone reading the trading and economic clauses of the Treaty will realise the highly restrictive, even autarkic motivation of the Community. Non-discrimination within the area, yes, but a whole panoply of tariff quotas, import levies and other methods to supplement the tariff provisions, if, contrary to the intentions of the signatories, outside products come in on any scale.

All this suggests that there will be a very formidable series of weapons designed to limit the imports into Europe, and into Britain, of the products of many Commonwealth countries. Free trade within the area, yes, but *vis-à-vis* the outside world – let us be frank about it – this is a highly restrictive, discriminating trading bloc. We should have no illusions about it. It is the sort of bloc which, perhaps, the Conservatives can join and perhaps, with the right safeguards and assurances, the Labour Party could support joining, but why in heaven's name the Liberal Party supports it I find it extremely difficult to follow.

It will fairly be argued that the agricultural proposals are still to be agreed and that we can do more to influence from the inside than we can from the outside looking in. It would be unrealistic, when talking of the influence we could exercise about Commonwealth imports over this panoply of tariff walls and the rest, to assume that on this issue Denmark and the Netherlands would necessarily be on our side. This is the most important of the matters for negotiation on the economic side.

We are told that the Commonwealth will not suffer. Last night, the President of the Board of Trade[1] sought to console us – and, I suspect, to console himself – with the rather meaningless piece of fluff which he held out to us –

> We must not get into the frame of mind of choosing between the Commonwealth and Europe. It would be tragic if this country were forced to make that choice.

I would like to be certain that we are not to have to make that choice.

[1] Reginald Maudling.

I would like to be certain that the Government have not already made that choice in their own mind.

Let us strip the problem of all these fair words and get down to realities. I want to put this question, because the Government ought to put it in the negotiations. In, say, seven years from now, on the assumption of going in, do we expect to see as much Australian and Canadian wheat coming to Britain as today, or will it be wholly or substantially replaced by French wheat? The French make no secret of their aim to be the granary of Europe.

This question should be put, for it is the acid test of the words about the Commonwealth. Shall we have as much of those commodities coming into Britain seven years from now – or coming in to Europe seven years from now – as at present? Will there be the same amount of New Zealand meat, or will it be replaced by French production? New Zealand butter? This question must be put and answered, because it is the only criterion by which these fair words about the Commonwealth can be judged.

This question and the answer to it are vital for us, and many of our friends in Europe recognise that. I understand that some of them, some of the most powerful figures in Europe, are now privately talking of a five- or seven-year contract for New Zealand butter and other Commonwealth commodities, just as Germany concluded a seven-year agreement – secret agreement as it was then – with Denmark when the two parted company on the formation of the Common Market.

If measures on those lines could be taken, they would greatly assist the solution of the problem, at any rate for a time, and I hope that the Government will not be put off with words, but will ask the question which I have asked and will get a firm answer to it, and that, if the answer is not satisfactory and if some measures of that kind are not suggested, such as long-term purchase from New Zealand, they will come here and frankly tell the House.

There is one other equally fundamental question I would like to ask. We have not been told about this. Yesterday, the President of the Board of Trade referred to the position of the French territories as associated members, what the Prime Minister calls 'country members'. Do the Government intend to press for self-governing Commonwealth countries to be admitted on a basis of association with the Community. Is that suggestion being put forward?

Although Article 237 of the Treaty restricts full membership to European countries, Article 238 makes no such restriction and under the Treaty it would not be inappropriate for Commonwealth countries outside Europe to enter this obligation. Can we be told whether the Commonwealth countries told the ministerial visitors that they wanted to be associated with the Common Market in this way? I hope that we shall be given a clear answer to that tonight.

I turn to the third aspect of the Commonwealth problem, the problem of tropical agricultural products. What pledges have the Government given, or what are they willing to give, about the Commonwealth Sugar Agreement? That is a clear question and we must have an answer to it. This is one of the vital pillars in the structure of Commonwealth economic prosperity and the establishment of colonial economic prosperity after the war.

There was a great fuss in the Chamber, before the change of Government, about the 'Black Pact' with Cuba[1], but at the same time as that was negotiated we had the Commonwealth Sugar Agreement, which owed, and owes, a great deal to the statesmanship and negotiating ability of our right hon Friend and former colleague in the House, Arthur Bottomley[2], whom we miss and whom the Commonwealth misses from this debate today, as he was largely responsible for that measure.

The Government have continued the Commonwealth Sugar Agreement in their peculiar manner – through free enterprise and operated through a monopoly with a levy and a subsidy and all the rest of the very clumsy and complicated Heath Robinson machinery, but at any rate in a form they have continued it. Will they give a pledge that they intend to maintain it after these negotiations with Europe are completed? Also, what do they intend about citrus fruits, on which the economies of important Colonial Territories depend?

We are entitled to know, because it really is nonsense for the Prime Minister to talk about a holy war against Communism. He did not quite use that phrase, but it was sticking out from a lot of what he said yesterday. It is nonsense for him to talk in those terms if he is wantonly embarking on a course which by undermining, for example, the Commonwealth Sugar Agreement and the citrus fruits arrange-

[1] 'Black Pact' with Cuba: a 1951 agreement increasing sugar imports.

[2] Re-entered House of Commons, 15th March, 1962 as MP for Middlesbrough East.

ments will knock out the props which underpin the prosperity of struggling colonial economies.

I have stated these Commonwealth problems in terms of hard economic facts, but I should be the last to disagree with those hon Members on both sides of the House who put the problem in yesterday's debate in terms more of sentiment, kinship and bonds of a less materialistic character than those that I have been describing.

The public Press has inevitably been filled with countless articles and letters for months past about all these problems, but for me – and, I think, for many others – the most pointed and moving of all of them was the letter written to the *Guardian* by my right hon Friend the Member for Middlesbrough, East (Mr Marquand)[1], about three weeks ago. My right hon Friend was Secretary for Overseas Trade immediately after the war. I followed him in that capacity, and I know the kind of problems with which he was dealing. In the letter he referred to the difficult negotiations this country had in the immediate post-war years when we sought to get the food and raw materials that we needed with very little to offer in terms of the steel, chemicals and engineering goods that other countries so desperately needed and that we could ill-afford.

My right hon Friend wrote:

> Then one day I sat down with the New Zealand delegation. I expected a bargaining session as difficult as any other. Instead, the leader of the New Zealand delegation –

a very good friend of this country's, Walter Nash –

> opened the proceedings in words I shall never forget. 'We have not come to ask you "What can you give?" but simply "What do you need?" When you stood alone you preserved our freedom for us. Now tell us what butter, what meat, what grains you need, and – whatever the sacrifice may be for the New Zealand people – we will supply it.'

Hon Members: Hear, hear.

I submit to the House that we cannot consistently with the honour of this country take any action now that would betray friends such as those. All this and Europe, too – if you can get it. The President of

[1] Resigned his seat in 1962 and was succeeded by Arthur Bottomley – see Footnote [2] Page 106.

the Board of Trade last night seemed to think that we can. I hope that he is right, but if there has to be a choice we are not entitled to sell our friends and kinsmen down the river for a problematical and marginal advantage in selling washing machines in Düsseldorf.

Before I leave the economic aspects of the problem – I do not want to go on for more than a few minutes more – there are two other questions that I want to raise. The first is East–West trade. The Common Market, whether we are inside or outside, is restrictive in intent. We all know that Eastern Europe, too, has its common market, a tighter and still more restrictive bloc than anything we are thinking about. All the same, if joining the Common Market means a reduced ability to trade with the Soviet Union or other Eastern European countries, or China, I submit that this will be detrimental to our economic welfare and to the prospects of full employment – and it will make real peace more remote.

So, when the Prime Minister talks in terms of a political grouping against the Communist threat, when I recall the way Dr Adenauer last year forbade us to trade with East Germany while his own businessmen flocked across the frontier to filch our orders, I must admit that I am apprehensive about East-West trade relations. I therefore trust that the Government will tell us that they will seek assurances on this question.

The other question relates to the Coal and Steel Community and Euratom. This is a problem which was dealt with by my hon Friend the Member for Houghton-le-Spring (Mr Blyton) last night in a speech which drew, I think, a great deal of support from both sides of the House. Presumably it is intended that we should join both these bodies as well as the Common Market, though little has been said from the Government Front Bench about either of them. We ought to be told a lot more about it.

Hon Friends of mine have made it clear that there is great anxiety in the coalfields about joining the ECSC[1], probably far more than there is about our joining the Common Market. I am bound to ask: what safeguards would we have, if we are to go in, that British coal will not be sacrificed to the special discriminations which will be introduced in favour of Saharan oil? That is a problem – subsidised pipelines, and all the rest of it. We know that there will be com-

[1] European Coal and Steel Community.

petition between British and European coal. That is a problem which has to be faced in one way or another, but against subsidised Saharan oil. This raises some very fundamental questions on which I hope we shall get an answer tonight.

Also on the broader question, we should like much more specific assurances than the Treaty gives against the growth of private or even Government-supported cartels in Europe. Some Continental industries take to cartelistic activities like ducks to water, and there are some British businessmen who would be only too anxious to get in on that kind of organisation. I hope that this is very much in the minds of the Government.

Before I sit down I should like to turn briefly to one or two of the wider issues which have been raised in the debate, because it is clear that, for the Prime Minister at any rate, the motive is not economic but political. I think that was clear from his speech. Important as the economic issues, of course, are, and the Commonwealth issues with which I have been dealing, I think that our expectations or fears about the political aspects are even more fundamental.

First, I should like to take issue straight away with some right hon and hon Gentlemen, sitting below the gangway opposite[1], who quite simply regard it as an issue of sovereignty. I respect their arguments, but they – and even the word itself, I think – are really out of harmony with this modern age. The whole history of political progress is a history of gradual abandonment of national sovereignty. We abrogate it when we have a French referee at Twickenham. We abrogated it – some would say that we did not abrogate it enough – when we joined the United Nations. One cannot talk about world government in one breath and then start drooling about the need to preserve national sovereignty in the next.

Mr John Biggs-Davison (Chigwell) *rose*

Mr Wilson: I will give way when I have finished this. Perhaps the hon Gentleman will wait a moment. All of us have the difficult task of trying, as far as we can, to speak for Britain, but not all of us can speak on behalf of some of the Ancient Britons who sit on the benches opposite.

[1] Group of Conservative MPs, led mainly by Lord Hinchingbrooke, now Earl of Sandwich, and Rt Hon Derek Walker-Smith, MP.

Mr Biggs-Davison: I am hardly one of them. Will the right hon Gentleman give way?

Mr Wilson: In a moment. It may satisfy the hon Gentleman in what I am about to say.

The question is not whether sovereignty remains absolute or not, but in what way one is prepared to sacrifice sovereignty, to whom and for what purpose. That is the real issue before us. The question is whether any proposed surrender of sovereignty will advance or retard our progress to the kind of world we all want to see.

Mr Biggs Davison: I am much obliged to the right hon Gentleman for giving way. I do not want to intervene on behalf of ancient Britons nor about nineteenth century Liberal ideas on supranationality or world government. But what about the new Britons spread around the world? What about the modern Commonwealth, whose common principle is national sovereignty?

Mr Wilson: I have been discussing the economic problems of the Commonwealth countries. In a moment I hope to say a word or two about the political aspects and importance of these new countries. What I am objecting to is the old-world style of talking of national sovereignty when really we should be dealing with much more fundamental issues in this debate.

Equally, I do not join with those extremists who have been trying to estimate what Britain will become if we do or do not join the Common Market. Stay out, some say, and we shall be powerless and become another Sweden or Portugal. Go in, say the others, and we shall become another Idaho. But I think that these arguments grossly understate the position and role of what Britain is and what Britain could be under the right kind of leadership. The vital issue in the political sense is whether to join the Common Market explicitly or implicitly means a move towards a federal Europe. There is nothing in the Treaty of Rome enjoining federalism, although there is a great deal of supranationalism.

But we are right to be concerned about the express intentions of many leading figures in the Six. Yesterday, the Prime Minister quoted President de Gaulle concerning the *Confédération des Patries*. We all welcome that phrase when it was used by the French President, but there are the cautious, but far from meaningless, words of Dr

Adenauer who said that political unity remained the common aim of the Common Market countries, but that he favoured a pragmatic rather than a theoretical approval. One day, he said, it would be found that European unity had been reached. On 8th February the *Guardian* reported him as aiming at a federation

> with one Prime Minister and a unified policy towards the rest of the world.

Monsieur Spaak, on 14th June, made a statement and Professor Hallstein has said many times that the final aim is the integration of Europe. On 22nd May, Professor Hallstein said:

> We are not in business to promote tariff preferences, or to establish a discriminatory club to form a larger unit to make us richer, or a trading block to further our commercial interests. We are not in business at all. We are in politics.

In view of these statements and others – and it is for us to select which of these various statements we should accept as correct – it is a little myopic of the Prime Minister to refer to it as

> a purely economic and trading negotiation and not a political and foreign policy negotiation.

But, all the same, we warmly welcome his statement of yesterday associating himself with President de Gaulle's approach and I repeat the declaration of my right hon Friend the Leader of the Opposition yesterday, when he said:

> there is no question whatever of Britain entering into a federal Europe now.

I hope that the Government will be clear about this. There should be no doubt on this federal issue. There should be no double talk with Europe about it. Our position should be stated so that there is no accusation of bad faith, of dragging our feet, of perfidious Albion, if, subsequently, Europe seeks to move towards federation and then, and only then, we make clear our opposition to it. Whatever view may be taken concerning these economic negotiations, I hope that we make it clear that we shall not go into a federal system.

I very much welcomed the Prime Minister's condemnation of what the right hon Gentleman called 'little Europeans'. We must be outward looking. The Prime Minister is right. This is an issue on which every hon Member must make up his mind. We have a role to play in the world, perhaps a decisive role, at some historic moment; in building a bridge between East and West – between America and Russia, perhaps America and China, and we must search our hearts and ask whether going in, or not going in, will best help in that role.

It is no secret that the United States Government feel that Britain must retire from the task of organising summits. They have told the Prime Minister that. They consider our role to be in Europe. I would not deny that that is an important role. No one who recalls that the two world wars have begun on the Franco-German frontier will underestimate it. If that is the role that the Prime Minister has chosen, can we, playing a leading part in Europe, fulfil the role of bridge builders in the second half of the twentieth century?

I have referred to the position of the American Government and I understand that it is the firm view of the United States that negotiations aimed at a modification of the Rome Treaty would appear unacceptable to them and that they would be opposed to such a step. Protocols yes, but a redrafting of the Rome Treaty – and I understand that this is being said in Washington officially now – would be ruled out as far as they are concerned. I realise that they are not in the negotiations, but they have a veto in GATT. It is, therefore, extremely important that we should understand what the position will be.

But what of our role in the Commonwealth, particularly the newly emerging Commonwealth in Asia and Africa, where our partners will be, and already are being, called upon to play a leading part in Afro-Asian and United Nations politics? These are the questions – the ultimate decisions – which will be as momentous as any in our history.

I repeat, we do not oppose the negotiations, but on the Government's success in meeting the economic and political anxieties which my right hon Friend and I have expressed – and we wish the Government well in the negotiations – we utterly reserve our position about the package that the Government will bring back. On the Government's success in this will depend not only our decision on joining Europe but, I believe, the future standing and influence of this country in meeting its decisive and unique contribution to the peace of the world.

LET THE PEOPLE DECIDE[1]

THIS WEEK'S CONFERENCE OF PRIME MINISTERS has made one thing clear beyond doubt. Practically the entire Commonwealth is against Mr Macmillan's plan to take Britain into the Common Market on the terms proposed.

A year of negotiations has produced a set of conditions which, where they are not vague beyond belief, are downright unacceptable.

This is not just a question of economics, or the prosperity of individual Commonwealth countries. What of the effect on the Commonwealth as a whole, this unique multi-racial community of 700 millions, the greatest guarantee of peace and security in this divided world? All Mr Macmillan's honeyed words will not banish the fear that the Commonwealth, as we know it today, cannot survive if Britain continues her breakneck rush into Europe on these unacceptable terms.

Week by week, public opinion polls, echoing MPs' postbags, show that the British people are ready to make their view felt.

Has Mr Macmillan, then, the power and the moral right to take this fateful step without seeking the approval of the British electorate?

The power? Yes, if he can bulldoze his divided and reluctant party into voting for it in the House of Commons.

The moral right? The answer is plain. If, when the final terms are known, they are unacceptable to a substantial section of the British people, then *I say that a dying Government does not possess the right, constitutionally or morally, to take a divided nation into the Common Market.* That right belongs only to a Government which, on an issue as important as this, has fought and won an election in which its intention was clearly submitted to the final decision of the British electorate.

Mr Macmillan had no such mandate. In the 1959 Election, when his only battle-cry was 'You've Never Had it so Good', the only mandate he received, if he received one at all, was to stay out of the Common Market. For, long before that Election, he had told Parliament:

> I do not believe that this House would ever agree to our entering arrangements which, as a matter of principle, would prevent our

[1] This article appeared in *The Sunday Express*, 16th September, 1962.

> treating the great range of imports from the Commonwealth at least as favourably as those from the European countries . . .

Or again,

> We must remain free to continue to give this great volume of imports the preferential arrangements we have built up over the last 25 years.

Equally, Mr Maudling, now Chancellor of the Exchequer, had said

> we have given a clear undertaking to the Commonwealth countries to maintain their position in our markets for foodstuffs, drink and tobacco.

Again, a few months before the Election:

> I cannot conceive that any Government of this country would put forward a proposition which would involve the abandonment of Commonwealth free entry.

It was on these pledges that Mr Macmillan and Mr Maudling sought the votes of the electorate. Their honour was pledged, and, like Brutus, Mr Macmillan and Mr Maudling are honourable men.

Where do they stand now?

In last week's Conference, Mr Macmillan, we read, embellished his speech with copious, if misapplied, examples from world history. I commend him now to study the history of our constitution of which, as the Queen's First Minister, he is currently the custodian. He will find that, on issue after issue, a Prime Minister planning to change the direction of the country's policy, or to alter our constitution has sought the consent of the British people.

In 1923, even Stanley Baldwin, after only 12 months as Premier, thought it right to go to the country before introducing a limited but controversial system of tariff protection for British industries. In 1910, Mr Asquith went to the country – for the second time in a year – to seek authority to curb the powers of the House of Lords. There are many more examples – does Mr Macmillan consider them less important than the course on which he is now set?

For, as he well knows, his plan to enter Europe means a whole series of consequences, every one of which involves this country in commitments he has no mandate to make. The economic and political future of the Commonwealth, the danger of handing over control of Britain's own foreign and economic policies to other nations, the future of British agriculture – these are only part of the problem. Mr Spaak has made it clear that if Britain joins she is committed to joining the political union of Europe.

To all these I would just add one other question, of supreme importance to our freedom and our conception of democracy.

Mr Macmillan is seeking to involve us all in a decision which will for all time fetter and cripple the working of our British Parliament, without seeking the authority of those who elect that Parliament.

For centuries our liberties have been guaranteed by the fact that Parliament is supreme in deciding the policies of this nation and the laws under which we live. No Parliament has the right or the power to dictate to any future Parliament.

But, what is Mr Macmillan demanding? The right to sign a Treaty, irrevocable, for all time, which provides that 'regulations' made by the institutions in Brussels, shall override anything the British Parliament may decide. Article 189 of the Common Market Treaty says in plain terms 'Regulations shall have a general application. They shall be binding in every respect and directly applicable in each Member State'.

I emphasise those words 'directly applicable'. There is no iota of a suggestion that the British House of Commons will have any say in the matter. At no time in the past year has the industrious Mr Heath sought to amend this provision, or to suggest that British entry would be conditional on scrapping it.

So, by one decision of his Cabinet, by one vote of a now unrepresentative but well-whipped majority Party in the House of Commons, Mr Macmillan is seeking to take away, for all time, rights which Parliament and the nation have enjoyed for centuries. I have reminded the House of Commons that we, the present Members, are trustees, sitting between those who have made our Parliaments in the past and those who are to come in future generations. We have no power to destroy institutions of which we are the custodians.

Mr Macmillan has scorned these arguments. In three major Parliamentary debates in one year, in Question Time after Question Time, he has not ever bothered to reply. Now we have the right to demand an answer.

There is still time. Time for Mr Macmillan to think again, to heed the warning voices of his Commonwealth colleagues and of British public opinion. Time to seek better terms, acceptable to the Commonwealth and to Britain.

But, if he decides that he will not listen, that he will not even negotiate, one last duty remains. He may rate his judgment higher than that of all those who are warning him to think again. But, he has no right to follow that judgment regardless of the British people in whose name he exercises power. This decision goes far beyond any power with which he has been entrusted. His duty is to let the people decide.

EXTRACT FROM DEBATE, HOUSE OF COMMONS, 8TH NOVEMBER, 1962

MR HAROLD WILSON (HUYTON): I think that this debate for the last two days has justified what was said about it by my right hon Friend the Member for Belper (Mr G. Brown) this afternoon – that it has been practical, constructive and detailed and has not been a striking of general philosophical attitudes for or against the Market.

There has still been some misrepresentation, even on the Government Front Bench, about the position of the Opposition on the subject. Perhaps I should first make it clear what our attitude is not. We are emphatically not against the European Economic Community or against the greater unity which has been achieved in Europe in the past few years. We have welcomed it, and we have welcomed it clearly. The first sentence of our policy statement, issued by the National Executive Committee of the party and overwhelmingly accepted by the Labour Party conference at Brighton[1], reads:

> The Labour Party regards the European Community as a great and imaginative conception. It believes that the coming together of the six nations which have in the past so often been torn by war and economic rivalry is in the context of Western Europe a step of great significance.

[1] 1962 Conference.

This is our view. No one in any part of the House will under-rate the work which has been done to guard against the danger of further conflict between France and Germany, which twice in our lifetime has plunged the world into war. We all welcome what they have achieved and what they may achieve. Some time ago I criticised the present Chancellor of the Exchequer, during the period of his negotiations, for failing to realise what was inspiring the Six and driving them forward. I said that he was approaching these problems with the posture of a greengrocer. But the question, of course, is not what we feel about the Six. It is whether and on what terms we can join the Six.

The second thing which I have to say is that none of us has said – and if any of us had done so it would have been a complete denial of the whole development of our policy on this issue – that we are against Britain going in. We regret the two extreme points of view – that we must go in at any cost, which is one view, or that we must stay out whatever the terms. Our document makes it clear, and my right hon Friend repeated it yesterday. I hope that there is no doubt where we stand on this issue. Our position is that if we can get the terms, then we go in.

The third thing which I must say – and it is perhaps a pity that I need say it, but our position has been misrepresented so much – is that our attitude is not based on national sovereignty. We are not clinging like woad-painted aboriginal Britons to outmoded concepts of national sovereignty. In our first debate in August, 1961, I said:

> The question is not whether sovereignty remains absolute or not, but in what way one is prepared to sacrifice sovereignty, to whom and for what purpose. That is the real issue before us. The question is whether any proposed surrender of sovereignty will advance or retard our progress to the kind of world we all want to see.

That has been our attitude right through.

Of course we should be willing to surrender national sovereignty to create an effective system of world government for the outlawry of war. We should surrender it gladly for the sake of a comprehensive disarmament agreement. We have made it clear that we would surrender our rights to our so-called independent nuclear deterrent as part of an international treaty preventing the spread of nuclear weapons. This jibe, which has frequently been thrown at us, particularly in the Press, is too cheap. It certainly would not lie in the mouths of right hon Gentlemen opposite to talk about sovereignty after their unequivocal refusal to accept the option clause for the reference of international disputes to the International Court at The Hague. It would not be for them to talk about sovereignty.

So much for what we are not saying. Now for what we are saying and what our position really is. We say that we should go in if, and only if, the five conditions which we have laid down are achieved in negotiations. My right hon Friend made it clear yesterday that he feels that these terms could still be obtained, and, as he said, we hope that they are obtained. But we must equally say that on the negotiations so far, on the outline which we have been given, on the terms which were so flatly and brutally put to the Commonwealth Conference, we are nowhere near securing the minimum on any one of the five issues which we have raised. The negotiations in Brussels are one long record of surrender.

The White Paper of August, which was set against the clear and specific pledges made by the Prime Minister and all his colleagues, was a humiliation for this country. Let us be clear about it. If the situation looked bad at the time of the August White Paper, it has got a good deal worse since. Since Llandudno, the Six have toughened their attitude still further.

We read the accounts of what happened at Llandudno – Ministers of the Crown stationed on the 'prom', glad-handing bewildered delegates to manoeuvre them into supporting entry into the Common Market. What a role for them. There was the last minute flood of Central Office propaganda. There were the buttons which were issued marked 'Yes'. 'Yes' to what? Perhaps the Lord Privy Seal[1] will tell us. [*Interruption*[2]]. I might have guessed that it would be quite impossible to explain to hon Members opposite the workings of party democracy. It would be like trying to explain the principles of vegetarianism to a tribe of cannibals. I am sorry that the Prime Minister is not here. He was democratically elected to his position by the Marquess of Salisbury, and he lost the confidence of that electoral

1 Rt Hon Edward Heath, MP

2 Earlier in the evening the ballot had been declared in the contest for the Labour Party's Deputy Leadership when George Brown defeated me. The interruption referred to this.

college within six weeks. I shall not mention the right hon and learned Member for Wirral (Mr Selwyn Lloyd).

I hope that the Lord Privy Seal, at least – perhaps he is a little more serious – will tell us what these buttons marked 'Yes' meant. Was it 'Yes' to entry on any terms? Was it 'Yes' to the terms so far negotiated? We were told yesterday that they were only provisional. I do not suppose that anyone really knew at Llandudno what he was saying 'Yes' to. They just said 'Yes' because they were told to do so.

The impression created, not least by the Prime Minister – this is the serious aspect of it – was of a Government party falling over itself to get into Europe at almost any price. I should sympathise with the Lord Privy Seal in the impossible negotiating position into which he has been put as a consequence were it not for the fact that he was one of the main organisers of the demonstration. He went along and addressed the agents and told them all about it, telling them to say 'Yes'.

Our charge is that the Government began to negotiate at a time of economic crisis in July, 1961, in such a way that the impression was given that we had no alternative way out of economic crisis except entry into Europe. Our charge is that this posture has been maintained throughout. At all times since then the whole range of Ministers' speeches in the country, particularly those of the Prime Minister stressing the political and cold war aspects of his approach, have given the idea that we are determined to go in at virtually any price. How can the Lord Privy Seal negotiate on that basis? No one could negotiate the purchase and sale of a chip shop on a basis like that.

I come now to the five conditions. I shall not repeat all that my right hon and hon Friends have said. As regards the EFTA[1] I say only this. We think – we hope – that we got from the Lord Privy Seal yesterday a clear repetition of the pledge. We take it from what he said – the Lord Privy Seal will make it clear if I misrepresent him – that Britain will not enter the Common Market or make any commitment or irrevocable step in that direction unless and until – I stress the word 'until' because there is an important question of timing – our EFTA partners are satisfied that their legitimate interests have been met in their own bilateral negotiations whether for full member-

[1] European Free Trade Association.

ship or associate membership. I should like the Lord Privy Seal to tell us if we have got that right.

Secondly, on economic planning, I am not going to repeat all the anxieties we have expressed in previous debates, but we are concerned about three things. First, the distribution of industry. We are anxious – I hope that we are wrong about this – lest the system that we have today of location certificates, inducements and all the rest, inadequate though it is and even more inadequately implemented by the Government, will be inoperable under the Treaty of Rome. I hope we shall be told about this. There is no power, as far as I can see, left to our Government under the Treaty of Rome to prevent take-overs by foreign interests which the Government might consider undesirable. I do not want to raise unnecessary bogies. It is only too easy here, but is it possible, under the Treaty of Rome, for the firm of Krupps, which should not have been allowed to raise its ugly head again in Germany anyhow, to come here and take over a vital British steel or engineering firm without any power of intervention by the Government? If that is so, I should be even more worried.

The next point concerns our anxieties about our balance of payments. We are genuinely concerned that some of the terms of the Treaty of Rome make it impossible for any Government – Tory, Labour or any other kind – to take the action necessary if we should get into balance of payments difficulties, particularly when there is free movement of capital, and, perhaps, at a very tricky time, soon after we enter the Market, if some of our Sterling Area partners should decide – which I hope they will not do – that we have written them off and want to cash their sterling into some other currency.

We have been told that we can nationalise steel and that coal will remain nationalised, but there is all the difference in the world between the form of public ownership and the substance of it – the right to nationalise and the right to use nationalisation as an instrument of national planning. That is what we want to know. Will the Lord Privy Seal tell us? Is it a fact that the Six have objected to the structure of the National Coal Board, and that we may be forced back to setting district against district in some move to stimulate competition? Is it a fact that even the Steel Board, that shadowy and useless substitute for national ownership which this Government set up, will have to go if we join the Common Market? I was worried when I read a few weeks ago that Dr Erhard, who has been a good friend towards Britain's entry, said at Russelheim on 15th August last:

> A nationally planned economy is incompatible with membership of the Common Market.

Perhaps the Lord Privy Seal will tell us. I wonder whether members of a Tory Government would be able to follow a Tory planning policy. We are not very sure. Could they, without challenge, impose the 7% Bank Rate midway between general elections, which is a vital element in their economic planning? We got it for four years; enough deflation, enough elbow room to make reflationary handouts look respectable in the 12 months before an election.

Thirdly, I come to agriculture. Neither the Lord Privy Seal nor the Minister of Agriculture[1] has achieved a fraction of what, in June, they regarded as their minimum terms. The August breakdown was bad enough, but last week's was even worse. Let us be quite clear about this. What we are up against here is not the Treaty of Rome; it is the agricultural policy and structure agreed upon last February. I cannot find any enthusiasm for this Common Market agricultural structure even among strong supporters of the Common Market. I do not think that anyone can regard this as anything but a monstrosity. This agricultural system is not a system of free trade but of market rigging and manipulation dependent upon entirely untried methods and untried men. It can fairly be said that the industrial part of the Treaty of Rome is, if we like, free trade over a limited area, and there is nothing to stop it being outward looking. But the agricultural system – this is not free trade. It is mercantilism on a European scale. How does the Liberal Party feel about it? I must tell its members that the inspiration of the agricultural system of the Common Market is not Adam Smith or Cobden, or any of their heroes. It is pure Schacht[2]. Last June, the Minister of Agriculture proclaimed in ringing tones all he was going to demand in the negotiations. I will not quote what he said; it would not be kind. He said three times that we must get a period of adjustment and that deficiency payments would continue. He made those remarks in columns 596 and 597.

What is the position now? There is very great doubt about the production grants. It is very doubtful whether we shall be allowed even to have hill farming subsidies and the rest unless they are agreed on

[1] Rt Hon Christopher Soames, MP
[2] Hitler's Minister of Economics.

for the whole European area. It is virtually certain that fertiliser subsidies will go. The Minister of Agriculture entirely failed to answer our questions about whether even the marketing board system could remain. What did he tell us? He said that there would be room for marketing boards. Of course there will be room, but are there going to be marketing boards? Is the right hon Gentleman banging the table at Brussels and saying, 'There are going to be marketing boards or else'? This is the way in which he should be negotiating.

There will be no guaranteed markets and no deficiency payments and not even a period of transitional assistance. The right hon Gentleman may say a lot about his little consolation prize. They have given him his annual review. But there is no guarantee that action will follow it. He was very vague about this. He is committed to the proposition, because he said on 6th June that a review without action is meaningless. He also said:

> An annual review is not an end in itself.

He told us then all the grave things which would follow the review.

I put this to the Lord Privy Seal and to the Minister of Agriculture. Suppose that farm incomes were to fall between one little review and the next. Would action follow? The Lord Privy Seal yesterday made a great deal in the Commonwealth context about this concept of the 'reasonable price' for foodstuffs, whatever that may mean. But suppose that a 'reasonable price' is fixed for these agricultural commodities at a level which, as the Government hope, will mean some continuance of imports from the outside world. Suppose we get that reasonable price and suppose that the Minister of Agriculture's annual review shows that farming incomes are below a reasonable level, what will happen? Will prices be raised? Obviously, he hopes so. But what happens if they are raised to what the Lord Privy Seal considers to be an unreasonable level?

This is the whole problem. We are trying to run an agricultural policy on the basis of a single price, and we cannot do it. The whole basis of our agricultural policy for the past 15 years has been that, for this country apart from Europe, there is no reasonable price, no single price which allows in a fair proportion of imports from the Commonwealth and elsewhere and at the same time provides adequate standards for the farming community in this country.

For 15 years we have operated a two-price system – a higher price for British farmers with a lower price for imports from the Commonwealth. We have bridged the two prices – under the Labour Government by guaranteed markets and under the Conservative Government by deficiency payments. The essence of these negotiations is that the two-price system must go. We must have a single price system, and I tell the right hon Gentleman that it cannot work. He has not even secured interim arrangements for cushioning the shock.

This brings me to the problem of the Commonwealth. This has been very fully dealt with in the debate and I shall not go over the facts so clearly set out by my right hon Friend the Member for Leeds, South (Mr Gaitskell) and by my hon Friend the Member for Leeds, East (Mr Healey). Our Amendment, which shows a great deal more courage than the Government's Motion because, after Llandudno, they have gone right back to their resolution of August, 1961, says that

> the terms so far provisionally negotiated do not satisfy either these conditions –

that is, our five points –

> or the binding pledges given by Her Majesty's Government.

Can right hon Members opposite deny that they have gone back on every pledge that they have given about the Commonwealth?

Yesterday, my right hon Friend referred to possible elections. Let us be clear about what Ministers said on this subject before the last election, the arguments with which they won their votes. The Prime Minister said:

> I do not believe that this House would ever agree to our entering arrangements which, as a matter of principle, would prevent our treating the great range of imports from the Commonwealth at least as favourably as those from the European countries.

Yet the arrangement that the Lord Privy Seal has made is one of outright discrimination in favour of Europe and against the Commonwealth. No hon Member can deny this. The Prime Minister went on:

> We must remain free to continue to grant to this great volume of imports the preferential arrangements we have built up over the last 25 years.

Are we now free to do what the Prime Minister said?

Or let us take the Minister of Defence[1], when he was President of the Board of Trade. He said:

> We cannot enter into a Customs union because that would mean that we should have to put up tariffs, where no tariffs exist today, against a whole range of Commonwealth goods.

That was the Minister of Defence. Or what about the Chancellor of the Exchequer[2], when he was at the Board of Trade, who said:

> As the House is aware, we have given a clear undertaking to the Commonwealth countries to maintain their position in our markets for foodstuffs, drink and tobacco.

Does the Lord Privy Seal think that we have maintained their position in our markets for foodstuffs, drink and tobacco?

Again, let us take the Chancellor of the Exchequer, who said only a few months before the last election:

> I cannot conceive that any Government of this country would put forward a proposition which would involve the abandonment of Commonwealth free entry. It would be wrong for us and for the whole free world to adopt a policy of new duties on foodstuffs and raw materials, many of which come from underdeveloped countries, at present entering a major market duty-free.

That is a clear and solemn pledge made by a Minister of the Crown and that was the kind of guff that the right hon Gentleman and his colleagues were talking at the last election. That is what they got their votes for saying.

Of course, there was a more recent pledge by the Secretary of State for Commonwealth Relations[3] at his party's conference last year, and he repeated it in similar terms in June this year. This was the theme of the party opposite that we would not – we could not – surrender the principle of free entry for Commonwealth foodstuffs and raw materials; we could not dismantle preferences.

That was where the Lord Privy Seal started from in his negotiations. The preference horse, however, fell at the first fence. So the

[1] Rt Hon Peter Thorneycroft.

[2] Reginald Maudling.

[3] Rt Hon Duncan Sandys.

Government backed another. They backed 'comparable outlets' as the way out. If Commonwealth countries were to lose some of their market here, they would be compensated by an equivalent increase in their sales to Europe. This was the theme of the Lord Privy Seal's speech of 10th October, 1961, paragraph 45.

That horse went down, too. Now we hear nothing about comparable outlets. Then we backed commodity agreements. That is fine. We on this side have always pressed for commodity agreements. We took the initiative when we were the Government against fairly strong American opposition. We insisted on the drafting of Chapter VI of the Havana Charter on inter-governmental commodity agreements. I had a lot to do with the first drafting of the International Wheat Agreement. As late as last February, however, the present Government were voting against commodity agreements at the GATT conference in Geneva.

We on this side want commodity agreements. There is no guarantee, however, that we shall get them. Merely to say that we want them will not give them to us. Other countries are involved besides the Six; there is the United States. Certainly there is no prospect of getting commodity agreements before the negotiations are supposed to reach finality. If that is so, if we have whittled down these solemn pledges made by the Prime Minister – which I quoted before the right hon Gentleman was able to join us, as he has now done – and there is no more than a vague hope for commodity agreements, why are we dismantling our defences before we get them? Why give away the card of preferences before we are sure of getting these?

As I have reminded the House before, commodity agreements do not solve the problems. The Government are still involved in the International Sugar Agreement, but everybody agreed that that agreement did not provide the guarantees required by West Indian and other sugar producers. On top of that we had to put the Commonwealth Sugar Agreement. The Lord Privy Seal has never told us whether we shall be able to carry on with the Commonwealth Sugar Agreement if we join the Treaty of Rome. Has he negotiated this yet? Is the Commonwealth Sugar Agreement one of the fish that he has landed safe and dry on to the bank? There are not many of them, but we hope that he has got this one.

Where do the Commonwealth negotiations stand? We have been promised – this was the great thing offered to us yesterday by the

Lord Privy Seal – a reasonable price policy. The Six have generously said that their price policy will be reasonable. The idea is that if the price for wheat, dairy produce and other commodities is low enough, there will be a margin for third countries to export into Europe – and, of course Commonwealth countries will be able to scramble for their share of this. But how low is such a reasonable price? On a single price system – I come back to the point I was making about the inoperability of a system of this kind – when the price is low enough, if it is reasonable enough for the Lord Privy Seal's definition, to allow a continuance of Commonwealth imports, the Minister of Agriculture will have apoplexy, because it is far too low to meet the requirements of the farmers. He is counting on a high price. He told us so in June.

The Lord Privy Seal has secured his negotiating triumph, but all he has got, after 12 months of negotiation, and after the solemn pledges I have read from the Prime Minister just now, is a form of words that they will allow us to pursue a 'reasonable' price policy. Did he expect the Six to say they would be 'unreasonable' about the price policy? Has he got so much? A brilliant negotiator always says he will be reasonable. The Chinese have just asked India to stop resisting aggression and to start negotiating reasonable terms. Would any hon Member, buying a second-hand car, or a house, would one of the growing number of hon Members involved in mergers and take-over struggles, drop his guard and dismantle his defences in return for a promise by his negotiating partner that he will be reasonable about the price he was going to be paid? Of course they would not. Not one of us would do that in his private life. But the right hon Gentleman would. He did. In the Yorkshire phrase, 'They saw him coming'.

I hope he will tell us tonight what would be a reasonable price for wheat, because everybody who knows these figures knows perfectly well that if we get a price for wheat somewhere near the European price there will be a tariff of as much as 62½% against the British farmer's price, and it would mean a move of anything between £10 and £13 per ton – and the right hon Gentleman said it was inconceivable that this House could ever agree to scrapping the free entry of Commonwealth products.

So with all this uncertainty, with nothing at all secure for the permanent basis after 1970, and with virtually nothing for the transitional period up to 1970, why, I ask the right hon Gentleman, why give away his one negotiating card and agree to scrap the preference system and to scrap free entry till he has got something in return? This is not negotiation. This is unilateral disarmament.

The same applies to the whole question of Asian manufactured exports: give away the principle and try to salve a few reassuring words about the future. I understand that the Hong Kong talks are starting tomorrow and I hope that the right hon Gentleman will say something about them. These words about exports have no gold backing. The right way to ensure gold backing for them is to hold on to one's negotiating card till promises are matched by performance.

Independent foreign policy I shall refer to only very briefly. It was dealt with by my right hon Friend. We are very worried about the Government's ambivalence on this. It is not only causing concern in this country but it may lead to grave charges of bad faith in Europe if we go into a federation which is moving quickly to political union and then, after we have got there, we start dragging our feet over political union.

The Government have blown hot and cold. On the eve of the Conservative Party Conference the Prime Minister's pamphlet[1] – an extraordinary thing to do on the eve of a conference – played it down; but after his speech which won that 'Yes' he played it up, but there is no doubt in the minds of many of our European friends that to join the Common Market does mean a commitment towards federation. The Chancellor of the Exchequer, whom I have already quoted, and who spent the best years of his life negotiating in Europe, was never in any doubt. A few months before the election he said that

> we must recognise that for us to sign the Treaty of Rome would be to accept as the ultimate goal, political federation in Europe, including ourselves.

The Times, in a leader on 18th October, regarded it as axiomatic that joining the Common Market would mean some form of European Government, and it said:

> With the power to formulate a common foreign policy this in turn will have to be supported by a common strategy.

Is the House really ready to surrender the right to our independent foreign policy? The mere fact that we were not consulted over Cuba

[1] **Britain, the Commonwealth and Europe.**

does not mean that an independent foreign policy for Britain is already dead.

As I argued last week, that was merely a measure of where the Government have brought this country. We have a role to play in issues going far beyond Europe. In the past we have looked at the problems – African and Asian problems, becoming more important every day – not through European eyes but through eyes whose vision has been sharpened by years of active partnership in the greatest multi-racial system in the world. That is what is at risk now.

Before I conclude I want to refer to one myth which has been brought out, that of the declining Commonwealth. Commonwealth imports are rising. It is our ability to hold our market there which has been at fault. From 1953 to 1960 Australia increased her imports to us by 83%, but Britain's exports to Australia rose by only 22%. India increased her imports to us by 57%, but our exports to her rose by only 32%, despite the fact that loans in her case were tied to purchases in this country. Pakistan increased her imports to us by 86%, while Britain's exports to her increased by only 22%. The fault lies not in the Commonwealth but in ourselves.

That is why if the terms are unacceptable to us we have a real job to do in mounting a determined export drive to the Commonwealth. We must have a link with other Governments at governmental level in their Commonwealth development plans and must by every means open to a modern government recast our industrial development so that we get less expansion in the soft-centre industries and more in the hard-centre industries which are capable of making goods which the Commonwealth wants and for which so often Commonwealth countries turn to Germany, Japan and the United States.

The other thing that we have to do if the terms are unacceptable is to look at trade problems not on a narrow European basis but on an Atlantic basis – indeed, on a free world basis. I commend to the House the Report by Mr Herter and Mr Clayton published a year ago in the United States[1]. If we could have something on those lines bringing in the Commonwealth and Latin America – the whole free world – we should be on the right lines. We hear about the economic value of a market of 200 million people. What about a market provided by 1,200 million people?

[1] Herter-Clayton Report – a report to the Joint Committee of Congress on Foreign Economic Policies.

I hope that, in viewing the future, the Government will realise that one card that we have in our hands if Europe turns us down, if the terms are unacceptable, is that we have still to go to GATT. Do not let us forget that, because the agriculture proposals of the Six are absolutely contrary to the whole letter and spirit of GATT and can go through only if they have the support of ourselves and others.

Finally – perhaps I should refer to this – the challenge of the European negotiations was the theme of the Prime Minister's speech at Llandudno. We read it with interest. He said, 'We are to be the leaders of change. We must make the best use of our brains and of the traditional skill of our people'. How could he say that when skilled craftsmen are unemployed in increasing numbers, when school leavers in wide areas of the country are unable to get jobs which will enable them to be trained for skill, and many of them cannot even get jobs at all, when scientists are emigrating in droves to America and when world class scientists are seeking jobs at the employment exchanges?

We must accept change. We have said that. I said it at the TUC conference this year. We have stressed it on this side of the House in every economic debate in the last few years. We have heard before from the right hon Gentleman about change. We were heartened five years ago to hear his speech about the 'wind of change' in Africa. What have the Government done about the 'wind of change' in Africa? – Arms to South Africa, the Southern Rhodesian Constitution, Northern Rhodesia, Katanga, and Pilate washing his hands over Portuguese atrocities in Angola and Mozambique. [*Interruption.*] This has everything to do with the Common Market.

No one will deny that the change at home, to which the Prime Minister referred, is relevant to the Common Market. Change at home means more than nostalgic perorations about how bad unemployment used to be in Stockton under the Tories. In any case, Stockton opted for its change in 1945 when it threw the Prime Minister out. But, no, the right hon Gentleman tells us – I quote him – 'As a nation we are too set in our ways. We are too apt to cling to old privileges. We are too apt to fear new methods. We are often too unwilling to abandon old practices which have outlived their usefulness.' That is true – such as appointing one's nephews and in-laws to Government posts. That may not matter in this Government. I do not think it does. I do not think it either raises or lowers the level of the average quality of the Government. But it matters when it is happening in British industry or when qualified young men are being held back by the prevalence of industrial nepotism.

The Prime Minister calls for an attack on privilege. There was no sign of an attack on privilege in the Gracious Speech; on fiscal privilege where a favoured few, by one legal means or another, are able to evade their fair share of taxation – the farce of capital gain. Are the Government going to change what a Tory delegate at Llandudno called this 'property developing plutocracy', this stop-go system, red light after the election and green light in the last twelve months?

The Prime Minister's indictment of our economic and social system is the most telling indictment that I have read of Tory society and Tory freedom. This is Britain after eleven years of Tory Government, more than half of it, God forgive us, under the right hon Gentleman. We all of us know that the change that we need is a change that must come in this country, in our industry. We agree about that. We agree with the right hon Gentleman. There is no more dangerous illusion than the thought that entry into Europe is going to be a gimmick solving all our economic problems, giving us back our lost economic dynamic.

All of us know that that dynamic will come only from our own efforts in industry and our policies in this House. If we make the changes we have nothing to fear whether inside or outside Europe, but, if we fail, the only choice is whether we are to be a backwater inside Europe or outside Europe. Change we need, and here we agree, but the right hon Gentleman must know that the first prerequisite is that a change must be made in the leadership given to this country.

EXTRACT FROM DEBATE, HOUSE OF COMMONS, 13TH DECEMBER, 1962

MR HAROLD WILSON (HUYTON): The House will be grateful to the Lord Privy Seal[1] for this last of his series of statements to the House

[1] Edward Heath.

on the successive phases of the negotiations. Even if he never has very much success to report to us, at any rate he always reports with the greatest courtesy and gives us as much information as is possible in the time that he takes.

Before I come to the detailed negotiations, the first thing I must do tonight is to underline the very significant change of tone in Ministerial pronouncements about the Common Market during the past few days. We have had the President of the Board of Trade[1] and we have had the Chancellor of the Exchequer[2]. Enthusiasm for joining EEC on anything like present terms now seems very strangely muted. It is certainly very different from the halcyon days of Llandudno. I have referred before to the button marked 'Yes'; the President of the Board of Trade was not wearing one last Saturday.

Now Ministers are falling over themselves to stress that it would 'not be the end of the world' if we failed to get in. When I used these very words on 7th June, the Secretary of State for Commonwealth Relations[3] took me to task at once from the Box and said that it would be a great misfortune. Ministers are now even hinting that there is a possible alternative – as we have urged at all stages in these negotiations. I wonder whether they troubled to inform the Prime Minister about this possible alternative before he read out his Llandudno speech. After all the jibes we heard in October, I feel that even Ministers are now coming to recognise that it was the speech at Brighton[4] and not that at Llandudno which was realistic and responsible on this subject.

Obviously, tonight's statement was an interim report, and I was interested that the Lord Privy Seal said that next week the institutional arrangements are to be discussed. I hope this means that at long last he will come to the vital question of voting and the question of qualified majorities. I hope he will tell us about that tonight, because my right hon Friend and others of us have emphasised the vital importance of the size of the vote required for a veto in view of the far-ranging effect of qualified majority decisions over the whole economic life of this country. I hope that tonight he will talk about

[1] Frederick Erroll.

[2] Reginald Maudling.

[3] Duncan Sandys.

[4] Hugh Gaitskell's speech: Labour Party Conference, Brighton, October, 1962.

the position of this House and of Parliament under the Treaty of Rome.

We have raised this subject many times. We have been promised answers – we had a promise from the Prime Minister in July – but we have never had a single cheep out of the Government Front Bench on this question. All we have had is a rather meaningless statement by the noble Lord, the Lord Chancellor[1], addressing someone down in Bristol during the recess and leaving us in worse confusion than we started.

Tonight, I do not intend to deal with general issues, with arguments for and against going in, which we have debated so often in the past eighteen months. Nor do I want even to restate our own five conditions, the five safeguards, which we have laid down before Britain can consider entering. I propose to deal only with the details of the negotiations over the past month and to assess the position which we have now reached. I will take some of the points in series as the right hon Gentleman did.

I come first to Asian manufactured goods. The Lord Privy Seal has secured minor concessions – I do not depreciate them – minor reductions in the Common Market external tariff for items such as hand-knotted carpets, coir mats, jute bags and East Indian kips – he had quite a fight over the last. But on textiles, which the whole House recognises as absolutely vital to any programme of Asian economic development, there has been no concession.

The negotiations for trade agreements with these Asian countries, we are told, will open three months after Britain's entry in, say, April, 1964, at the earliest. But when these negotiations open all our defences and all India's defences will be down, because by that time discrimination in the British market in favour of Asian Commonwealth manufactured goods will have ended and discrimination in favour of Europe against the Commonwealth will already be in force.

I ask the Lord Privy Seal – and he has never answered this question – why did he not insist on maintaining these preferences and on relating any concession from us to progress in these negotiations for a comprehensive trade agreement. Why did he not say, 'No progress in the negotiations, no concessions in this matter'?

[1] Lord Dilhorne, formerly Reginald Manningham Buller.

Now there is a question of what the White Paper called *décalage*. I rather regret this Brussels jargon coming into British White Papers. I looked up *décalage* in a dictionary and found that it did not mean what I thought it did – it is much less interesting. I found that it means 'unwedging; throwing a machine out of gear; shifting a pulley off a shaft; or generally getting out of phase'. I would have thought that the right hon Gentleman could have found an English word to express all that in a White Paper.

On this question of what he calls *décalage*, so far as I can understand it, and the Lord Privy Seal has not given us full details of this, it would appear that Asian textiles have one programme for the application of the tariff, Asian manufactured goods yet another and other Commonwealth manufactured goods a third. I hope that when the right hon Gentleman winds up tonight he will tell us what those three ranges are, because there is a feeling, on studying the White Papers and trying to correlate them, that in certain respects at least Asian manufactured goods will be worse treated than some of the goods coming from more advanced Commonwealth countries. The right hon Gentleman realises in any case that to slow up relative *décalage* will simply mean a very heavy imposition of tariffs in the later years before 1970, and what we have been concerned with all along is not how we get to 1970 but what the 1970 position will be when we get there.

The next point is on raw materials. There is still no agreement on aluminium, newsprint, wood pulp, zinc and lead from developed Commonwealth countries. Negotiations on aluminium and newsprint were held in November, but, to quote the White Paper,

> the Conference reached no conclusions.

There are reports – I hope that the Lord Privy Seal will comment on them – that the Six have rejected abolition of tariffs, but have agreed to concede a tariff-free quota for Britain for newsprint and either a tariff-free quota, or a tariff reduction, for aluminium. I hope that tonight the right hon Gentleman will tell us whether this statement, which has been widely reported, is true. Will the right hon Gentleman also tell us whether the quota, if there is a tariff-free quota, for example, for newsprint, is intended to equal the whole present level of newsprint imports from the Commonwealth into Britain, or only a small proportion of them, and whether that tariff-free quota is merely a temporary transitional arrangement, or whether it is going to be permanent?

Turning to processed foodstuffs, we have had the Kangaroo meat and canned rabbit, but will the right hon Gentleman tell us something about the processed foodstuffs on which agreement has not been reached and how he sees the chances of agreement on them? As I understand it from the White Paper, there are about 29 quite important processed foodstuffs on which agreement has not yet been reached, and we would like to know not only whether that is so but what is the total volume at the moment of the trade in these processed foodstuffs coming into the United Kingdom.

This list includes canned fruit. I think that the House knows the importance of canned fruit in the Australian economy. These large areas are settled by ex-Servicemen of World Wars I and II, and the importance in the minds of Australian people and the Government far transcends even the value of the trade in monetary terms. I remember negotiations in the GATT conference eleven years ago when the Americans were willing to offer a substantial reduction in their tariff on raw wool from Australia, which ought to be one of the biggest prizes the Australian Government could have, but they set against that a reduction – not an abolition, not a reversion transaction – of Australian canned food, and the Australian Government said that they could not accept even that reduction in the preference on canned foods because of the social importance of this settlement, even though in return they would have got a substantial opening of the American market for raw wool. If that was how they felt then, and I suspect that they have not changed their position on this, I hope the right hon Gentleman will tell us tonight what he is doing to secure free entry for canned fruits.

We would also like to know about Canadian canned salmon. Again, there is a story that there have been some assurances or hints about tariff-free quotas for Canadian salmon, for Australian canned fruit. Is this so? Again, is it proposed that tariff-free quotas would cover a volume of trade equal to the present volume of trade into this country from those areas?

Before I come to the fundamental issues of agriculture and the Commonwealth countries – and really these are two sides of the same medal, and the sooner this is realised the more progress we will make

– there are three other questions arising out of the negotiations which I should like to put to the right hon Gentleman.

First, the right hon Gentleman referred to Article 234[1]. I gather from Press reports that some of the Six at any rate had unworthy suspicions about the Lord Privy Seal's good faith in regard to Article 234. They thought that, having come to a final settlement about the Commonwealth, he would use Article 234 relating to prior commitments to maintain Commonwealth arrangements that he had agreed in the general negotiations to scrap and would insist on keeping the EFTA agreement in being whatever else he might have agreed in Brussels. There was a lot of briefing to the Press from the Brussels powers last week that the Lord Privy Seal must be tied hand and foot on Article 234 lest he gets in by the back door what he has failed to get in at the front door of the negotiations. I understand that he has properly denied that he had any such intention, and I think that he was right to do so, because if he cannot win his points about the Commonwealth and EFTA in the main negotiations by a frontal attack, he should pull out of the negotiations. He should not use the back door, and I am glad that he has made his position clear.

When he gave his assurance about Article 234, did he raise the question of one prior commitment which is affected by this, one of the most important of all the prior agreements, namely, the Commonwealth Sugar Agreement? When I have raised points on the Commonwealth Sugar Agreement before, the Lord Privy Seal, has said, rather tetchily on one occasion, that he had not yet got as far as this. Perhaps he has not, but in view of its vital importance for the West Indies and other parts of the Commonwealth he ought to have, because I think he will realise that neither an offer of association to the West Indian countries, nor any development of the present sugar commodity agreement, will solve this problem. These areas must have the Commonwealth Sugar Agreement, and this must be a *sine qua non* of any settlement in Brussels. I wonder whether when he gave his assurance on Article 234, which he properly gave, he at the same time specifically reserved the Commonwealth Sugar Agreement?

Would he say a word on Article 234 about East-West trade? Is it the intention that any trade agreement we have with Eastern

[1] Article 234 provides that all existing national commitments in trade and economic matters must be made to conform with the provisions of the Treaty of Rome.

European countries would have to lapse, would have to go, if Britain entered the Common Market? It is, one understands, a fact – the right hon Gentleman will perhaps tell us whether this is true – that the Government are refusing to enter into long-term agreements with Eastern European countries and are only prepared to negotiate on a twelve-month basis because of the fact that we should have to scrap and curtail all this trade if we entered the European Economic Community. I hope the right hon Gentleman can deal with this point. If he cannot, perhaps he might consider publishing in *Hansard* the text of assurances that he gave on Article 234.

We would like to know the position on EFTA. We were a little reassured by what the right hon Gentleman said, because there were inspired stories last week that the Six were holding back even on the Norwegian and Danish applications until we were in. This has been dropped by the Six, but we still have the problem of the neutrals. I was glad to see a Press report that the Lord Privy Seal has been completely firm about the EFTA position in Brussels. From what he said tonight, that is the impression he was trying to give the House, that Britain cannot enter until the requirements of all our EFTA partners, neutrals and others, have been specifically met, whether by membership or by association, and I hope that the Six are now in no doubt whatsoever about the British Government's position on this, because we know that the British Government are fully committed.

I have a list of twelve detailed and specific commitments made by Ministers on the subject of EFTA in this House and elsewhere. Some had to be got out of them, but we got them in the end, and if I thought there was a danger that Her Majesty's Government might go back on the commitments I would read them tonight, even at the risk of wearying the House, but, despite the fact that the Government dishonoured their Commonwealth pledges, I think that the right hon Gentleman intends to stand firm on the pledges to the EFTA countries[1]. I am assuming therefore that the Government will stand by their word, and this relates not only to Norway and Denmark, but refers also to the neutrals, and that as regards the neutrals the Government will stand firm not only on the acceptance of the

[1] EFTA pledges: Government's assurance that Britain would not enter the Common Market until the vital interests of all our EFTA partners had been safeguarded.

neutrals as associates, but will stand firm on the timing of that acceptance.

On the question of associated overseas territories, the Government have rather given the impression that they have some concessions, that this convention on AOTs[1] is remaining open for the African countries to think again. That is what the Convention said. It stands permanently open, so there is no real gain here so far as we can see, and I hope that the Lord Privy Seal will make this clear. If one of the African countries, say, Nigeria, does not accept AOT status – and this is a matter which must be decided by Nigeria alone – and if some separate form of association is negotiated which goes less far than AOT status, does not this mean that Britain, on entry into the Common Market, would then be forced to erect discriminatory tariffs against Nigerian produce while allowing free entry of produce from ex-French territories in Africa, in other words, discriminate against Nigeria in favour of, say, Senegal, or other French territories? I hope that that will be made quite clear tonight.

I want to come to the main issue of the negotiations on which we have now come very near deadlock – the issue of agriculture. As I understand the position – if I may try to summarise it – the Lord Privy Seal, having first sold the pass by accepting the Community's agricultural problem, still hopes that the prices fixed, commodity by commodity, will be reasonable – that is, low enough to permit a full inflow of Commonwealth imports; while the Minister of Agriculture[2] has sworn by Ceres and Pomona, or whatever gods and goddesses a Minister of Agriculture may swear by, that prices will not be low enough to permit any such thing.

Having accepted the EEC agricultural system, I understand that negotiations have reached near deadlock on two things – and I am still only summarising the position. The first of these is the Community's insistence that our two-price system, and its concomitant system of deficiency payments, will be wound up, cut up, dead, the moment that we enter the Common Market – as against the insistence of the Minister of Agriculture of a more lingering death. I have quoted in the House the very, very clear and categorical insistence by the Minister of Agriculture, in that very brave speech of his on 6th June – which I now think that he would like to forget he ever

[1] Associated Overseas Territories.

[2] Christopher Soames.

made – that the deficiency payment system must continue for many years.

The second thing, as I understand it, is that although a working party has now been set up we may again be very near deadlock – and here the disagreement is perhaps as much between the members of the Six as between the Six and ourselves – about the financing of the Common Market Agricultural Fund and the ultimate disposition of the hundreds of millions of pounds of which British and other consumers are to be mulcted by the operation of this iniquitous import levy.

That is the position on agriculture, as I understand it. I hope that that brief summary – and I have put it with deliberate restraint – will be accepted by the House as a fair statement of the position that we have now reached.

Let me take these three issues one by one. First, the agriculture programme. Once again – and I am amazed at him – the Lord Privy Seal confirms that he has walked right into it as soon as they drafted it. Why? Has not it occurred to him that by accepting it he has made it impossible to get a price low enough to allow Commonwealth imports except by driving British farmers into bankruptcy? I gave him the whole argument on 8th November[1], and I repeated it in a letter to *The Times* last week. It is significant that the vast and highly articulate pro-Common Market lobby, never slow to rush into print, has not raised a single word of disagreement with the argument that I put forward in that letter. Not a single hon Member of pro-Common Market persuasion, or a single pro-Common Market supporter in the whole country can defend or justify the Common Market agricultural system.

For 15 years in this country we have reconciled the apparently irreconcilable requirement of cheap Commonwealth food imports with a fair measure of security for the British farming community. We have done it by this two-price system, bridging the gap between the two prices by guaranteed markets and price averaging when we were in power, and by deficiency payments by right hon Gentlemen opposite. Now we are to have a single price if we go into the Common Market. Ministers delude themselves if they think that we shall get a price which will allow in Commonwealth imports and be fair to

[1] Debate in House on Common Market, see pages 122-3.

British agriculture, because, on a single price system, there is no such price. And for most agricultural commodities European prices are a good deal higher than ours.

Let us take wheat, for example. The French target price for wheat at present is about £35 9s per ton. In Germany it is £43 3s. Comparable Australian wheat is coming into this country at between £20 and £25 a ton at present. That means that if the Common Market price is no higher than the French price there will be an automatic import levy of at least £10, or 40%, on Australian wheat coming into this country, and if the final price fixed is anywhere near the German price the levy will be at least £18, or 72%.

We have accepted the agricultural programme with the certainty of harming if not destroying either Commonwealth trade or British agriculture. But we have also accepted the likelihood of an increase in food prices of between 8s and 10s per head per week. The Lord Privy Seal gave some very revealing figures recently, which were published in the *Daily Telegraph.* I do not know whether they were meant to be published, but, on any calculation, they suggest an increase of from 8s to 10s per head per week. If this happens, what do hon Members think will happen to wages and industrial costs?

Then there is the effect of this levy on our balance of payments. It has been estimated that this would be £250 million a year, and possibly more. The right hon Gentleman has accepted all this. For what? For fair words – and even some of those fair words have been qualified in the past two months. So we do not know what they meant. We had some fair words on New Zealand in August. Since then, however, the French have made it clear that they do not accept what we thought was the general interpretation of those offers to New Zealand.

Having swallowed the camel, Ministers are now arguing about the question of transitional provisions. We have been told that the deficiency payments will end on the day that Britain enters the Common Market. There may be an easement for one or two products, where British prices are above the European level. That goes without saying. The Lord Privy Seal hinted that a possible extension will be allowed for a month or two in order to carry the Government up to the election without a too obvious repudiation of yet another pledge to British agriculture.

As for the agricultural fund – here we have a really monstrous proposal. The levies on our food would not accrue as tariff revenue to the Chancellor of the Exchequer. If they did he might use them for paying increased pensions, or for partial compensation of higher living costs, by cutting Purchase Tax on essentials – although, being a Tory, he would probably give the benefit to the Surtax payers, on the ground that they would need better incentives if we entered the Common Market. But he will not have a chance of making this decision, because this enormous revenue will have to go to the European fund, and it will be used partly to subsidise European agriculture and partly to subsidise exports of high-cost European produce in third countries, and so have the effect of penalising still further Commonwealth producers who have already been pushed out of the British market.

Let me tell the Lord Privy Seal what he should have done, and what he should still do. He should recognise that negotiations on detail, from now till Domesday, cannot solve the agricultural problem. We cannot accept the agricultural programme so long as it is based on this penal import levy, and if the Six persist we should join with the majority of the GATT countries, including the United States, in declaring it invalid. That is what the right hon Gentleman should be doing.

On 8th November[1] I reminded him that this policy is contrary to the letter and spirit of the GATT. He disagreed. I ask him now, who was right? Ten days later the 18-member Committee of the GATT condemned the EEC programme out of hand, and fourteen days later the United States Secretary for Agriculture subjected it to a blistering attack. Why does the right hon Gentleman, having this weapon in his hand, insist on always negotiating from weakness when he could negotiate from strength and insist on accepting something which he must know to be wrong when he could be fighting for what he knows to be right. It is because of this posture that the Government have adopted from the outset; because of the ministerial speeches; because of the spirit of Llandudno[2], and because of a Prime Minister who insists on treating these vital negotiations as an electoral gimmick, that we are in this weak position.

Let the right hon Gentleman think again. Let him recognise that while the industrial Common Market can be outward-looking and liberal – and I believe that it is intended to be – the agricultural

[1] Speech in House of Commons, see extracts, page 129.

[2] Conservative Party Conference, Llandudno, 1962.

Common Market is restrictive, autarkic and Schachtian and is an offence to the trading interests of the free world. It will divide, not unite. We should have no part in it. I do not want to rub salt in by saying too much about the Acheson speech[1]. I think Lord Attlee was right yesterday in saying that the Acheson speech was an attack not on Britain but on the Government of Britain. Ministers reacted against that speech last week, and I was rather surprised, because the Acheson speech was in fact Macmillan in an American accent. It was the same thing, the same theme, that we are nothing without Europe. That was the main theme of the Prime Minister's TV broadcast and his Llandudno speech. And there was his reply to Lord Chandos[2]. After all the jibes at my right hon Friend's thousand years of history, we got the lot from the Prime Minister – we got four hundred years of it at any rate, going right back to Philip II of Spain. I ask you!

I do not think that it is quite a parallel. I do not remember the Lord High Admiral of those days, Lord Howard of Effingham, negotiating with another Power for the weapons with which to defeat the Armada; or saying that we must have them if we were to have an independent defence policy. No. While I disagree with the Acheson speech as a description of the real mood and temper of the British people, and I disagree still more with his conclusions, one can see how anyone who has watched this country and the right hon Gentleman from July, 1961, onwards could get the wrong idea of that temper and that mood. A lot of it derives from the posture of the Government.

It is from this posture that Ministers – I warned the House last May that this would happen – are trading defence and foreign policy for supposed economic advantage. We sabotaged the chance of preventing the spread of nuclear weapons by defending a French nuclear policy for which Ministers in their hearts had nothing but contempt. I make this further forecast. The Minister of Defence will be offering to save President de Gaulle £300 million and four years in time by offering him plutonium, if the Lord Privy Seal thinks this necessary to get another concession on preserved food stuffs.

I began by saying that one or two Ministers – not, of course, the Lord Privy Seal – are beginning to lisp the language of alternative

[1] Dean Acheson speech: 5th December 1962, West Point.
[2] Formerly Oliver Lyttelton.

policies. We welcome it, but it is a bit late. Eighteen months ago we told the Government that they would negotiate from greater strength if they worked out credible alternative policies to strengthen their hand; policies to fall back on if our negotiating partners proved too obdurate. Earlier this year we indicated more than once what they should do. We set it out in our Brighton document[1]. Let me conclude by opening the eyes of the Lord Privy Seal to wider horizons than those to which he has been confined for the last few months and to the basis of real negotiating strength.

First, whether in or out of Europe, we should turn our eyes towards an Atlantic trading community, indeed, one covering the whole of the free world rather than a community covering part only of Europe. In the last debate I referred to the Clayton-Herter Report[2] to the US Congress which I believe holds the key to the future in this respect. President Kennedy's trade expansion Act envisages negotiations within the spirit of GATT with the enlarged Six, including Britain on one side of the table and the United States on the other. So be it, if we get in. But if entry becomes impossible, I recognise that there will be a big traumatic shock in Washington, though – let us be frank – more and more Americans are becoming worried about the implications of the EEC policies especially in relation to agriculture.

When we have all had time to get over the shock, why not have the same negotiations with the United States, with, perhaps, a different shaped table; with the United States, Britain, the Commonwealth and Latin America and the EFTA countries on one side and the Six on the other? I know that this would mean a small change in the United States legislation by including the Douglas Amendment[3]. But after all the Chairman of the Ways and Means Committee of the House of Representatives made it clear that this was envisaged if the Brussels negotiations foundered. Out of the breakdown we could then erect a freer trading community for the whole of the free world, with, one hopes, agreement at long last on measures to increase the

[1] Labour Party document on Common Market presented to 1962 Conference at Brighton, and endorsed.

[2] See page 128.

[3] Provided that the freedom given to the President of the US to negotiate trade agreements with other countries should apply whether or not Britain entered the Common Market: the Act as passed by Congress was based on the assumption of British entry.

volume of international liquidity; with commodity agreements – after all the initiative did not come from the Six in Brussels; it has been an international agenda for many years – with provision that if the Western world insists on having higher prices, and we do, for agriculture, any resulting surpluses should be made available to the hungry nations of the world. It may be time to reconsider Lord Boyd-Orr's pronouncement regarding world food[1] which was made many years ago at a time when it would have been more difficult to accept it.

It may be said that this is visionary and that American protectionists will never agree. Perhaps I have had as much experience of this kind of negotiation with the United States as anyone in this House. I am not sure, however, that the kind of negotiations which I have mentioned need be more obdurate or difficult than the kind of negotiations which the right hon Gentleman has been having in Brussels all this time.

Because of this fear that these negotiations may not succeed or because of the greater likelihood that they will take a long time, my second point is that we should consider it all the more urgent that the Government should press on more urgently with improving the links of Commonwealth trade. By this I do not mean a Commonwealth free trade area. I have advocated that in the past and I wish that we had one. I believe the Government should have made all-out efforts to get one. But I also believe that now the opportunity has passed.

The shock to the Commonwealth resulting from Ministerial treatment of their pledges this year has been too great to be able to get a Commonwealth free trade area now. But I believe that the atmosphere, particularly if the Brussels negotiations break down, would be such that a British Government – may I say that a new British Government would have a hundred per cent better chance of success than this one – could then call a Commonwealth trade conference, and we could begin with the development plans and see what we could do to help with essential equipment.

I am not only talking of plans for the underdeveloped areas. What about a big development scheme in New Zealand where a textile mill has just broken down, for which we have some responsibility?

[1] Lord Boyd-Orr: proposal in 1946 to the Food and Agriculture organisation of UN for a World Food Board.

What about a development scheme in Australia such as the scheme in the last decade, the Snowy River scheme? Experts and engineers should sit down together to see how our productive capacity could be integrated in these various production schemes. This could lead to a substantial increase in Commonwealth trade. Let us recognise that it could not be a one-way trade. It could not be unilateral. We should have to give guarantees about buying goods both from advanced Commonwealth countries and underdeveloped Commonwealth countries.

If we are to do this, it would mean reversing this laissez-faire attitude of the past ten years, and it would mean forsaking our ideological worship of speculative commodity markets and a return to guaranteed markets at fair prices. I have said again and again that I do not accept the decline in Britain's trade with the Commonwealth as due to historically inevitable factors. Our decline in recent years, our relevant decline in Commonwealth trade, has been due first to Conservative ideology and a succession of wrecking measures breaking the links of Commonwealth trade – such as the futile restoration of the Liverpool cotton market, which has never worked anyway.

Secondly, it has been due to the miserable failure of large sections of British industry – there have been honourable exceptions – to capture Commonwealth orders which were open to us. In the last debate I gave the House some figures showing that the decline has not been in Commonwealth imports as a whole. They have increased steadily. The decline has been in our share. We have lost the markets, despite preference, to exporters from Germany, Italy, Japan and the United States. If we are to win these markets, it will mean a major re-deployment of our industrial resources on hard-core goods; the production of the goods which the Commonwealth and other countries want. We shall not win back the markets which we have lost with a soft-centre economy.

I will not develop my third point because it is more appropriate to another debate. It is the need for a virile reconstruction of our economy and industrial life on lines which we have urged for so many years. Every hon Member in this House knows that, in Europe or outside, we shall be a backwater unless we ourselves, both sides of industry, Government and Parliament, effect a transformation in our economy so that we can recapture that lost dynamic; so that we can get British industry sparking again on all six cylinders instead of idling and misfiring.

I suggest this three-point alternative which we should be preparing. If the Government would even now at this eleventh hour seriously apply themselves to such an alternative, recognising all it would mean for both the external and internal economic policy, they would, at one and the same time, strengthen the hand of the right hon Gentleman in negotiations and provide an alternative and viable policy to fill the vacuum, the dangerous vacuum, which we may face if, in January or February or March, we are faced with the clear realisation that the terms dictated to us in Brussels cannot be accepted without national humiliation. By failing to prepare such an alternative, the Government, on their own argument, are driving us into a position where there may be no alternative to unconditional surrender.

DEBATE IN THE HOUSE OF COMMONS, 11TH FEBRUARY, 1963

MR HAROLD WILSON (HUYTON): I beg to move, to leave out from 'House' to the end of the Question and to add instead thereof:

> has no confidence in the ability of Her Majesty's Government to formulate or to carry through a programme which would bring about the necessary changes in our policies for international trade and for economic and political co-operation; and does not believe that it has the capacity to arouse in Great Britain the sense of urgency and national purpose so necessary to meet the situation created by the breakdown in the negotiations in Brussels.

No words of mine could be more eloquent in support of that amendment than the speech which we have just heard.

I do not intend to spend a lot of time on it, but what does the Prime Minister think that he has achieved by that speech? He got a lot off his chest about President de Gaulle. We understand that, but the speech did not provide a breath of justification for his policies over the past eighteen months and gave no indication of a Government with either the ideas or the capacity to chart a course out of this Sargasso sea in which they have found themselves becalmed. Looking for any positive policies and for any inspiration, the nation, when it comes to study his speech, will find nothing but defeatism, a certain amount of peevishness, and a complete policy vacuum.

There were one or two parts of the right hon Gentleman's speech which I think the House will have found interesting. There was his appeal on behalf of an understanding for Dr Adenauer. I find it hard to give the right hon Gentleman the support for which he asks in that direction. We have read Dr Adenauer's speech this weekend. He does not want us in because he calculates, rightly, that at the next General Election this country will go Socialist. Hon Gentlemen opposite, with no confidence in their own ability to stop it, now look to Europe to stop it. Dr Adenauer went on to say, and on this occasion he was wrong, that at the next election this country will go neutralist. We shall not.

I was moved also by the right hon Gentleman's reference to Commonwealth trade. Quite early in his speech he said that during the last 18 months the Government have studied with greater care than ever before these problems of Commonwealth trade. What were they doing for the 10 years before that? No doubt during those 18 months they were studying Commonwealth trade with great care, but for what purpose? For the purpose of entering into agreements that would have destroyed a great part of it. There was plenty of care. Oh, yes! It was the same care with which an intending burglar studies a house. I think that it is called 'casing the joint'.

At any rate, I will say for the right hon Gentleman that this afternoon he did not try, as in his broadcast, to evoke a Dunkirk spirit. I am glad that he did not, because it does not lie in his mouth, the man who fought the last General Election on a materialist 'Never had it so good' philosophy, the man who has preached the doctrine and whose Government have encouraged other people to follow the precepts of an 'I'm all right, Jack' philosophy. In any case, I should remind the right hon Gentleman, although I am sure that he does not need reminding, that the success of the Dunkirk appeal from the right hon Gentleman the Member for Woodford (Sir W. Churchill) was that that right hon Gentleman had no responsibility for the state of affairs that had led up to Dunkirk.

There is, at any rate, one central theme which was clear again this afternoon and which is already passing into the corpus of Conservative mythology. This is the idea that the Government were within an ace of achieving a satisfactory agreement only to find the prize snatched from their grasp by an intransigent Frenchman. Let this myth be nailed once and for all. Even ignoring the long list of unsolved problems – from the Commonwealth Sugar Agreement to New Zealand butter, the association of Commonwealth African countries, the price level for food and agricultural prices, transitional provisions for British agriculture and, still more important, a permanent settlement for British agriculture; quite apart from all these unsolved issues, the fact is that the terms which have been negotiated, the accumulated totality of vital national and Commonwealth interests, already surrendered by the Government, already constituted a national humiliation.

We on this side of the House had laid down a series of broad conditions and detailed requirements which we felt must be met if this country could reasonably be asked to enter into the Community. We were agreed on them and we believe that the country supported them. Again, I ask the House now: where was the greater realism to be found and the greater sense of national interest shown – in Brighton[1], or in Llandudno[2]? When we debated the state of the negotiations and the outcome of the Commonwealth Prime Ministers' Conference in the two-day debate on 7th and 8th November[3], we moved an Amendment saying flatly that the terms obtained up to that time were not acceptable. Since that time, there have been unacceptable concessions on agriculture, on net tariffs, and a total collapse of what should have been our position on voting rights and on the extent of the veto. We therefore utterly reject this account of a satisfactory agreement sabotaged by President de Gaulle.

The right hon Gentleman spent a lot of time on President de Gaulle. What we should have liked from him would have been more information on his meetings with the French President. It would have been interesting if the veil could have been lifted on the *tête-à-tête* at the Chateau de Champs and at Rambouillet. Last May we warned the right hon Gentleman against throwing a cloak of

[1] Brighton Labour Party Conference, 1962.
[2] Llandudno Conservative Party Conference, 1962.
[3] See pages 116–130.

respectability over President de Gaulle's nuclear ambitions in return for help in getting into the Market. No one – not even the Prime Minister – can now be in any doubt about what the French nuclear go-it-alone, do-it-yourself policy means either for the unity of the Western Alliance or for world-wide hopes of preventing the spread of nuclear weapons. But it is now becoming very clear from President de Gaulle's disclosures last week that the Prime Minister last year not only condoned French nuclear plans, but encouraged them.

When the right hon Gentleman, in the defence debate a fortnight ago, spoke of fighting a General Election on the line that Labour's policy would mean that France would be the only nuclear power in Europe, and when the Leader of the House[1] dutifully took up the call in a speech in East Anglia, and when no doubt, the printing presses at the Tory Central Office are already grinding out propaganda material on this theme – we can trust the Leader of the House to see to that – do not hon Members opposite ask themselves who, above all others in the alliance, were responsible for encouraging France in becoming an independent nuclear Power? They have only to look at President de Gaulle's comment on that to find the answer.

What is much more important now than who was responsible for the breakdown is the total failure of the Government to produce any plans for the future. All we have been able to deduce from the Prime Minister's speeches and actions since Brussels is that the only concrete reaction, the one dramatic piece of policy following the new situation, is the petulant cancellation of a Royal visit to Paris[2]. When I interrupted the Prime Minister to ask him about the misleading statements which have been put out, he said that it was in accordance with the usual diplomatic courtesies to tell lies.

If that is his idea of diplomatic courtesies, it is about time that someone else was in charge of diplomatic courtesies. At any rate, I will say this for the right hon Gentleman. We are quite used to getting two accounts put out by the Government. We usually get the true one given to the Press and a false one given in the House. What we have had this time is a false one given to the Press and the true one given in the House.

This highlights how serious the situation is, for we have had from

[1] Iain Macleod.

[2] Cancellation of visit by HRH Princess Margaret to Paris.

the Prime Minister no plan and no proposal either in the world economic field or in any measures at home to reassure our sense of national purpose in domestic economic policy. Why? Why is it that no preparations were made long in advance of the possibility of the Brussels negotiations breaking down? It was certainly not for want of advice. In every debate on the Common Market that we have had my hon Friends and I have stressed the need to prepare alternative policies: first, to strengthen the Government's hands in the talks – because negotiations without a credible alternative are liable to lead to unconditional surrender – and; secondly, simply as a measure of prudence, to prepare for the situation which would arise if the negotiations broke down – the situation with which we are now faced.

I will not worry the House by repeating the warnings, proposals and alternative policies we put forward in debate after debate. If any hon Member doubts that we did so, I can give him a full list of references – from *Hansard*, articles and speeches in the country – which will indicate exactly what the Government were told. But the Government – the Prime Minister and his right hon Friends – were so convinced that we had no alternative but to go into Europe that our warnings went unheeded.

We remember the Foreign Secretary[1] asking in another place, on 21st June, 1961, whether we could afford to stay out, with only one answer in mind. We can remember speech after speech which the Prime Minister made and that broadcast of his last September in which he wondered what would happen if we did not go in but stood outside. We should not be able to develop our true strength, he said, or be able to compete in a world of giants.

Does the right hon Gentleman accept that as a true description of the position in which we find ourselves now? In that broadcast the right hon Gentleman went on to discuss the economic reasons for our going in and he described the products of which British industry was capable of producing. Would we be able to sell those goods either to the Europeans in the Common Market area or outside in other markets in the world against competition? How would we sell them in the home market which is only a quarter the size of theirs? That was his argument in September. Really, have we now no hope

[1] Lord Home (now Sir Alec Douglas-Home) in House of Lords Debate.

of selling them? The right hon Gentleman, in that broadcast speech, said:

> I know that there are some people, however, who talk as if there was an alternative system to the Common Market.

and, in the rest of his broadcast, he went on to prove how foolish and short-sighted they were.

Then we had the pamphlet[1] issued to the nation, or Conservative conference, a week before Llandudno, a somewhat undignified proceeding, one would have thought, for the Prime Minister. It contained one idea: that if we did not go in, we were finished. No wonder the Prime Minister was so defeatist this afternoon if that is what he really thinks. What has collapsed is not only the Common Market talks, but the whole system of Government policies based on them. From July, 1961, onwards the whole complex of economic, trade, defence and international policies revolved around entry into Europe. It was meant not only as an electoral ploy – and the Prime Minister made no secret of that – but an economic solvent as well, to call Europe into existence to redress the balance in British industry, to enforce the pay pause, to solve the industrial problems which the Government had failed to solve – and so, with the breakdown, the whole edifice of Government policy collapsed.

I do not intend to say much more about the Government's record over the last eighteen months. It would be easy for me to go on, and, I must confess, it would be tempting to go on, but where the Government have so manifestly failed leads my right hon and hon Friends and I to accept that we not only have a right but a duty to say what we believe should now be done. What we are putting forward we are not going to call an 'alternative'. Much of it – such as the need for more dynamic policies at home – has been, and would have been, equally necessary whether or not we entered Europe. Again, the same applies to world commodity agreements. These would have been necessary irrespective of whether or not we joined the Common Market.

What we are really discussing today is not a packaged alternative to the Common Market, but a plan for the future of Britain in world trade and economic affairs. To approach this we must get the facts

[1] 'Britain, the Commonwealth and the Common Market'.

clear. First, the Prime Minister was a little nostalgic as to whether or not the talks were on or off. They are off. We had better understand that. While we are not slamming the door to proposals to advance European unity – indeed, we do not rule out the possibility of further proposals on this – we must understand, agree and resolve that we cannot hang around in European antechambers for a further period of months or years in the hope that the Brussels temperature will become warmer.

We certainly do not rule out the possibility of further negotiations in Europe at the right time and under the right auspices. (HON MEMBERS: 'Oh?') Hon Members opposite should be a little more patient. I intend to say what they are. In any further negotiations in Europe we cannot again allow ourselves to get into the posture of suppliants. It was in that posture that the Six regarded us, even if we did not so regard ourselves. If at any future time we enter negotiations in Europe we must not start from the catalogue of concessions granted by the Lord Privy Seal which, we felt, went far beyond any authority granted by the House of Commons, and which, in our view, would have been rejected by the country.

Secondly, we must get clear which markets are and which are not affected by the breakdown in Brussels. The markets of the Six? Yes, undoubtedly this is affected, though we are selling there today and we are selling in the United States, despite a considerable domestic tariff. The Commonwealth? Our trade with the Commonwealth has received a merciful reprieve. Harm has been done – great harm, in our view – not only by the clear willingness of Ministers to sacrifice their interests to the scramble to get into Europe but, no less, by the whole manipulation of the Commonwealth Prime Ministers' Conference, the calculated leaks by British Ministers to the Press – and the guiltiest of the lot the Secretary of State for Commonwealth Relations[1], who, I see, making notes – designed to isolate and, even on occasions, to discredit individual Commonwealth leaders. The whole sorry history of this was given in the debate on 7th November last by Hugh Gaitskell and has never been answered or denied by the Government.

Because of this we certainly need a new Commonwealth Prime Ministers' conference to restore confidence, but we must ask whether

[1] Duncan Sandys.

the Government has not gone too far now to have any hope of success. Nevertheless, there is good will in the Commonwealth countries despite all this. As to the efforts of our exports, and apart from the fact that some Commonwealth countries have already redeployed their trading arrangements because of what they thought we were going to do in Europe, the markets are there.

The dollar areas? Our trade with them is unaffected completely by the breakdown. EFTA? Our links there remain and, as I think the Prime Minister tried to indicate, these links can and should be strengthened – certainly until something better comes along. The third countries? From Latin America to the Far East these markets are unaffected for our exports. Eastern Europe – East-West trade – remains open to us.

Indeed, we have escaped a twofold danger which was presented in the talks, as we warned: first, adoption of a common European trade policy, which would have limited our freedom to complete trade agreements with Eastern Europe; and, secondly, the effect of the Market's agricultural policy of placing penal import levies on agricultural imports from Eastern Europe, which would have prevented those countries from buying engineering and chemical plant from us.

There is scope for East-West trade, and we are now free to develop it. While not exaggerating the prospects – the House will recognise both the possibilities and the limitations– we can now achieve a substantial increase above all in those products of heavy industries where orders are so urgently needed to get back to full employment in our northern industrial areas. Nothing would be further from the truth than for the idea to get about that our export trade is finished or that we face an inevitable decline. We do not. The upward trend of our exports is, as it always was, a matter uniquely dependent on our own endeavours.

One thing further is that we no longer face, as some of us felt we faced with the concessions which the Government had made, a choice between the Commonwealth and Europe. Nor are we faced with a choice between Western Europe and some of our partners in EFTA. There is no ground for defeatism provided that we seize the opportunities presented to us.

What about the political position in Europe? The position here is undoubtedly more sombre. Our task, avoiding all bitterness and recrimination, is to ensure that existing political relations, and, in particular, the Western Alliance, are not further endangered.

What, then, are we to do? I begin with Europe. Our European initiative should be on the basis of an area of Europe wider than the Community, wider than the Six. The Six, EFTA and we in any such initiative should leave the door open for other countries, such as Yugoslavia. We shall make more progress, whether in economic or political co-operation, the less we aim at federal or supranational solutions, the more we work within an inter-governmental framework.

In our view, OECD[1] provides an adequate forum for this. We should take the initiative at OECD, making clear our willingness to discuss any proposition which covers the whole European area of OECD. The position is obviously too fluid to have any hard and fast plans about what is to be done, but we ought not to rule out an idea which was put forward from this Box four years ago – the idea one day of a free trade area in which the Six would join as one integrated country.

The main reason for the failure of the Maudling Committee[2] was the feeling of the Six that we were working in the hope of destroying the unity and integrity of the Six. Readiness to accept the Six as an integrated unit might create a new and more favourable climate – I do not know, but it is worth trying and it is better than sitting down and criticising what President de Gaulle has done.

We should be quite ready, too, to examine any French proposal, if such there be, for an industrial free trade area. I do not know what de Gaulle backing there is to this proposal and there would certainly be difficulties about an industrial free trade area – Denmark is one. However, I thought that the Lord Privy Seal rejected the idea rather too hastily. It was a fortnight ago and we could understand his feelings at the time – heaven knows that we could understand them – and I certainly would not have excessive hopes that this would be a satisfactory solution.

But at any rate let us keep an open mind and, if they are willing to talk about an industrial free trade area, let us have a look at it, provided only that we are not to be kept hanging around again and

[1] Organisation for Economic Co-operation and Development.

[2] A Committee set up shortly after the establishment of the Common Market aimed at the creation of a 13-nation free trade area to replace the Common Market.

provided only that such discussions do not exclude action on all the other fronts, including the Commonwealth and including the Atlantic area with which I shall be dealing.

On the political side in Europe, so far as the alliance is concerned, we must base our stand fairly and squarely on NATO. Cynicism and bitterness about the recent French action must not be allowed to endanger NATO still further. As we urged in the defence debate, a great initiative is open to us by taking the lead and improving the effectiveness of our conventional contribution to NATO. There is equal urgency about proposals which have been made from this side of the House for strengthening the political arrangements and the political control of NATO.

However, that is not the whole answer, of course. Some of our friends are not in NATO, including Sweden and Austria. They are not in WEU. That is why I am rather doubtful about the Prime Minister's first thoughts of working through WEU, which, I gather, he indicated last week. We must realise that we are considering a number of possible courses of action in Europe. It is not yet clear which of them, or which combination of them, will be the right ones, but at any rate we should consider these.

We could show our determination not to turn our backs on Europe and we could show our desire for greater European unity of an acceptable pragmatic kind if we made a formal proposal for regular meetings of heads of Government of all the countries of Western and Northern Europe, not with the idea of imposing a federal constitution or common foreign and defence policies on the basis of majority decisions, but to get the widest measure of agreement possible on international questions.

This is not a dramatic proposal, but some of the most significant advances in international co-operation began far less dramatically. In the present condition of Europe, we might have to be content with a step at a time. But in our negotiations and groupings and in all we try to do in Europe we must be constantly looking outward to wider horizons, and this brings me now to a subject touched on by the Prime Minister – the trade and tariff negotiations on an Atlantic scale – indeed, wider than Atlantic; on a two-oceans scale.

For many of us, one important test of the Brussels negotiations was whether the resulting Community at the end of the day would be restrictive and protectionist and inward-looking, or whether it would pave the way for a wider zone of freer trade – the Prime Minister expressed the same thought this afternoon. President Kennedy's Trade Expansion Act was directed to this very end. As the House knows, President Kennedy was given power in the negotiations with the enlarged Community, including Britain, to reduce any tariff by 50% and, in the case of commodities where the enlarged Community plus the United States accounted for 80% or more of world trade, to negotiate with full powers to reduce the tariff to nil, a provision which realistically took account of the fact that under GATT any tariff concessions mutually agreed in bilateral negotiations had to be extended on a most-favoured-nation basis to all other signatories of GATT.

We have been pressing for some time – we said this in the debate in November and again in December – that we should not regard any breakdown in Brussels as a disaster, but that we should go forward with the Kennedy Round. We know that the United States legislation specifically refers to a state of affairs in which Britain is in the Common Market. The Douglas amendment[1] was accepted by the Senate and, in the conference which followed between the two Houses, it was clearly said by the Chairman of the Ways and Means Committee, Mr Mills, that if Britain did not get in the matter could be put right quite simply by an amendment.

What is now required, as we argued in December, is the same negotiations as were already planned, the Kennedy Round, but with a different table plan. Instead of a confrontation with the United States on one side and the enlarged Community, including Britain, Norway and Denmark on the other, we should have the Six on one side – as soon as we can get them to sit down together again – and the United States, Britain, our EFTA partners and the Commonwealth on the other. It may be that the United States will insist on Latin America; so be it.

Talks on these lines should be pressed urgently. I was glad that the Prime Minister appeared to feel that this was the right course and I hope that when Mr Herter was over here last week, talking to the Government, the Government gave him the green light for these talks to go ahead. There are some who may say that these talks, too, will founder on the rocks of French obstructionism, but if we are to

[1] See page 142.

initiate nothing because of those fears the outcome is certainly predictable – we shall achieve nothing.

Now, the problem of Commonwealth trade. The Prime Minister said very little about this. He told us that the Trade Ministers were to meet together before the GATT ministerial meeting. But is not this common practice? Has it not been the position all along, wherever there is a ministerial meeting in the GATT, in the International Monetary Fund, or whatever it may be, that the Commonwealth Ministers get together first? It always used to be so under the Labour Government. Has it changed, or is the Prime Minister just taking what is normally common form and scratching it together to make something to put into his speech? I say frankly that, after the handling of the Commonwealth Prime Ministers' Conference, we shall need something more than a routine meeting to restore confidence.

I come now to specific measures to develop Commonwealth trade. We have been urging these measures for 10 years, because we simply do not accept the relative decline of Commonwealth trade as a historically necessary secular trend. Commonwealth imports have not been falling; they have been rising sharply during the past few years. I gave the figures in our debates last year and I shall not repeat them now. What has fallen has been not Commonwealth imports, but Britain's share of the trade going into these markets. We have lost ground year after year to Germany, the United States and Japan, despite our preferential advantage, simply because we failed to demonstrate a willingness and ability to seize the trading opportunities which are open to us.

We have lost ground, also, because of Government policy, the systematic dissolving of the links of sterling area inter-dependence, destroying, in the interests of speculative commodity markets, the system of long-term contracts and bulk purchase[1] which, in my submission, did more for Commonwealth trade than the preferential system ever did. Government policy bears a heavy responsibility for the relative decline in our trade with the Commonwealth. During recent years, the heat of Government policy and exhortation which has been turned on to British exporters to trade with Commonwealth countries has not been a tithe of 1% of the heat directed to trade with the dollar area or trade directed towards Europe.

[1] Under the 1945–51 Labour Government.

What we now suggest for Commonwealth trade is not an alternative to OEDC or to the Kennedy Round. It can go on simultaneously; there is nothing incompatible. I suggest that we begin by sitting down with Commonwealth Governments and their public purchasing agencies and discussing their development plans in detail. I do not mean only with the underdeveloped countries. In 1949, Board of Trade officials, special missions appointed from industry and the Government spent months sitting down with the authorities responsible for, for instance, the Ontario hydro-electric scheme and the Toronto subway, seeing where we could help and considering what could be done to channel major equipment orders to this country.

There was the Snowy River scheme in Australia. There were vast development programmes in New Zealand. More recently, under this Government, we abdicated from the Canadian coast-to-coast pipeline project without a struggle. There is the Volta River scheme and a score of lesser projects in Asia and Africa. These projects are going on all the time in both advanced and underdeveloped countries.

Despite the grave harm done during the past 18 months, there is still enough good will so that these countries would welcome our representatives sitting down with them and getting down to cases to see where we can help. These things could lead to quite spectacular orders, but, of course, they involve obligations upon us as well. We must, in return for a greater willingness to take our products, be completely forthcoming in our willingness to buy, on a long-term basis from them, guaranteed quantities of Commonwealth primary products.

This will mean – we must face it – interference with speculative markets. It will mean bulk purchase or equally effective alternatives. We cannot afford to let ideology stand in the way. [HON MEMBERS: 'Oh'.] If hon Members opposite are not interested in getting these orders from Commonwealth countries, I pity them. I am telling them how to do it. What I am saying may or may not be ideological, but it will get the export orders. It did last time, and it will next time. The method of right hon and hon Gentlemen opposite has failed.

I remind the House that, in the days of the Anglo-Canadian bulk purchase wheat agreement, which many hon Gentlemen opposite viciously criticised but which was one of the finest bargains ever recommended to the House, the Saskatchewan Wheat Board was the best ambassador for British exports to Canada that we ever had.

These things could happen again. Commonwealth planning of this kind would have another implication for this country, too. We must ensure, by purposive economic planning at home, that we expand those sectors of our industrial system which are needed to supply the particular types of development capital needed.

We shall not do this on the basis of a laissez-faire, soft-centred, speculative, hire-purchase, advertiser-controlled, stop-go, three-year freeze and a false thaw every election year, sort of economy. We have had a lot of experience of this now. We must have the changes in our industry which are needed to meet these markets. Hon Members opposite know perfectly well that these markets are there, and the reason why we are not getting them is that we have not created the industry capable of meeting their requirements. If that is not true, why have we not been as successful as other countries, when we have had the preferential advantage, in getting into these markets?

What this all means is not only a national plan for Britain – hon Members opposite are supposed to believe in this now – a target of 4% or whatever it is every year, but the means of enforcing that plan, not just a global financial plan but detailed industrial expansion plans for the sectors which have to expand to meet Commonwealth requirements and the requirements of world trade generally, for transport, for earth-moving equipment, for irrigation equipment and the rest. This will require a whole range of action on the part of the Government. My hon Friend the Member for Cardiff, South-East (Mr Callaghan), if he catches your eye tomorrow, Mr Speaker, will deal with that.

It will require tax incentives. It will require State-guaranteed orders. Hon Members opposite should not scoff at this. I can tell them of cases under the Labour Government when business firms or consortia came to us with world-beating inventions, but were afraid to go into production because they thought that the markets might not be there. They asked us to provide a guaranteed order, that the Labour Government would buy any which they failed to sell. We gave that guarantee, and what they then produced has been one of the finest of our lines in the export market ever since. Sometimes, the Government must give guaranteed orders to private enterprise so as to get the production lines laid down.

It will mean more than this. It will mean State initiative in building, equipping and running factories to fill the hard-centre gaps in our economy. We must have State factories, too, to provide some of the goods which the Commonwealth will want.

I turn now to the measures on a world scale which will be needed. Again, most of these are not alternatives. They are certainly not panic measures thought of after Brussels. First, measures with regard to world liquidity. We all agree now on the urgency of means to ensure that world trade does not seize up through a shortage of the necessary monetary lubrication.

World commodity agreements. I am glad that the right hon Gentleman gave his blessing to this. It is a new thing for the Government. One would have thought, when the Six proposed this as a means to enable the Government to escape some of their Commonwealth commitments, that no one had thought of it before. But, of course, the Havana Charter[1] negotiations, largely on the initiative of the British Government, prepared a complete chapter of agreed enabling provisions. Year after year we have pressed for them both as a Government and an Opposition. The Prime Minister is now converted to this idea, yet only last year, in GATT, his Government voted against commodity agreements when the proposal was made on Commonwealth initiative in Geneva.

One of the difficulties has been that there has been United States opposition to the idea of commodity agreements. Now, for the first time, we have an American Government in active sympathy. They see, if others do not, the futility of beggaring the primary producing countries of Africa and Latin America and then having to spend millions of dollars on military means to fight the Communist threat there. This quest of stability and security in primary cereal crops is absolutely vital to these areas. All the advanced countries today, all of us, have painfully raised our total contribution of economic aid to the underdeveloped areas to a total now of almost 3½ billion dollars. The whole of this and more was wiped out by the fall in the purchasing power of the recipient countries through the fall in commodity prices over the past two years.

Thirdly, and linked with this is the problem of surpluses. It seems to be a political law of advanced countries that our concern for our

[1] The agreement to establish a world free trading system negotiated in 1947. With the failure of the US Congress to ratify the Charter the temporary, interim General Agreement on Tariffs and Trade (GATT), was put into force which despite its provisional nature has become a permanent body.

own agricultural producers is such that, taking advance countries as a whole, there is a permanent endemic surplus of agricultural goods and, of course, the Brussels agricultural programme will swell this surplus still further. In food production we are no longer affluent societies; we are surplus societies. Commodity agreements for temperate foodstuffs must provide machinery for channelling the overspill of our advanced countries into the hungry countries on the lines of the World Food Board proposed years ago by Lord Boyd-Orr. I led a delegation to a four months' conference to examine that. That scheme did not go through because of a peculiar post-war condition, but times have changed, and it should be revived as an essential proposal in the world after Brussels.

But why food only? There is a surplus of steel in many advanced countries, and in this country the steel mills are working at 60% capacity. We all want to help India and a score of other developing countries. Apart from money, why not send them a million tons of ingot steel? We might go further. Our railway workshops stand idle through a combination of Government ideology and the end of steam as a means of locomotion. But those of us who have had to deal with the problems of developing countries know that the biggest bottleneck in many of them is rail transport, and for them steam is not obsolete. Why, then, should there not be international plans for mobilising some of these workshops in Britain and elsewhere to produce the locomotives and the rolling stock? Why not mobilise the steel mills to produce tracks?

Next year the United Nations is holding a conference on world trade and development. I should like to see the Government propose that that conference be advanced a year – held this year – and that at that conference proposals for the mobilisation of surpluses of food, steel and rolling stock, and the rest, be considered and put into action. Of course, the other priority on a world scale is that of providing markets in advanced countries for Asian, and later African, manufactured goods. This was one of the issues on which the right hon Gentleman had a lot of difficulty in Brussels.

Britain, as Lancashire and Cheshire hon Members know, takes more than her fair share of Asian textiles and other manufactured goods. To talk of world development and then to refuse on an international scale a planned access to our markets is hypocrisy. That is why not only the Six, whose record in the matter is abysmal, but all advanced countries should agree on quotas to allow a reasonable flow of these goods into their markets. The George Ball proposal[1] is one that we should support.

I have not dealt in detail with the implication for British economic and industrial policy of the post-Brussels challenge because, as I said, my hon Friend will deal with that matter tomorrow. But I must emphasise the need to maintain intact our foreign exchange controls, and, if need be, to strengthen them. We know that this would have been impossible under the Treaty of Rome, and we have frequently expressed our anxieties about this. Doubts and uncertainty at any time may lead to sudden and perilous flights of capital, including British capital, from the City of London.

The breakdown of the Brussels talks, with the certainty now of a discriminatory tariff against our exports to Europe, may well increase the number of firms seeking to establish plants in Europe. In such cases this will be of value to our balance of payments, but it is essential that full control be maintained case by case. It is appropriate in every case to use exchange control.

Nearly two years ago, when we produced our statement 'Signposts for the Sixties'[2] we said that whether we went into Europe or not the case for a purposive plan for economic expansion was equally strong. If we did not achieve such an expansion the only choice was between being a backwater inside Europe or a backwater outside Europe.

I think that the events of the past few weeks have underscored that warning. The veils have been torn away. One thing is clear. Our future lies now clearly in our own hands, on our sense of purpose, of dynamism, of self-discipline, of sacrifices, if sacrifices there must be, fairly shared. If this failure of the Brussels negotiations has brought this home to us as never before, I thank God for it, because this is the first condition for reasserting our national strength and our national independence.

What has been brought home in these past few weeks with almost sickening clarity is the total incapacity of the Government to produce the policies capable of mobilising the energies of Britain in the 1960s. The right hon Gentleman's speech today was one of abdica-

[1] Put forward at a Geneva Gaat Conference and suggested that all advanced countries should take agreed reasonably liberal quotas of Asian-manufactured textiles.

[2] Labour Party policy statement, 1962.

tion on behalf of a whole Government. The recovery of Britain's lost dynamic is a task that must and will now pass into other hands.

SECTION V

Foreign Policy and Defence

Five of the six speeches in this section were made after I became Opposition spokesman on Foreign Affairs in November, 1961, the last two of them as Leader of the Opposition.

The first was the winding-up speech for the Opposition in the memorable Blue Streak debate in April, 1960. As is explained in the speech the Government after the Suez débâcle instituted a major change in defence policy by announcing its intention to switch from manned bombers to a genuine British independent bomb-carrying missile – Blue Streak. Long before it was ready to leave the drawing board, but after the expenditure of getting on for £100 millions, Blue Streak was scrapped, largely because military technology made a fixed-base, liquid fuelled rocket highly vulnerable to a pre-emptive strike by the enemy. Labour speakers, (the debate was opened by Mr George Brown, then Opposition Defence spokesman), had good reason to feel that the Blue Streak project had been continued long after most experts had recognised that it should be cancelled, and that the unhappy story had a great deal to do with Ministerial rivalries. Be that as it may, the cancellation of Blue Streak was the end of Britain's attempt to maintain a genuinely 'independent' British means of delivery.

Mr Watkinson's decision to rely on the American 'Skybolt', a stand-off aerial missile, which was criticised by Labour speakers, had an equally unhappy outcome, Skybolt being scrapped by the American Government in December, 1962, Britain then transferring its reliance to Polaris, which as my speech makes clear, had been rejected in favour of the Blue Streak in 1959.

The speech in the defence debate on 6th March, 1962, foreshadowed the cancellation of Skybolt, a forecast which was vehemently rejected by Ministers. It also contained a detailed outline plan for the disarmament talks projected for the summer of that year.

The Berlin speech on 5th July followed a mission of over 40 Labour MPs to Berlin the previous month.

The speech in the Nassau debate on 31st January, 1963, two weeks after Mr Gaitskell's death, and two weeks before my being elected as Party Leader, was the concluding Opposition speech in the two-day debate on the agreement signed by Harold Macmillan and President Kennedy at Nassau the previous month. This agreement followed the US cancellation of Skybolt, and provided that Polaris weapons, and the know-how for building Polaris-carrying submarines, should be made available to Britain. Mr Macmillan undertook that these weapons be incorporated in a NATO deterrent, but secured the agreement of the American President to a clause under which they could be withdrawn in case of urgent national need. It was this clause on which Mr Macmillan relied for his claim that Britain would still possess an 'independent' (sic) *'British'* (sic) *deterrent.*

This speech contains the definitive Opposition viewpoint on the so-called independent deterrent and on Labour's attitude to 'European deterrents' and any proposals involving German participation in a joint nuclear deterrent.

The speech at the National Press Club, Washington, (*see page 207*) *was made when I visited Washington in March–April, 1963 to meet President Kennedy and other US leaders.*

Finally, the speech in the Foreign Affairs Debate on 3rd July, was made shortly after my visit to Mr Khrushchev and other Soviet leaders about the prospects for a test-ban agreement. It was in this debate that I made clear that the Western Governments should drop their insistence on an inspected ban on underground tests and concentrate on a ban on tests in the three 'environments', the atmosphere, space and under-water, the only type of test ban to which, I felt, Mr Khrushchev would be likely to agree. The agreement reached at the end of the month was in fact on these lines.

CHAPTER SEVEN

*

Blue Streak Debate, House of Commons, 27th April, 1960

I PROPOSE TO DEAL IN THE MAIN tonight, following the terms of our Motion, with the unhappy story which culminated in the announcement by the Minister of Defence[1] on 13th April. The main facts have been recounted by my right hon Friend the Member for Belper.

While, of course, missile research goes back a good deal further this story goes back to about 1957, when we had a new Defence Minister, now the right hon Gentleman the expensive Minister of Aviation[2]. Really, it goes back to the Prime Minister and to the post-Suez situation, as my right hon Friend said. Suez, besides being a moral crime and an international blunder, was universally admitted to be about the most inept military operation in the whole of our long history. So the right hon Gentleman the Prime Minister, who boasted on television, on his appointment, that he would make Great Britain great, tried to find a short cut to greatness, and, as he hoped, a cheap short cut to greatness. The means he chose was to sacrifice the whole of our defence resources to keep up with our nuclear neighbours.

That was to be the means and the right hon Gentleman the Minister of Aviation was to be the instrument. We had the H-bomb; the problem was the delivery. The V-bombers would serve until the mid-'sixties and then we should need an independent missile, hence Blue Streak. The then Minister of Defence, the present Minister of

[1] Harold Watkinson.

[2] Duncan Sandys.

Aviation – I think that he was the eighth Minister of Defence that we have had under this Government – told us last year how Blue Streak came to be chosen. These were the words he used:

> Before coming to our decision, I can assure the House that we made a searching examination of this problem with the help of our scientists and military experts and with the full co-operation of those engaged on this work in the United States. . . . In making the choice of the Blue Streak rocket we considered a wide variety of operational factors – thrust, range, vulnerability, size of warhead, spare-carrying capacity for various future developments and, finally, date of delivery. . . . But in the present state of knowledge –

this is last year when he was speaking –

> I am confident that our decision to continue with the development of Blue Streak is the right course, and, in fact, that any other course would involve a wholly unprofitable 'gamble'.

That was his phrase – 'wholly unprofitable gamble'. We had the bill this afternoon for avoiding that gamble.

The then Minister of Supply[1], who addressed us this afternoon – they were all in it up to the neck, the whole lot of them – said in last year's defence debate that Blue Streak was not a duplication of American development. It was a necessary intermediary between the American single-stage missile and the multi-stage missiles they were working on. Blue Streak was, he said, essential. He used these words which I think the House should take account of today – this was the then Minister of Supply, the right hon Gentleman the Member for Hall Green:

> I do not see how we can lightly turn round to the United States and say, 'No, we have not the talents nor the skills, nor the resources to do this. We must look to you to develop something in addition to what you are doing'.

The right hon Gentleman said that we could not go cap in hand to the Americans to provide a means of delivery: no, we needed our own independent means of delivery. What he then said that we could

[1] Aubrey Jones.

not say to the United States is exactly what the Minister of Defence is now saying to the Americans.

The then Minister of Defence went on to refer to the need for 'a margin of additional power and payload. . . .' He said:

> The Blue Streak, with its powerful thrust and large capacity, will, we believe, provide this margin, and sited underground it will be very difficult to knock out.

The then Minister of Supply had no margin at all, whether of thrust or capacity, and he was knocked out himself soon after.

The Minister of Aviation went marching on. Although he was laconic in the House, it was outside the House that he became really lyrical about his pet project. In February, 1959, on the eve of the Prime Minister's visit to Moscow, the right hon Gentleman held a Press conference, and the whole of the Press were left in no doubt of his enthusiasm. To quote only one of the papers involved, the headline in the *Evening News* was:

> Blue Streak wins. Go-ahead for 3,000 mile missile. Now Macmillan will talk from strength.

The newspaper went on, obviously quoting the right hon Gentleman:

> The Blue Streak which can be developed for space exploration . . . adds up to the fact that when Mr Macmillan goes to Moscow next week he will be able to talk to the Soviet leaders from a position of impressive strength.

I have a large number of cuttings from different newspapers, and they are all practically identical in their wording. At the same Press conference, to judge from the Press, the right hon Gentleman made some scathing criticism of Polaris, with which Ministers, or, at any rate, some of them, are now flirting as a possible substitute for Blue Streak. A year ago the Minister of Aviation utterly dismissed Polaris as a possibility.

He said that it was unlikely to remain undetectable. Perhaps Russian powers of detection have deteriorated since a year ago. He said that its movements could be closely watched by an enemy. According to the right hon Gentleman, all this is presumably no longer true.

However, the newspapers came out with the headline: 'Polaris out.

Blue Streak in', on the basis of what the right hon Gentleman told us.

That is one of the troubles of having nine Ministers in less than nine years, each of them with a new costly project, scrapping his predecessor's project and launching out on another.

We opposed the gamble. My right hon Friend the Member for Belper was very blistering about it year after year. It was clear, certainly to this side of the House and to informed sections of the Press 16 months ago, that the project should be scrapped. However, the right hon Gentleman went on with it and was still going on with it this year. In February of this year the Government were still standing firm. On 8th February, the Minister of Aviation accused my hon Friend the Member for Bosworth (Mr Wyatt) of harbouring dangerous thoughts when he conceded even the possibility that Blue Streak might be abandoned. The right hon Gentleman said on 8th February:

> I know of no intention to discontinue the development of Blue Streak.

All these intricate mergers in the aircraft industry, all the right hon Gentleman's shotgun weddings between one aircraft firm and another, were based on the assumption that Blue Streak would go on, and on the division of labour between civil and military work in the various firms being integrated.

Now I come to the Defence White Paper of two months ago. This said:

> The development of the British ballistic missile Blue Streak is continuing.

Then, of course, it started to hedge:

> However, it may be decided –

and I quote what my right hon Friend the Member for Belper quoted this afternoon –

> not to rely exclusively on fixed-site missiles as the successor to the medium bomber armed with the stand-off powered bomb. Therefore, the possibilities of mobile launchers, whether aircraft or submarines, for long-range delivery of nuclear warheads are being investigated.

The key word there, if words mean anything, is the word 'exclusively', but the Government have entirely changed their policy since the White Paper was debated in the House only a few weeks ago.

The Minister of Defence[1], the present Minister – No 9 – opening the defence debate gave the House this encouraging message and perhaps one or two hon Members actually believed it. Commending the White Paper to the House he said at the very beginning of his speech:

> the Government's plans for defence are clear, comprehensive and, I believe, give good value for money . . .'

And there are actually some who say that the right hon Gentleman has no sense of humour.

Just six weeks later, and, of course, about two days after the Press had got the story, the Minister came to the House and pronounced the funeral oration on Blue Streak. What the House and the country have the right to know is why it took 16 months and £100 million to take a decision which most informed people knew had to be taken as early as January, 1959. The Minister of Defence has not given us the answer today in his lame and limping list of excuses. He did not speak as if he had his heart in the job. The only time that he spoke with any assurance at all was when he was sheltering behind his civil servants – when he was whining at the Box that civil servants had not advised him last September that the scheme should have been dropped. Let me tell him that Lord Crathorne, when he was Sir Thomas Dugdale, did not do that[2].

The right hon Gentleman told us why the scheme was not dealt with earlier. Some cynical people, among whom I am not to be found, might have thought that the reason was the election, that it was a costly fiasco on the eve of a General Election and that it might diminish the enthusiasm of those ageing young Conservatives who went from meeting to meeting shouting 'Groundnuts' every time any Labour candidate tried to emphasise to the electorate the need for expanding the development of the underdeveloped areas.

Perhaps it was not the election. In my view, it was not. Frankly, the reason for the refusal to write off Blue Streak when everyone else saw what the position was, the reason for the waste of tens of millions of

[1] Harold Watkinson.

[2] A reference to Lord Crathorne's resignation on the Crichel Down affair.

pounds was one thing only – to save the face of the then Minister, the present Minister of Aviation[1]. This is the most expensive face in history – certainly since that of Helen of Troy launched a thousand ships, and at least they were operational.

This is not just our view. Let me quote the *Financial Times*, the voice of the City:

> Blue Streak survived as long as it did simply because Mr Duncan Sandys is an extremely obstinate man. He based his defence policy on the deterrent, and he based the future delivery of the deterrent on Blue Streak. So long as he was Defence Minister he was a jealous patron of the project against all comers and, indeed, against all arguments. Even after he had left the Ministry of Defence his ardent advocacy in Cabinet, backed by muttered threats of resignation, kept Blue Streak alive – though on sufferance only – in this year's Defence White Paper.

There we are – 'muttered threats of resignation'. The right hon Gentleman should speak up. Let us be clear. It was not, of course, considerations of cost that caused the project to be dropped. The sudden change was the admission that fixed sites, even holes in the ground, were extremely vulnerable to enemy attack.

I have quoted the *Financial Times*. Now I will refer to an important article which appeared in *The Times* last February written by its Defence Correspondent, whom hon Members on both sides of the House regard with great respect as a defence authority[2]. I apologise for having to quote so many newspapers, but Ministers give us so little information in debates that the House is launched on a projected expenditure of £500 million or £600 million on the basis of a dozen lines of explanation in Hansard. So we have to rely on what Ministers opposite tell the newspaper correspondents, who produce their stories afterwards.

It was clear from the account in *The Times* that at the very time when the Minister of Aviation was announcing in February of last year the victory of Blue Streak, the end of Polaris and the rest of it, a high-powered committee had been set up by the Ministry of Defence, under its Permanent Secretary, to decide all these issues,

[1] Peter Thorneycroft.

[2] Alan Gwynne Jones.

and the right hon Gentleman was going out on his own, making his announcement and prejudicing its decision. However, the Powell Committee went on meeting and finally produced the decision of 13th April this year, as we understand it.

Before I turn to the finance of this matter, I will examine some of the arguments put forward by the present Minister on 13th April and repeated today. The right hon Gentleman now admits that my right hon Friend was right on 13th April when he said that the estimated cost was certainly over £100 million. What has the Minister to say? The Minister says that the cost of completing it would be between £500 million and £600 million. In other words, he says that the project has been stopped when about only one-sixth of the expense has been incurred, so that we have not wasted £100 million, we have saved £400 million or £500 million. You lucky people!

What an argument for defending a policy, a policy which is involving £100 million going down the drain. It can only be compared with the argument of the man who banged his head against a wall for 10 minutes and, in answer to queries as to why he was doing it, said that it was because it was so nice when he stopped. Not satisfied with this, the Minister continued:

> If we are to keep the peace for an occasional expenditure of £60 million-odd, it is very cheap.

Yes, but how does the Minister argue that this £60 million or £100 million has helped to keep the peace? It has gone on research and testing structures and projectiles, which were not, in any case, due to be operational until 1965, and now never will be. How can he say that this has had any bearing on the maintenance of peace? Of course, if he really believes this, if the abortive expenditure of £100 million has kept the peace, then on his argument he should have gone on and wasted the lot.

The Minister of Defence tells us again that the decision to make Blue Streak was based on the best military and technical and scientific advice. So, incidentally, was the groundnuts scheme – on the advice of Unilever. But the then Minister's chief adviser, Sir Frederick Brundrett, on whom great reliance must have been placed, said recently that the alternatives of airborne or seaborne missiles are still a long time off, and it will be 1970 at the earliest before Britain can have a mobile independent deterrent.

So here we are. In 1957, we were told that we must have rocket delivery of an independent British missile because V-bombers would be going out of business by the mid-1960s. A start was urgent because eight years would be needed. Now, with three of the eight years gone, we are told that there is time to look around. If that is true, why did we have to take this desperate and costly plunge three or more years ago?

Why was it that eight years ago we needed every month to be ready by 1965, but now, in five years, we have plenty of time to look around? The Minister of Defence said today that we have Skybolt. Have we? We do not know about that.

This is the trouble. Every new Minister of Defence has a pet project. He finds a goose and tells us in one White Paper, that it is a swan – until we have finished paying for it and then it is a dead duck. Are we, in fact, getting Skybolt? Does it exist? The Minister was only able to tell us that the United States Government would give it full priority. Is that not what the British Government did with Blue Streak? Is this a guarantee?

The *Observer* of 10 days ago carried an interview with a high Pentagon officer. It is worth quoting:

> Pentagon sources are saying that the logic which forced Britain to abandon the Blue Streak missile will compel her to abandon an independent deterrent. 'We have reason to think this is what London plans eventually', a United States Air Force general said.
>
> He and other senior officers contend that if a fixed-base missile, like the Blue Streak, is too vulnerable to missile attack, the airfields from which the V-bombers would take off are even more vulnerable.
>
> If the bombers can be destroyed on the ground in a surprise attack it makes little sense to buy the American Skybolt for them. Even with the ballistic missile early-warning station at Fylingdales Moor, Britain would have only a three-minute warning against rockets from Eastern Germany bases 600 miles away.
>
> 'To avoid having her bombers destroyed on the ground, Britain would have to maintain an airborne alert. And you don't seem to be able to afford that', the American general said.
>
> 'If the Blue Streak is too expensive, then an airborne alert and the Skybolt are too expensive for you. As a matter of fact, you

> already are in the position of not having an independent deterrent, and by deterrent I mean the threat that you will hit back if you are hit'.
>
> 'Because of distance they may not catch us on the ground, but they could catch you now'.
>
> 'The Skybolt will not change matters much because it will not be ready for six years and, in any case, it is too big for your V-bombers'.

This is a Pentagon general talking. Members opposite will find that Pentagon generals very often have great power with the State Department, and some of the optimistic accounts which we have had today may not be so optimistic when we debate this next time. The *Observer* article added:

> As for announcing that Britain may acquire the Skybolt, this is considered here as a face-saving step, half-way to abandoning an independent deterrent.

If it is not Skybolt, is it Polaris? Does the Minister of Defence agree with the devastating criticisms made by his right hon Friend the Minister of Aviation at a Press conference a year ago, when he used such phrases as 'extremely costly', 'unlikely to remain undetectable', 'its movement could be closely watched by an enemy', and so on.

Reference has been made to space research. We were all impressed by the speech of my hon Friend the Member for Bosworth[1]. The Government must not try to use space research as a way of riding out of this situation. If there is a good case for space research – and we should like to know – the Government should come honestly to the House, make a full statement of what is intended and give a full and accurate account of what it is to cost and, for once, let the House of Commons know what it is to be committed to.

The other problem is that of those engaged on this work. I wish to say that all our criticisms of the Government today are no reflection on the technicians, designers and scientists who have done a wonderful job on Blue Streak. They have solved thousands of problems that might have been thought to be insoluble. The complaint and the attack are not on them, but on the Minister for his misdeployment of

[1] Woodrow Wyatt.

his valuable scientific resources. Let me remind the Minister that the total spent on civil research in this country is about £60 million a year. We have had £100 million going down the drain on Blue Streak for the past four or five years, with all that that could have meant if it had been properly deployed.

The Minister of Aviation will no doubt announce the new deal which he has fixed up in Germany – the supersonic jet airliner. I hope that he will not try to sidetrack his responsibility for Blue Streak by a thing like that. If he is to announce a programme of joint missile research and production with Western Germany, involving strategic missiles, we on this side of the House will view it with very great anxiety, indeed. As we have shown in the Lobbies, we are already most anxious about the supply of nuclear arms to Western Germany. If there is to be any question of missile production, we shall want to go into the matter very thoroughly indeed.

I turn for a moment to the financial aspects of this problem. Grave criticisms were made by hon Members opposite, including the noble Lord for Dorset, South (Viscount Hinchingbrooke), before and during the Budget debate, about the growth of Government expenditure. I suggest that this is a subject to which they should give their minds. How they vote tonight will, perhaps, be a good test of their sincerity in this matter.

This is a dramatic and expensive illustration of a wider problem, that of Parliamentary control over expenditure on defence. In the sense in which the House understands it, control of public expenditure no longer works. Before the war, we could order a battleship and we could know what the cost would be and what we were getting, and there could be investigation, if it cost too much and it could have specific descriptions and was an identifiable animal. Now there can be no accurate estimates and, therefore, no control of expenditure. The whole business is done on a cost-plus-research basis and the contractor himself is the custodian of the public purse. It is difficult for the House, even *ex post facto*, to find out what has been happening.

If one could imagine the Government doing something so useful as sponsoring a system of cancer research, a wonderful thing to do, as with missiles one could never say for what one was looking and it would all have to be done on a cost-plus basis. That is another reason to add to those given to my right hon and hon Friends for demanding an independent inquiry into what has happened to Blue Streak as a guide for the future.

The Government have so far been completely frivolous and irresponsible about this gross waste of public money. The Minister of Defence[1] today said that £500 million was not an excessive economic burden on the country. The Minister of Aviation[2] arrived at London Airport last week with such helpful phrases about £100 million as, 'It will all come out in the wash', and 'We will be on the side of the angels'. There was not one word or suggestion of contrition for the way in which he has been responsible for this monstrous waste of Government money.

What of the Chancellor of the Exchequer? I should have thought that he would have been sitting in on the whole debate. Was he not concerned? We were told that the right hon Member for Monmouth (Mr Thorneycroft) resigned over £50 million. Since then, £100 million has gone down the drain.

We used to hear a lot from hon Gentlemen opposite about groundnuts, but at least that scheme left some abiding assets of value in East Africa – hospitals, roads, ports, and harbour installations. I remember Lord Crookshank – there is no time for all the quotations from those groundnut debates, but how I would like to make them tonight – reminding the House that the House of Commons was responsible for the waste of £35¾ million, which would be chicken feed by the calculation of the Minister of Defence. Lord Crookshank went on to say

> although we have got a new Minister, it is still the same Government, I am sorry to say, and they still have the same collective responsibility, and they still have the same Prime Minister . . .

He added:

> This House regards as essential and urgent a full inquiry into the present situation and the future prospects . . .

We do not get – [HON MEMBERS: 'Was there an inquiry?'] Yes, there was a full inquiry. We do not get this attitude from the Government when it is a question of social expenditure. We did not get it just

[1] Harold Watkinson.

[2] Peter Thorneycroft.

before Easter in the censure debate on old-age pensions. We would not get it if it were a question of more money for a hospital. We do not get this idea when it is a question of finding £5 million to get rid of prescription charges on the old-age pensioners and the chronic sick. What has gone down the drain on this scheme would pay for the full restoration of housing subsidies for 20 years.

The trouble is that there is no sense of guilt. The attitude of right hon Gentlemen opposite is out of keeping with the tradition of the House. I began by saying that the House would want a much wider debate on these issues, because what we have seen today, as my right hon Friend the Member for Belper indicated, is the end of the independent nuclear deterrent. From now on, there is no sense in any defence talk about independence. From now on the word will have to be 'interdependence'.

We have had nine Ministers of Defence and we have spent more than £15,000 million, and yet the whole of our defence policy today is in shreds. Hon Members opposite, who will be trooping into the Lobby in half an hour, know that as well as we do. Today's debate is a censure on the Minister of Aviation and those who bear joint responsibility with him, but in a wider sense the facts which have been disclosed today reflect most gravely of all on the Prime Minister.

Since the right hon Gentleman has been Prime Minister the country has spent nearly £5,000 million on so-called defence. When he became Prime Minister, he set out to keep up with his nuclear neighbours. Like so many other rather pathetic individuals whose sense of social prestige outruns their purse, he is left in the situation at the end of the day of the man who dare not admit that he cannot afford a television set and who knows that he cannot afford it and who just puts up the aerial instead. That is our situation, because without an independent means of delivery, the independent nuclear deterrent, the right hon Gentleman's cheap, short cut to national greatness, is an empty illusion.

As the *Financial Times* said:

> We should leave to General de Gaulle the fatuous search for national prestige through the belated and the technologically inferior production of weapons that belong in the arsenals of powers richer than ourselves.

After the disaster which we have debated today, does the British deterrent, based on Blue Streak, impress our nuclear neighbours any more than France's Sahara bomb impresses us?

I have given reasons, as have my right hon and hon Friends, why the Minister of Aviation should make a short speech, apologise and resign – but I am not certain that he should resign alone.

DEFENCE DEBATE, HOUSE OF COMMONS, 6TH MARCH, 1962

LAST YEAR, THE MINISTER OF DEFENCE[1] said – and the House should mark these words:

> There is only one answer to the threat to mankind posed by armaments. This is to reach a satisfactory agreement on general disarmament....

Those were the words of the right hon Gentleman in opening his 1961 Defence White Paper. Today's debate takes place on the eve of what may be well the most momentous conference in the world's history. If we believe, as we have all said – the Government have said it, too – that there is no security except in disarmament, I do not apologise for spending a few minutes dealing with this subject in this year's defence debate.

I begin from what I regard as one of the finest declarations on this subject: the communiqué of the Commonwealth Prime Ministers, last spring. Disarmament, they said, was

> the most important question facing the world today.

They called for 'total world-wide disarmament' and asserted that

> in view of the slaughter and destruction experienced in so-called 'conventional' wars, and of the difficulty of preventing a conventional war, once started, from developing into a nuclear war, our aim must be nothing less than complete abolition of the means of waging war of any kind.

[1] Harold Watkinson.

I do not question – nobody will question – the sincerity of the Commonwealth Prime Ministers' Conference. Our duty as a House, however, is to ensure that that aspiration is turned at the Geneva talks into a reality.

The House certainly welcomed the announcement yesterday that Mr Khrushchev had finally agreed to the convening of the Foreign Ministers' conference to precede the 18-Power talks. I hope that Britain and the United States will match this decision with a flexible and constructive approach. We have to recognise that the Soviet Government do not accord to a Foreign Minister the same standing as we do in this country, or as the Americans do to the Secretary of State. Mr Khrushchev has called Foreign Ministers functionaries.

I hope, therefore, that if we are disappointed at the opening talks, the President and the Prime Minister will stand ready to go to Geneva at short notice if their presence is needed to break a deadlock and to get things moving. I hope that the Prime Minister will not rule out the possibility of two visits, one early on, if that is needed, and another, if progress merits it or if failure demands it, at a later stage in the 18-Power talks.

We all know the difficulties about organising Summits. We well understand the President's feeling after Paris and Vienna. There would, however, be a great deal to be said for systematising the subject of Summits so that we can expect the world's leaders to come together more frequently.

I once more press upon the Government our suggestion that a special disarmament department be created in the Foreign Office, adequately staffed, under a full-time Minister of Cabinet rank, to prepare a British initiative, not only for this summer, but for all the vast and complicated work which lies ahead, a department which would not only call upon the great and partially untapped expertise which there is, both in civil and defence Departments, but which could bring in on an advisory basis scientists, defence experts and others who might help.

I hope that the Minister of Defence, who is to reply to the debate tonight, will take what I say now in the spirit in which it is made and pass it on to the Prime Minister. The job at Geneva cannot be done by a Foreign Secretary[1] or by a Minister of State[2] on an in-and-out

[1] Lord Home.

[2] Joseph Godber.

basis. Throughout the conference the British delegation ought to be led by a senior and respected leader, or Minister, I have even heard it suggested – and I hope that right hon Gentlemen opposite will not mind my passing on the suggestion – that the Prime Minister should bring back someone like Derick Heathcoat Amory, now Viscount Amory, who was respected by us all, irrespective of political differences. Someone of standing would then lead the delegation throughout the period, and we should not just have it headed by a Foreign Minister who, inevitably, had to dash off for two or three days at a time.

I want to turn for a moment to the conference itself. I suggest to the Government the importance of having, instead of a different chairman every day, a permanent chairman; not a national delegate – someone respected by all the delegations, who might, perhaps, aspire to the position and standing of the late Arthur Henderson in previous disarmament talks. Assisted by an independent secretariat from the United Nations, a chairman like that could do a great deal behind the scenes to break up the log-jams and try out new initiatives. I might also suggest one impartial Press report each day, issued by the chairman or the secretariat, rather than a series of inevitably slanted national versions.

As to the content of what might be achieved, we have, first, the problem of the nuclear test ban. That is urgent. The West have rightly made it a test of good faith. Even if there were no danger whatsoever from fall-out – and, of course, although the fall-out in both the Russian and American tests has been greatly reduced it is still a great problem to the world – an effective ban on nuclear tests is needed to avoid giving further twists to what can become an arms race of indefinite duration and infinite danger.

We all know the problem. From the American side, faced last autumn with the Russians' breach of their undertakings not to resume tests, they now believe that the Russians have made some advance in those tests – not enough, they feel, to reach equality with the Americans, but in the absence of guarantees against further tests, the Americans fear that a further Russian series of tests – after, say, nine months of preparation – might create a very perilous situation to the West. That is why a voluntary self-policing moratorium, with one partner possibly preparing tests while the other feels bound not to prepare them, is ineffective.

But let us be frank. A test ban can and should only be part of a wider and more comprehensive disarmament agreement. The Prime Minister and his colleagues know that one cannot go into nuclear disarmament on a limited liability basis, and that if one gets the inspection and verification needed to enforce a test ban, including the control of preparation, one has already crossed the threshold of national secrecy; one has made a major break-through, and is on the road to an agreement. That is why I suggest that both the East and the West must set their sights well beyond a test agreement.

If that fails, if the West feels that the Russian objections to inspection continue to obstruct a settlement, I would still recommend with a heavy heart, as a third best, a *faute de mieux*, a self-policing moratorium. The progress so far made, even as compared with a year ago, in the technology of the verification of atmospheric tests is such that a breach of the agreement would be known even without inspection. It could not, of course, deal with the vital question of preparation which I have mentioned. It would hardly be enough to meet the conditions that President Kennedy has laid down and, with the possibility that the Soviet Union would be continuing preparations, the West would inevitably have to claim the same freedom, lest nine or twelve vital, dangerous months were lost.

Therefore, if we had a moratorium of that kind, it would have a very limited value. It could not and should not be expected to be able to deal with preparations on either side. It would be a poor second best, but it would be better than nothing, and if nothing better is obtainable I hope that the Government will not reject it out of hand.

I come to the general disarmament conference. I do not need to go into the various stages embracing tests, destruction of missiles, destruction of nuclear stockpiles, destruction of productive capacity, proceeding simultaneously with a phased programme of conventional disarmament, but I do want to say a word about the vexed question of inspection and control.

The joint American-Soviet statement of principles agreed on last September was valuable as far as it went, but, of course, both sides agreed to omit the vital question of whether inspection covered only the weapons to be destroyed or covered as well the weapons that were left. The Americans might well feel like a tax inspector who receives a voluntary cheque covering what the taxpayer thought he should send, with the taxpayer firmly refusing to send any details of what was left, or of new sources of income.

My experience of negotiating with the Soviet Union, which is not inconsiderable, has taught me that one has to get into their minds and see how they look at these problems. Just as a map of Western bomber bases looks very different on a Russian map, with Moscow in the centre, so their attitude to inspection and secrecy – their identification of inspection with espionage – needs to be understood if one is to be able to combat it in negotiations.

During the past four or five years the whole nuclear balance has changed. The days when Foster Dulles could talk of massive retaliation, or of rolling the Russians back, confident in a first-strike ability that could not only destroy the main Russian targets, but also paralyse Russia's power to hit back – those days have gone. One cannot now knock out one's opponent's cities and his power to retaliate at the same time. The balance of terror now depends on the certain knowledge that an aggressor must face a merciless counter-stroke against his main cities. Neither can win.

Now that neither the East nor the West is any longer dependent either on bombers or the equally vulnerable, obsolete, Thor-type bases – which ought to be scrapped – their missile-launching sites are now capable of complete protection. That is the big change that has overcome the disarmament problem in the last year or two. Most American missiles, especially the Minuteman, are now in hardened underground sites which can survive blast pressures of what the scientists call 100 psi – that is to say, they can withstand the pressure of the blast caused by a 10-megaton explosion at a distance of 1·3 miles. In those circumstances, even if one's sites are only three miles apart, one needs a 10-megaton blast for each. I imagine that the Russian sites are equally well protected.

The fact is that the Russians are conditioned to fear what they regard as American aggression. Some of them, perhaps, expect American aggression. We may dismiss their fears as groundless, but that is what they have been brought up to believe. They believe that inspection, revealing all their missile sites – and there is reason to think that they have not as many sites as all that, but that they have used their large shop window for the space show – would make it possible for them to be knocked out on a first-strike aggression, and their power to retaliate would be gone.

We have to take account of those fears, however groundless we may think them. This is the main obstacle, as I am sure that the Minister will agree, to a disarmament agreement at present. That is why we commend to the Minister one proposal that is well worth studying – the Sohn plan, under which each country divides its territory into, say, twenty zones of equal military importance, and gives the numbers, but not the location, of strategic weapons and installations in each zone. The other side can then – say, once in every six months – select one zone for complete inspection on the spot – to test the honesty of the manifest; rather like a Customs officer inspecting one of five suit cases, the owner not knowing which one it will be.

That could be a very important step forward, and in the first six months the location of only, say, 5% of the sites would have been revealed; in a year, 10%, and so on. In that first six months, only 5% of the Russian or American installations would have been located or made known, and they would not, therefore, feel that the espionage problem was as difficult as they would on the basis of a hundred per cent inspection. Nevertheless, it would be a complete test of the accuracy of the statements put forward.

I should like, very briefly, to summarise the rest of the agreement we should like to see come out of Geneva. After the nuclear test and nuclear disarmament agreement, there should be an agreement to set up a United Nations Disarmament Agency, first to study, later to play its part in controlling, as the Prime Minister once suggested, the enforcement of the agreement. I believe that the nucleus of this agency should be set up now to help service the talks in the next few months.

We should seize the opportunity – better now than ever before – to stop the spread of nuclear weapons. On the initiative of Sweden and Ireland, the United Nations, on 4th December, passed two resolutions calling for the restriction of nuclear weapons to the existing countries. As I have said, this is in the back of the American Government's mind, and we in the Labour Party, who fought the last General Election on the non-nuclear club policy[1], have the right now to ask that our British deterrent – the right hon Gentleman's decaying

[1] The Labour Party advocated that Britain should be prepared to become a non-nuclear power as part of a world agreement under which each country, other than the US and USSR, would bind themselves not to make or possess nuclear weapons.

asset – should be offered as a contribution to a world agreement.

Do we want to see Israel, Egypt, China or Cuba as nuclear Powers? This is a tremendous problem and a tremendous danger to the world. Twelve countries, we are told, have already the economic and technical resources to make these bombs. China will soon make the thirteenth. I therefore hope the Government will be prepared wholeheartedly to make their contribution to a plan for the limitation of nuclear arms among the countries of the world by surrendering our own nuclear deterrent as part of such an agreement.

For the reason that I have just mentioned, China must be brought into the nuclear disarmament negotiations if we are to have any security for the future. The agreement should provide, we believe, for the establishment of guaranteed non-nuclear zones. Would it not make a big difference to the world if Africa were to become a complete non-nuclear zone free from the dangers of nuclear installations or nuclear explosions? Central Europe, also. If, in Central Europe, on each side of the Iron Curtain, we had a non-nuclear guaranteed zone, this could be, as the Minister knows, a very powerful solvent to the Berlin problem and meet Russian anxieties, which are almost obsessional, about what is their greatest fear – nuclear arms for Germany.

There should be international agreement to study the economic effects of disarmament, to supplement and co-ordinate the work of national agencies, including the one that I have suggested for this country. At all costs we must avoid the creation of a vested interest, or the suggestion that any nation has a vested interest on grounds of either full employment policies or private profit, in the maintenance of the arms race. There is a tremendous task to be undertaken by national Governments, and internationally, to ensure that the resources released by disarmament do not lead to unemployment and surplus capacity, but are converted to measures required for raising living standards all over the world.

This is the sort of agreement and approach that we believe might be fruitful. Naturally, we on this side of the House are sorry that it is hon Members opposite and not ourselves who are to be in charge of the negotiations – that will come. But the world's opportunity and the world's danger will not wait. This conference begins next week, and we tell the Government – I think they know this – that this is not the time for weary repetitions of outworn ideas and approaches. The world and history are looking for a new initiative. They will be quick to judge any statesman of any country who regards the occasion as just one for propaganda tricks or short-term debating points rather than constructive ideas and practical concessions.

While we condemn, as we have condemned, this White Paper and the defence policies which over five years have so utterly broken down, we nevertheless see hope in one paragraph only, and that is the paragraph relating to general disarmament; and on behalf, I am sure, of right hon and hon Gentlemen on both sides of the House, we not only call on the Government to take every measure within their power to make a success of this disarmament conference, but, for our part, we wish them well.

BERLIN DEBATE, HOUSE OF COMMONS, 5TH JULY, 1962

MR HAROLD WILSON (HUYTON): We would probably all agree that a Parliamentary debate on the situation in Berlin is long overdue. But I make no bones about the fact that the occasion for having it this week is the fact that a considerable number of my hon Friends and I have just returned from a visit to West Berlin. This was a visit of perhaps the largest party of Members of Parliament[1] that has ever gone abroad. We were invited by the German Social Democratic Party, and I think that our visit enabled us to show the solidarity that we felt with the people of West Berlin at this critical time.

I should mention that we had full discussions with our colleagues in the SPD and the Parliamentary leaders of West Berlin, and a long meeting with Herr Willy Brandt. During the period that we were there we inevitably saw a good deal of Berlin, including a brief visit to East Berlin – and we saw the wall.

Those of my hon Friends who catch your eye, Sir Robert, will be able to give their impression of what they saw and of the wall. We

[1] 40 Labour MPs in delegation which I headed visited Berlin in June, 1962.

have probably all seen photographs, television films and descriptions in the Press, but to see the wall as we did, and as other hon Members on both sides of the Committee have seen it, came as a real shock. Hon Members who have seen it will agree – and although I have used this phrase before I make no apology for repeating it – that one has to see the wall in all its three-dimensional horror to appreciate what it means.

Various members of our party were moved by different aspects of it. There were the blocked windows, facing the West Berlin streets at the top storey and sub-basement levels. Perhaps it seemed rather worse to see, round the corner of a building going back into East Berlin, the windows blocked just far enough to prevent even the most athletic would-be refugee from leaping across the wall.

Others of my hon Friends were very much moved at seeing the Church of Reconciliation, which had been a place of worship for citizens of East and West Berlin alike, cut off from West Berlin by this wall, with the barbed wire and the armed sentries. Some were very much moved by two or three women of East Berlin who very tentatively and diffidently waved handkerchiefs to us, not quite sure whether the armed sentries would see them. In this localised sector of one divided city we have epitomised and dramatised, in drab, unfeeling concrete, the political division of the world in which we live.

Last December, when we debated foreign affairs, I said that the archaeologists of some future generation, digging up the relics of this wall, would probably find it difficult to produce a thesis explaining how it came into being. What they will have to explain is that, unlike so many of the walls in history – the Great Wall of China, and the walls in the North of this country – the Berlin wall was built not to keep people out but to keep them in. It was not a fortification or bastion; it was a prison wall.

One can well understand its impact on the people of West Berlin last August, and their demand that action should be taken. If the first reaction of some of us, fairly hard-bitten Members of Parliament, was a mad desire to drive a heavy demolition vehicle against it – and we were only foreigners – we can understand the feelings of the Berliners who were divided from their own families, when they saw the wall going up.

In this connection, I was reported in *The Times* and elsewhere in terms suggesting that I was in favour of driving a non-existent 100-ton tank through the wall and suggesting that I was therefore in favour of a forcible solution. As many of my hon Friends who were there will confirm, what I said was that if our first reaction was a desire to resort to some ponderous vehicle to knock the wall down, the restraint with which West Germans held back this natural impulse to take violent action was truly remarkable.

One of the first points on which we must comment is the restraint of the people of West Berlin and the leadership that they have had from Herr Brandt[1] in this matter. I was told of a recent meeting of West German police at which, in the course of a speech, Herr Brandt referred to the fact that East Berlin policemen had been shot. This statement was immediately cheered by a section of West German police, whereupon Herr Brandt stopped the cheering and said that that was not what he wanted. He said that he could never bear to think of one German being killed by another, and he reinforced his appeal to them for every possible restraint at this critical time.

I join with that tribute to West Berliners a tribute to the restraint and realism of British forces and their commanders during these very critical months. I cannot too highly stress that the need today is for calm in Berlin and a sense of urgency outside Berlin.

It seemed to my hon Friends and myself that there are three problems – or, more correctly, three facets of the same problem. First, there is the immediate problem of the serious rise in tension which has developed in the past few weeks, especially with the shooting of East Berliners seeking to escape to the West. This creates a very special problem of acute urgency for all of us, for everyone knows – to use the fashionable jargon of our time – how a shooting incident across this brutal and unnatural frontier could be escalated into a far graver crisis.

That is why I welcome the proposals made by the three Western nations 10 days ago for meetings of representatives of the four military Powers. Whether it be commandants, their deputies – military or civil – or some other representatives, matters not; such a meeting is urgent, and my delegation gave its full support to the proposals when it had a chance of making public comment on them, by Press, radio and television in Berlin. Putting it at its lowest, if there are two versions of these incidents – and there are – it is better to

[1] Socialist Mayor of West Berlin.

argue them out across a table rather than leave them to the dangerous arbitration of armed frontier police.

There is also the problem of easements of the present situation – easements to help the lot of individuals. For example, a proposal has been made that men and women of over 60 years of age should be allowed freely to cross to West Berlin to join their families; that children should be free to join their families, and that families should be free to travel across the frontier to see family graves in West Berlin. None of these proposals should be unacceptable to the East Berlin authorities. The main purpose of the wall was to prevent the migration of skilled labour, technicians, and so on, and I do not see that any point of principle – if 'principle' is the right word to use in this context – is breached if there is some easement to allow families to be reunited and to travel in that way.

Another proposal is that the police should be disarmed on either side of the wall for a given distance – a proposal that we heard referred to as the '100-metre Rapacki[1] Plan'. Here again, I should have thought that there was very great value in proposals of this kind.

I know that for many in the West, West Berlin particularly, these proposals would seem to imply acceptance or condonation of the wall. There is no such implication, I should have thought. The wall is wrong and must go at the earliest possible opportunity, but that is no reason for failing to mitigate individual and family hardship as long as the wall is there.

Another proposal which was made many months ago – it has been made by my right hon Friend the Leader of the Opposition, by myself and others – is the idea of establishing a special agency of the United Nations in Berlin. I hope that this will be strongly pressed by Her Majesty's Government and that it will be discussed with U Thant when he is in this country. It has also been suggested that it might be appropriate to establish a commission of human rights in Berlin. It was suggested in the debate on disarmament some months ago that this should be done when the new disarmament commission is set up, as we hope it will be, as a result of the disarmament negotiations.

I would make an alternative suggestion. I should like to see the FAO established there, because that organisation is of particular im-

[1] Polish Foreign Minister.

portance to representatives of the newly-developing countries in Asia, Africa, Latin America and elsewhere.

Since it is true, and I hope this will not sound cynical, that a great part of the Great Powers' battle is the struggle to win acceptance of countries of that kind, I should have thought that to establish FAO in Berlin, with regular visits to and from by representatives of the Afro and Asian countries, would be extremely valuable, because it would be difficult for FAO and the wall to co-exist in Berlin for long. I hope that the right hon Gentleman will say that this is in the thinking of the Government.

I turn from the immediate Berlin problem to the second and third facets; the problems of getting a viable solution to the immediate Berlin issue and the wider problem of co-existence and *détente* in Central Europe. Because there is a real danger – and this is natural and, in a sense, inevitable, but does not make it any less of a danger that anger and resentment should exist about the wall – this may turn Westerners, above all West Berliners, away from the search for a basis of co-existence. I believe that there is a real danger that people, upon seeing the wall, say, 'Co-existence is impossible'. The lesson of the wall is not that co-existence is made possible or undesirable, but that it is all the more essential.

The fact that one has in Berlin the whole East-West conflict concentrated and highlighted in one divided city is a challenge and not an excuse for cynicism, defeatism, or uncompromising hostility to those on the other side of it. My hon Friends and I have repeatedly made our position clear about the Berlin negotiations. We have said that there must be two non-negotiable conditions: first, freedom for the people of West Berlin to live under a system of society of their own choosing and, secondly, guarantees of access going beyond mere paper agreements. Associated with these must be the conditions necessary to ensure the economic viability of Berlin.

These are the absolutes of a settlement. To get them as part of a package deal which incorporates them we should be prepared to show flexibility, especially for example, by showing willingness to accept Germany's eastern frontiers with Poland and Czechoslovakia. We should also show flexibility in the matter of some measure of recognition of the East German administration as a purely factual arrangement pending, and without prejudice to, the ultimate reunification of Germany on a basis of free elections.

This is, of course, something which can be settled only outside Berlin. The right hon Gentleman will no doubt be reporting on the conversations which have been going on, first between Mr Gromyko and the United States Ambassador in Moscow and, secondly – after the problem came to a head in Geneva – between Mr Dean Rusk and the Soviet Ambassador in Washington. All hon Members will wish the negotiations well, disappointing and slow though the progress so far has been. I trust that the right hon Gentleman will associate Her Majesty's Government unreservedly with these discussions and with the desire to see them speedily and fruitfully come to a conclusion.

There can, I think, be no doubt that divided counsels in the West could have serious consequences. Last December, when I was attacking Her Majesty's Government for a lack of urgency over Berlin, I referred to the vital need for a NATO Ministerial Conference and the imperative need to get an agreed Western line on Berlin. I said that there was some reason to fear that Her Majesty's Government had sacrificed this to getting allies to support the lonely position they had then taken up at the United Nations on the Katanga issue. Certainly a sense of urgency was not shown on Berlin at those talks.

Since then the attitude of President de Gaulle and some of the pronouncements of Dr Adenaeur have put a heavy burden on the United States. It would have been understandable had the Soviet Union played on these speeches and statements and asked the United States how far they were negotiating on behalf of their Western Allies. The American position was made extremely difficult by some of those statements, although I do not want to make too much of this. It can certainly be argued that Washington's clear pronouncement on Dr Adenauer's speeches may have done more to create East-West confidence than anything for many years past.

As my hon Friend the Member for Coventry, East (Mr Crossman) has convincingly argued, one of the features of the cold war for many years was the feeling that Mr Dulles's[1] one guiding principle in European affairs was to back the Adenauer line, right or wrong. Now President Kennedy's declaration of independence could be a great step forward and lead to greater confidence in the negotiations. I trust that the right hon Gentleman will associate Her Majesty's Govern-

[1] American Secretary of State during Eisenhower Administration.

ment unreservedly with the line the American Government took in relation to the difficult situation that was then created.

We must all recognise that the Berlin issue cannot be settled on its own. The Russians are realists and they know that the adverse propaganda effect of the wall is incalculable. If the West were to spend 10 billion dollars and mobilise every public relations officer in the Western world they could not devise so powerful a propaganda weapon as the wall – and the Russians know it. At the same time, they know that East Germany's economy was in danger of bleeding to death through loss of skilled workers and technicians. Perhaps the real truth in all this can be summed up in a famous phrase of Aneurin Bevan's, who once said that the trouble was that the Soviet Union had expanded beyond her natural frontiers.

In the long run the problem is one of creating conditions in Central Europe which will provide the basis on which not merely the problem of the wall but the general problem of Berlin and West Germany can be solved. In previous debates we have asked the Government to adopt our proposals for a nuclear free zone and an area of controlled disarmament in Central Europe. We have stressed these proposals not only in the context of a general disarmament agreement, to which we think they are highly relevant, but also in the context of the Berlin situation. In one debate after another we have had no constructive reply to these proposals from the Government. We think that they could be a powerful solvent in easing the Berlin problem.

I have a fear – and I hope that the right hon Gentleman will do something to allay it tonight – that the Government and certain of their Western Allies have lost the sense of urgency they had last autumn over Berlin.

When we were threatened with immediate crisis, when Mr Khrushchev's deadline overhung the situation, there was intense diplomatic activity and every sign that something was going to be done. Once that deadline was removed, Western statesmen seemed to heave a sigh of relief and lose any sense of urgency about it. Leave the problem as it is, they seemed to say, no real harm is being done.

More recently, with other problems, with other sources of friction between Western countries uppermost in Ministers' minds – disputes about independent nuclear armouries, or about the precise means of achieving Western unity, arguments about the Common Market and the rest – with all these going on, one feels that Western leaders are perhaps in danger of becoming content to let the Berlin situation drift simply because they know that to press for a solution would add one more cause of friction within the Western alliance.

I hope therefore that we shall be assured tonight that this is not the position of Her Majesty's Government; for this problem, as all of us realise, could be inflamed to crisis level almost overnight, and if it were, the West would not necessarily face the new crisis with the unity and firmness which we all desire. Once again panic measures might be the order of the day. That is why we stress the need for urgency now. This crisis will not wait for ever. Nor, indeed, will the compelling requirements of the human tragedy which so many of us have witnessed in the past few weeks.

I hope that this debate tonight will be a signal that the resolve and the sense of purpose for which this tragically divided city calls will no longer be absent from the counsels of the West.

CHAPTER EIGHT

*

Nassau debate, House of Commons, 31st January, 1963

WE ARE APPROACHING THE END of the first of a series of vital debates on the state of the nation. Next week we are to debate unemployment and the economic position and the following week the breakdown in the Common Market negotiations. This debate, I think the whole House will agree, has been serious and grave and important. There has been relatively little attempt to make Party capital out of what is a grave national crisis. The Prime Minister will, however, at any rate allow me to say that of all the Government back benchers who have spoken only a minority have supported the Administration during this debate. While we shall go into the Division Lobby as a united party, the same cannot be said of the Government forces tonight.

This debate has raised three major issues, and it is to those that I want to address my remarks. First, there is the judgment of hon Members on the adequacy, the rightness, the correctness of the Bahamas Agreement and the exchange of Polaris for Skybolt. Secondly, the broader question, could Britain maintain the attempt to be an independent nuclear power and, if not – if the attempt is, as we argue, a costly illusion – what are our defence priorities to be? The third question, the question which I think underlies the whole debate, which underlies the whole reappraisal which recent events have forced upon every hon Member, of Britain's place in the world after Nassau, after Brussels and of its bearing on defence policy – I think this third issue is one which is relevant to what has been said by so many hon Members.

I turn first to the Bahamas Agreement itself. Speaker after speaker, certainly from this side of the House and some from the other side, has made clear that what we are debating is the end of an era – of an illusion if hon Members like to put it that way, certainly of the whole philosophy of the 1957 White Paper. Hon Members have dwelt on the history of the 1957 policy. I shall refer to it only briefly.

That White Paper was, as we know, the Government's reaction to Suez. It was a conscious decision by a new Government headed by a new Prime Minister to undertake in the defence field a fundamental swing to reliance on thermo-nuclear policies. Since that White Paper we have had three Ministers. As it has happened, each of them has been prepared to chance our whole security on a single terrible weapon. The Commonwealth Secretary[1] based everything on Blue Streak. The right hon Member for Woking (Mr Watkinson[2]) based his whole policy on Skybolt. The present Minister[3] now bases his policy, or tells us he does, on Polaris.

I must remind the House, because this is relevant, that four years ago, in February, 1959, the Government consciously and deliberately rejected Polaris as the weapon on which our defence policy should be based. They made no secret of their reasons for doing so. The then Minister of Defence[4] held a Press conference and briefed the Press very fully on why Polaris would be entirely unsuited to British defence policy. I have here an evening paper for 10th February, 1959, published just after the Prime Minister announced his mission to Moscow in February, 1959. 'Happy days', I suppose the right hon Gentleman feels. This is what the headline says: *Blue Streak wins. Britain rejects US rocket.* That was Polaris. *Now Macmillan will talk from strength. The Times* next morning told us on the authority of the then Minister of Defence: *Blue Streak is in. Polaris is out.* We were told why, officially. This was said:

> Too little attention has been paid, it is said, to the limitations of missile-firing submarines. Why, for instance, should it be assumed that they will remain undetectable and invulnerable? Their

[1] Duncan Sandys.

[2] Minister of Defence, October, 1959 to July, 1962.

[3] Peter Thorneycroft.

[4] Duncan Sandys, Minister of Defence, January, 1957 to October, 1959.

numbers will be comparatively few because of their great cost, and the movements of a very limited force could be closely watched by an enemy.

That was the considered judgment of the Government in 1959. Because of that considered judgment we have spent Heaven knows how much on the development of other weapons. Now four years, three Ministers and £6,000 million later we have come back full circle. With '*Faute de mieux*' emblazoned on his standard, the Minister now affects to believe that Polaris is the answer to any Defence Minister's prayer, that we always wanted it and that if we did not we should have.

Yesterday my right hon Friend the Member for Belper (Mr G. Brown) reminded the House of the warnings we have given. The speeches of all of us on this side of the House are on record – in the Blue Streak debate, for example. I will not go over those arguments. I hope the Prime Minister will study them some day. I certainly remember the cry of rage last March when I asked Ministers if they really thought we were going to get Skybolt. Immediately the Press were told that messages had been sent to Washington asking that I should be repudiated; Washington would make clear that everything that I said was wrong. The silence from Washington was deafening. There was no repudiation.

Now Washington has taken its decision. Hon Members have argued furiously for one or the other weapon system. Hon and gallant Members here with great ability and great energy have argued the case for the aerial weapon. I sympathise with what they feel, but if the air lobby in Washington cannot reverse this decision hon Members here have little hope.

Let me again state our position. We on this side of the House have not been arguing either for Polaris or for Skybolt. We support neither. However, I would ask the Prime Minister to be a little more forthcoming when he replies on the question of the costs that have been incurred, because the statement of the Minister of Defence this afternoon did not really satisfy any of our anxieties. The prospective British share of development costs on the A3, the 2,500 sea mile range weapon, throws great doubt on the optimistic figures given both by the Minister of Defence and by the Prime Minister on television when they returned from Nassau.

The Times only yesterday said this:

> The question of Britain sharing the development costs of the Polaris missile was not raised at the Bahamas conference, it was learnt in Washington today. Indeed, the expectation of the Pentagon that costs are to be shared appears to have caused as much surprise in other interested departments here as it did in London.

What is the decision? I think that the House has a right to know. For once, can we be told what we are in for before we start on the expense? I am a member of the Public Accounts Committee. Hon Members who have served on that hardworking Committee will agree with me that we have spent too long reporting on case after case of optimistic estimates of missile costs which turned sour at the end of the day and involved a very, very heavy cost to the taxpayer. This afternoon my right hon Friend the Member for Smethwick (Mr Gordon Walker) made what I thought was a damaging case on the question of costs. The Minister of Defence, if I may say so, was so busy with personalities that he never attempted to answer the points made by my right hon Friend. I hope, therefore, that the Prime Minister, who negotiated this agreement, will make the facts clear to the House tonight.

I turn to my second, broader question; should we, as a nation, maintain the effort – be it reality or illusion – to remain an independent nuclear power? The Government have presented their case – the whole of the Prime Minister's speech yesterday was really doing this – in terms of an answer to the question of whether the missile we should have from the Americans should be Skybolt or Polaris. That is the question the right hon Gentleman put and answered. Our criticism is not of the answer but that the question is wrong.

Let me restate our position. We can only make the contribution which it is our duty to make to Western defence if we cease these vain nuclear posturings. Britain's claim, her hope, of being an independent nuclear power ended the day the Blue Streak project was scrapped, and my hon Friends recognised that within a matter of hours. [*Laughter.*] It is on the record for hon Members opposite to read. They can study the speeches we made and the Motion we tabled. They can also see how we voted – and there were no abstentions on this side of the House. From that moment nuclear status for this country became a costly pretence. How can one pretend to have an independent deterrent when one is depending on another nation – a reluctant one at that – to supply one with the means of delivery? The Minister of Defence understands the point I am making. Although he is getting the means for his nuclear deterrent from the United States, only last April in Leicester he said:

> The Socialists and Liberals – there is little to choose between them –

How many hon Members opposite [Interruption from Conservative members] fought under the label 'Liberal-Conservative' or 'Conservative-Liberal'?

> intend to rely for their defence in the main on the United States of America.

That is what the right hon Gentleman said. Is that not what the Nassau agreement is all about? The truth is, and I think that hon Members opposite recognise this, that with the limited resources available to this country we cannot attempt all the separate and alternative missile systems one must go in for to have an adequate nuclear deterrent. The Americans can try 20 systems, and if three of them come off they are a nuclear power. We tried one, Blue Streak, and it failed.

What is the argument for pretending to be an independent nuclear power? Is it, firstly, because we want the right to use it in some private war of our own, independent of the Western alliance, against, perhaps, a non-nuclear nation – another Suez? Have not hon Members opposite learnt? Have they in mind a war without allies, without the Commonwealth, condemned, as it would be, by world opinion? For my part I acquit hon Members opposite of that intention, but is it that we think that this is the essential ingredient for Western defence? It represents a fraction, 1 or 2%, of the Western striking power and the Polaris fleet – perhaps flotilla would be a better word – will be an even smaller proportion.

We are told that the United States have a nuclear strength of 30,000 megatons TNT equivalent. That is 150 tons TNT equivalent for every man, woman and child in the Soviet Union. Are we really supposed to be making a significant contribution? Is there somewhere in the recesses of the Ministry of Defence a statistician carrying out his own contribution to the macabre calculus of megatons and mega-deaths, convincing Ministers that we are making a significant contribution to the defence of the West? If right hon Gentlemen believe that our contribution is essential to Western defence, let me say that there is not a single one of our allies, or anyone else, who believes that argument, or takes it seriously.

Or is it the view that if we are in the nuclear club we shall be consulted; that we can claim that we are not as other men are; that we are a nuclear power; that we shall be there when the big decisions are taken? Is that the argument? I should have thought that Cuba buried that illusion. Is it, then, the further argument that in this world of mutual deterrence we cannot trust our allies; that we must have the means unilaterally of triggering off a nuclear war that will ultimately force the hand of the Americans? If we thought that were the argument, we would reject it as fundamentally immoral – and, indeed, in this tightly-packed, vulnerable island, a prescription for suicide. That argument, again, I cannot think motivates right hon Gentlemen opposite.

I think that the answer is simpler – pathetic, perhaps, but not immoral. It is nostalgia. It is striving to relive our Imperial greatness. Within the lifetime of older hon Members we were once top nation, and it is not easy, even at heavy cost in terms of national security, to accept the facts of history, geography and of economics. I think that the Prime Minister understands this. Nassau was not a willing agreement between partners; it was a reluctant sop thrown by the Americans to a Prime Minister who knew in his heart that what he was asking had no defence relevance, but who knew that he dare not return and face some of his more atavistic supporters without it. Even *The Times*, in its leading article last Wednesday, at long last and very belatedly, realises the essential fact that we should cease our attempt at nuclear pretension.

Having dealt with the arguments for, as put to us in this debate, let me repeat why, in our view – and I quote our own defence statement – Britain should cease the attempt to remain an independent nuclear power. First, it is a wrong deployment of our national defence resources. Simply because we allocate our resources and equipment and our all-too-scarce scientific manpower to nuclear effort we have not the resources to honour our minimum national commitments. My right hon and hon Friends, and a number of hon

Members opposite, have in this debate, as they have in past debates, ruthlessly exposed the inadequacy of our conventional forces – their numbers, and the quality of their equipment – and all the evasions of the Minister of Defence will not conceal what our allies know to be true, and what a lot of hon Members know to be true – that we are not making anything like our full contribution to NATO.

The Minister of Defence knows that perfectly well, and I put this to him. If he has any doubt about it, if he still thinks that we are making our full contribution to NATO, that our forces in Germany are properly equipped, mobile, and properly balanced – if he pretends that for a moment, I would suggest that he appoints a committee of hon Members of both parties, and there are a number of them in all parts of the House who are widely respected for their military knowledge and judgment, from the Conservatives and Labour – and probably Liberals, too, for all I know. I suggest that he appoints that committee of hon Members who are respected for their military knowledge, and that he gives them full facilities to make a tour of military installations in Germany and report back to this House – if necessary supplementing that report with a secret report for the Government.

I hope that when the Prime Minister replies he will tell us what he thinks of that suggestion, because there is a clear contradiction between the Government's complacency about our contribution to NATO and the equipment of our forces, on one hand, and what every hon Member knows to be the fact on the other.

The inadequacy of our contribution to NATO is not disguised, either, by the fiction of our strategic reserve, this force supposedly so mobile that it can ensure that men are in two places at once. The strategic reserve which is required now in the Far East, now in the Middle East, now for some other trouble spot, perhaps in the Commonwealth, is going to be required at a moment's notice to be the balancing force needed to make our contribution to BAOR[1]. It can be one or the other, but it cannot be both. The old conception of a stage Army where half-a-dozen minor actors moving quickly behind the scenes can represent the whole of Caesar's legions may be all right for a second-rate repertory company, but it is not a sound basis for Britain's defence policy.

[1] British Army of the Rhine.

The events of this week have shown it. These moves of skeleton formations to the Far East may or may not be adequate for their task. I am not competent to say whether they are not, but once they are in the Far East they are not available to the Supreme Allied Commander in Europe. One cannot fight a bush fire in Borneo and be available at a moment's notice to fill a vital defence role on the Rhine – not at the same time anyhow. And crises have a habit of coming not singly but simultaneously.

Last March, in the defence debate, I warned the House against the facile assumption that we can solve our problems by depleting our garrisons in other parts of the world. I mentioned Hong Kong, and I wonder whether anyone would argue today that I was then too alarmist in referring to the problem of Hong Kong. We have a duty as a House of Commons. Our conventional troops are stretched out dangerously as a tenuous red line all over the world. Their security and their contribution to our still scattered defence effort should count more in the final reckoning than nuclear prestige.

Therefore, this is point No 1. We can, with our limited resources, either pay for the pretence of the nuclear deterrent or can honour our commitments in NATO and elsewhere. But we cannot do both.

Secondly, if we are laggard in our contribution to NATO we immensely increase the danger of a conventional outbreak in Europe, perhaps based on a mistake, a gamble, a misunderstood signal, or perhaps an impulsive intervention by West Germans to aid their compatriots in the East, as very nearly happened in 1953, or perhaps an incident across the Wall. Any one of these could rapidly escalate into nuclear war if there were not enough conventional troops for a holding operation. This is one of the big dangers. If Cuba had one lesson above all others, it was the need for time – for time to pause, to think and to realise. It is a barely disguised implication of British defence policy that a conventional attack in Europe would escalate quickly, too quickly into nuclear war.

Thirdly, and we have stressed this again and again, the insistence on a British nuclear deterrent, the French insistence on a French deterrent at which, let us be frank, we connived last summer in a vain attempt to buy our entry into the Common Market – these have been damaging, I hope not fatal, but certainly damaging, to the hopes in this country, in the United States and elsewhere of all those who believe that it is vital to stop the spread of nuclear weapons.

Because of us, and France, the hope is fast fading of an enforceable world agreement limiting nuclear weapons to the two major nuclear powers. That is what we feel ought to happen until, as all of us hope, we secure a world-wide comprehensive, multilateral disarmament agreement which outlaws the bomb altogether. When we think of Egypt with the aid of German rocket experts producing the means of delivering nuclear weapons over a distance of 350 miles and the inevitable reaction of Israel, when we think of China and other countries, we must recognise that any nation which, for an inadequate reason, insists on its own nationalist position in maintaining nuclear weapons is imperilling the chance of world agreement.

For these three reasons – because we consider it essential to fulfil our obligations to NATO and cannot, because we want to limit the danger of escalation from conventional to nuclear war, because we regard it as vital to stop the spread of nuclear weapons – we reject the very basis and inspiration of the Government's defence policy.

Before I turn to the third main subject of this debate, I wish to deal with one other much canvassed scheme, the idea of a European deterrent, with or without Britain. I am here referring not to proposals for a NATO deterrent but to the idea of a purely European deterrent developed and operated by European Powers only, whether including or excluding Britain. We reject this proposal.

We reject it, first, because it would lead to a dangerous diversion and would distract urgently needed resources of energy from NATO itself into the new nuclear grouping. Second, it would cause tremendous strains within the West, since there is nothing more debilitating than an alliance within an alliance. Third, it would speed the creation of what is already more than an embryonic danger, a third force in Europe, narrow, nationalistic, intransigent, irredentist, *revanchiste*. Fourth, it would face the Soviet Union with the most provocative challenge the West could in its folly devise, a nuclear force which included, and might be dominated by, Germany.

I think that we have all referred at one time or another, some of us from quite deep personal knowledge, to the Russian obsession – I do not apologise for the word; it is understandable when one considers their history and their 20 million dead in the last war – about the Germans. I believe that to endow Germany with nuclear status would mean the end to our hope of easing East-West tension and a successful conclusion to the efforts now being made in East and West to make co-existence work. In spite of our preoccupation with weapons systems, which we have been debating this week, let us keep clearly before us the paramount aim, to mount successful negotiations between East and West.

We have a right to ask where the Government stand on these proposals for a European deterrent, including the nuclear rearmament of Germany. I make perfectly clear now where we stand. We are completely, utterly and unequivocally opposed, now and in all circumstances, to any suggestion that Germany, West Germany or East Germany, directly or indirectly, should have a finger on the nuclear trigger or any responsibility, direct or indirect, for deciding that nuclear weapons are to be used. That is a categorical statement, and I most earnestly press the Prime Minister tonight to make his reply equally categorical.

I turn, now, to the third question, what should our defence policy be against the background of our position in the world? If I look at it against the background of wider foreign policy issues, the House will, I know, agree that this is right. There is always a danger of these debates becoming so enmeshed in the details of weapon potentialities that we may miss the broader realities. When defence becomes the master of foreign policy, as it sometimes has in recent years, vision and realism alike are banished from our counsels. I make no apology, therefore, for widening, as, I believe, most hon Members have in their speeches, the content of the debate to embrace our broader position and the foreign policy background of it.

First, as I have said before, and as all of us have said, we must make NATO the centre of our defence policy in Europe. I ask the Prime Minister to deal with this in all seriousness and to be frank with the House.

What is our contribution in real terms to NATO? How does the right hon Gentleman assess it? Certainly not the four divisions of the 1954 commitment. Is he satisfied that it is anything like three in real and effective terms, having regard to equipment, balance and mobility, making no allowance, of course, for dependence on reserves in some miasmal background. Can he say whether we really have, or are likely to have, three divisions? Is he satisfied that we have two divisions in real and effective terms? I know that many hon Members on both sides who have studied these matters would not answer categorically that we have effectively two divisions. This is why I press on the Prime Minister the necessity to send an all-party Committee to examine this and to report to the House.

I wish to ask the Prime Minister whether he knows that Germany's stated contribution to NATO is 12 divisions and that there is a danger that it may be raised to 18 if some people have their way. I beg the Prime Minister to tell us with all the authority of his office what in his view this would mean for Europe – for this country, too – if Germany has 18 effective divisions with or without nuclear weapons and we have barely one-tenth of this in real terms.

Secondly, in all the discussions about the future structure and armament of NATO – here I think we shall have a lot to discuss in future debates because the American proposals have not been fully worked out in any real sense – I think that we all agree that we must give a real priority to strengthening the machinery of political control. There is too much emphasis in current discussion about having more fingers on the nuclear button. This is the wrong approach. It is not more fingers on the button that we need; it is more fingers on the safety catch, more provision for consultation for what an American defence chief recently called the 'consensus' of the conditions in which the West's deterrent would be used, because we have to face this: Cuba proved our failure to devise methods of consultation in the West, and if the realities of the situation mean, as in our view they do mean, that the United States is the effective Western nuclear power, the need for America to consult her allies is not less but greater.

I make no apology for reminding the House again of the, to many of us, fearsome comment of *The Times* Washington correspondent at the height of the Cuba crisis, when he said:

> President Kennedy has dramatically emphasised his determination to act alone to defend United States and allied interests, wherever they may be threatened. The President has chosen to see the crisis as a direct confrontation of United States and Soviet power and, in effect, has assumed the supreme political authority that was always inherent in the American nuclear deterrent. If allies and neutrals should see a certain national arrogance in this posture, that is not the way the Administration views its actions. The firm

belief is that as the leader of the alliance, with control of most of the nuclear power available to the West, it has a right and a duty to defend itself and its allies – even to the extent of bringing about a nuclear exchange.

These are very grave words for all of us, and I think the implication of them is not that America should not have the nuclear weapon nor that Britain should have the nuclear weapon, because we had one then, so we were told, and it made no difference to consultation. The implication is the urgency that there is for getting political consultation and political control in NATO. We must ask the Prime Minister: was this question discussed at Nassau? We must be told. Our American friends well understand in this vulnerable area of Europe in which we in this House live our preoccupation with the maxim 'No annihilation without representation'.

Third and last, we must come to terms with our real status in the world, and I know that the whole House will realise that neither past greatness nor present illusions will earn us either respect or influence in the world. The Prime Minister – and I always enjoy his historical references – frequently refers to Philip II of Spain. There is a lesson to be drawn from Philip II. Spain was not able to live long on nostalgia or on its past greatness. The respect that we earn and the influence which we can exert depend uniquely on the efforts that we ourselves make – and only we can make them – to build up our economic, political and military strength, because these are the true foundations of a country's strength.

A great British essayist once said:

The most irrelevant thing in nature is a poor relation.

The plain fact of Nassau is that the right hon Gentleman was regarded as journeying there as a poor relation, and he need not have done and he need not have been, because in our view where Dean Acheson was wrong was to confuse the Britain we have become with the Britain we could be[1].

We shall soon be debating the lessons of Brussels. What we resent, and I am sure the whole House does and the Prime Minister showed it last night, is the spectacle of Britain being humiliated by nations which have exploited the image that we have given of a

[1] Dean Acheson speech – 5th December, 1962, at West Point.

country which is exhausted, which is stale, which is incapable of putting forth her real strength whether in economic or defence terms.

Naked in the conference room is one thing; naked and shivering in the cold outside while others decide our fate is an intolerable humiliation. I said 'image', for we do not accept that the image that they have gained of us is a picture of us as we really are. There is in this country an untapped resource of skill and craftsmanship, of science and technology, of design and ingenuity and of drive and determination which, if it could be mobilised by a calculated release of the nation's energies, could bring us once again to the leadership of the world. The same is true of defence policy. A wrong and pretentious defence policy leads to weakness. The right priorities in defence could immeasurably increase our influence.

A policy based on nostalgia means that we underrate where our real strength lies in the world today. I think – and I know that the Prime Minister does – that we could have a great deal more influence in Europe. One thing we have learned this week is that we have friends there as well as others. We could have a great influence in the Commonwealth. Our strength lies still in our potential leadership in the newly emerging world of nations which have come forward to nationhood in the last few years.

The Prime Minister has often said – and I am glad that he has said it and I do not mock him for it – that he desires to make Great Britain great. This is a noble aim and others share it. Our argument is about methods, not about the aim. We believe that a nation's greatness depends not on prestige military policies, but on the influence which we can exert in the forum of world opinion, and the forum of world opinion today is made up more and more by a lot of new nations not of the same colour as ourselves, but where we have the ability to influence decisions because of our unique contribution – and both parties have made it – to the retreat from imperialism, and because in the Commonwealth we have the greatest multi-racial community in the world.

This debate marks the collapse of a decade of policies which in our view have been wrongly conceived for the age in which we live. The Prime Minister in these last remaining months, or weeks, can make a unique contribution: he can make clear to the nation, with the authority which adheres to the office he holds, the true facts of our position in defence and in world affairs. He can do no more than that, because the crisis we face requires a united nation and a united Commonwealth, and for the past few months his Administration can no longer take the steps either to galvanise this nation, or to unite the Commonwealth. His Administration is now too tired and too stale and the task must now pass into the hands of a party which bears no responsibility for the past, a party which is ready and able to face the challenge of the future.

SPEECH AT THE NATIONAL PRESS CLUB, WASHINGTON, 1ST APRIL, 1963

I SHOULD LIKE TO BEGIN BY SAYING what I am here for. First, what I am not here for. I am not here to negotiate. An Opposition cannot negotiate with Governments. I am here as a leader of one of the great parties in our democracy to learn more about current thinking in the United States on the great issues confronting the Atlantic partnership. I was last here in January, 1962, at that time as the Labour Party's spokesman on Foreign Affairs. I would have come in January of this year, but had to return from New York to London on the day that Hugh Gaitskell died, without coming on to Washington.

So having said what I am here for I do not need, I hope, to repudiate the story which was featured in some papers last week under the title 'Wilson's Fourteen Points'. I haven't got 14. I haven't got any. A statement in one of Friday's papers that I 'announced' before leaving London that I was bringing a 14-point programme is quite wrong. The London story came as the responsibility of the pressman who wrote it and who at that time had not been to see me or had any discussion with me. It was a nice and amusing piece of imaginative writing but I cannot take any responsibility for it. I'm sorry.

I have not come to press any lines of policy on the US administration. To do so would be highly improper and unconstitutional. My purpose in coming is to learn and to listen – and to explain, when I am asked, the general trend of Labour Party thinking and policy on the main issues of world affairs.

But I have read a great deal of what has been written, and I should like to thank you for all the kind things you have said about me – I have in the process learned a lot of things about myself I didn't know before, and I have been asked by many pressmen a lot of questions about our approach. I should, therefore, like to try today in my talk to answer some of these questions.

I should like to begin with the economic problems the free world is facing.

All of us want to see a great expansion of trade, and a removal of trade barriers, between member-countries of the Atlantic Community. Equally we urgently need to see a steady and dynamic expansion of production within our respective countries. My fear is that anything we are able to do in freeing trade and expanding national production will run in a measurable period of time into a crisis of world liquidity. World trade has increased fourfold in monetary terms since pre-war: the monetary resources available to lubricate this trade have barely doubled. We have the position that the two greatest trading nations in the world both urgently need to expand production, in their own interests and that of the free world, and that both are inhibited by fear of balance-of-payments difficulties. We are moving more and more into the position that if sterling is strong, the dollar is weak, if the dollar is strong, sterling is weak, there are times when we face the danger that both are weak. And if Western nations show the degree of statesmanship which we hope for in reducing trade barriers, there is a real danger that trade expansion will grind to a standstill through a famine of liquidity. And we shall be reduced again to beggar-my-neighbour measures designed to export unemployment and deflation from one country to another. We are within a reasonable distance of a major seize-up in free world trade, beginning with a crisis in dollar and sterling trade, which at best will inhibit our hopes of economic expansion at a time when other nations are pressing remorselessly ahead, and which at worst could create another 1931. I am also deeply concerned at the growth of indebtedness in underdeveloped countries such as those of Latin America. Already the burden of servicing loans is preempting a high proportion of their overseas earnings; in four or five years many of them will reach breaking point.

In passing may I say with all the emphasis I can command that the answer does not lie in devaluation whether of the dollar, or sterling, or both. That would be a lunatic and self-destroying operation, neither justified by the problem nor relevant to its solution. The same applies to loose talks about floating rates. As an ex-Trade Minister[1] I have a built-in prejudice in favour of enabling exporters to quote fixed prices with reasonable assurance of monetary stability. Equally the answer cannot be found in a revaluation of gold, which would simply provide an uncovenanted benefit to two countries, South Africa and the Soviet Union, whose benefit should be low in our scale of priorities.

What is needed is a medium for the creation of international credit through the established machinery of the International Monetary Fund. The unparalleled American and British expansion in the 19th century was made possible by a new discovery, the power of commercial banks to create credit, free from the thraldom of gold. In the 20th century we have so far shown ourselves unworthy of the ingenuity and inventiveness of our grandfathers. We should now move toward a system in which the IMF[2] could create international credit *pari passu* with the development of world trade. If this could be combined with the Australian proposal for discriminatory credit facilities to be issued to underdeveloped countries to spend in debtor countries – such as, in present circumstances, United States and Britain, we could evoke increased production in our two countries, related to the needs of world development. This could be the answer to unused capacity in our countries.

The dangers – and the opportunities – we now face would justify the summoning of a World Monetary Conference, an economic summit for the free world.

Now I turn to the situation which arises from the breakdown of the Brussels negotiations. I do not want to go back over the past. What matters now is our response to a challenging and even exciting situation. It is above all a new, though not an unforeseeable, situation.

[1] President of the Board of Trade, 1947–51.

[2] International Monetary Fund.

For 18 months Western policies were directed to a consummation in Brussels. Now we have to start again.

The Labour Party was prepared to accept a solution which would have been genuinely outward-looking and be a stepping-stone to a wider free trade area embracing the Atlantic Community and the Commonwealth. There was nothing in the Treaty of Rome, as such, that would have precluded such an advance. What we were not prepared to join was an inward-looking, autarkic Europe which would sever Britain from our traditional channels of trade with the Commonwealth and the wide trading world. The adoption by the EEC of an agricultural policy based on restrictionism, of high prices policed by a penal import levy on imports from the outside world was a sign that perhaps Schacht, rather than Adam Smith, provided the inspiration for the agricultural planners of the new Europe. This policy involved a degree of interference with established market channels, a degree of rigging of prices and production, of internal self-sufficiency, far transcending the wildest dreams of any British or American Secretary of Agriculture, of any party, who ever existed, and in saying this I am speaking the language of superlatives.

At every stage of the debates in Parliament, Hugh Gaitskell and I and others of us stressed the need for the preparation of an alternative policy in case the talks broke down and Britain was presented with entry terms which proved intolerable. This was designed not only to strengthen our bargaining position, for negotiations based on the thesis that there was no alternative to entry were bound to produce stiff, possibly unacceptable, terms: it was designed to avoid a vacuum, a paralysis of policy in the event of breakdown. At all stages we spelled out a policy based on the concept of an Atlantic – and wider than Atlantic – community based on the United States, Britain and EFTA, EEC, the Commonwealth and probably Japan and possibly Latin America. As long ago as November 1961, when the Clayton-Herter report was presented to the joint committee of Congress, I said that this, rather than a narrow European conception, provided the key to the future.

President de Gaulle's brusque intervention faced us with the need for a constructive alternative. Paying every tribute to the breadth and vision of Mr Macmillan's reappraisal after Brussels, I could not feel that a policy whose constructive measures were limited to the cancellation of a royal visit to Paris could be said to be measuring up fully to the challenge with which we were faced. We, therefore, put forward the following:

First, urgent action to make the Kennedy round effective, on the basis I have mentioned including the United States, United Kingdom, the Commonwealth, EFTA, and those trading areas such as Japan and Latin America which are essential to US trade.

Second, urgent action to conclude international commodity agreements to provide stability in the prices and production of those commodities which enter into international trade, including products of temperate zones such as cereals and dairy produce, and those of primary producing countries such as cocoa, tin, rubber, sisal and tea. We are too apt to forget that all that has been done in the past 10 years in the development of economic aid from advanced countries to the underdeveloped areas, amounting now to $3½ billion, has been more than offset by the collapse in the export income of underdeveloped countries through the fall in primary commodity prices.

Three, associated with this, action to channel food surpluses from advanced countries to meet the needs of hungry nations, for example on the lines proposed by Lord Boyd-Orr in 1946 for a World Food Board, an imaginative concept 15 years ahead of its time, which was rejected because most of us hadn't the dollars in a dollar-hungry world. We must face the fact in our modern democracies, that built-in subsidies and support to our farmers will mean a permanent surplus of food, and this will be enormously augmented if the Common Market agricultural policy is not vetoed by GATT.

Four, planned international action to provide not merely monetary help for developing countries, but governmental and inter-governmental orders for steel, machine tools and transportation equipment – linking their needs with our industries at present working below capacity.

Five, measures to expand international liquidity.

Six, urgent action on the lines so imaginatively proposed by Mr George Ball[1] to provide planned quota outlets in all advanced countries for textiles and other manufactured goods from Asia and Africa.

Seven, on a Commonwealth basis closer integration of Common-

[1] see page 126.

wealth development plans enabling Britain to recapture markets we have lost through neglected opportunities in the past decade.

These are measures required on a world scale. For our part we are prepared in Europe to work to find a solution to the problem of an economic division between EEC and EFTA. Perhaps OECD will provide the right forum, perhaps, as we have suggested, regular meetings of European heads of government to seek close political unity and a solution of Europe's economic problems. We are prepared at the right time, and given the right conditions, to enter into fresh negotiations with the Six, provided this does not mean another 18 months with Britain sitting in the ante-chamber while the Six meet and wrangle about our fate, provided that no one regards the concessions made by Mr Heath as an acceptable starting point. We have stated the five broad conditions which should govern Britain's entry and we are prepared to negotiate on the basis of these conditions. But no one sees any immediate prospect of a new break-through, and that is why I stress the urgency of the other measures which are open to us.

Now I turn to some of the wider issues of world affairs: three in particular, Berlin, disarmament, and the defence of the West.

On Berlin, I recognise that reports of a speech I made in Cardiff five weeks ago have caused some anxieties. This is because the full text was never available. I do not blame the Press. I overloaded them. It was the night I made my first major speech as Leader of the Opposition. I had a full handout on our policy for housing and rents, and the position of slum landlords: in addition I had a few animad-versions on Mr Macmillan and his colleagues which news editors thought of some interest. So there was little space to report a speech I made earlier in the day at the university in which Berlin was mentioned. Our view, which I repeatedly stated in Berlin when last year I led 42 Labour MPs on a mission to Berlin, designed to show our solidarity and support for Willy Brandt and the citizens of West Berlin, is clear. Any settlement of the Berlin issue must provide two non-negotiable, inalienable conditions – first, the right of the people of West Berlin to live in a system of society and under a system of government of their own free choosing: second, guarantees of access to West Berlin from the West going beyond mere paper promises together with all other measures necessary to insure the viability of West Berlin. Third, we regard it as essential that for the foreseeable future Western forces remain in Berlin, as of right, and as custodians of the new agreement. Fourth, to secure such an agreement, we should be prepared to show some degree of flexibility in relation to recognising the existence of the authorities in East Germany and working out practical measures with them. Fifth, we should show a willingness to recognise on a factual basis Germany's eastern frontiers. Unfortunately some reports from Cardiff only repeated the fourth and fifth points of this package.

On disarmament I will say little because of the delicate stage of the negotiations, because we could be on the verge of a great break-through. My Party accepts and insists on the need for effective international verification and supervision. On the test ban there is not only the problem of the number of inspections, but also the means and effectiveness of the system of inspection. On this Russia still has to come through.

On the wider question of a comprehensive disarmament agreement, nuclear and conventional, we feel that the time has come when the Secretary-General of the United Nations might be asked to take the two drafts and examine the possibility of bridging the formidable gap which still exists between them.

We believe that a further step forward could be made – here I know that what I am saying will find little acceptance here today – by the creation in areas of high tension of nuclear free zones and areas of effectively controlled conventional disarmament. Such areas as the continent of Africa, the Middle East, Latin America, and central Europe, might be taken, perhaps in that order.

This would mean effective inspection. The Soviet acceptance of the Rapacki plan involves acceptance of inspection. But inspection must be effective. And, as the Swedish Government insisted in their December 1961 resolution at UN, we must have realism and no disturbance of the present balance of forces in Europe.

Now, on defence. Our position is clear. We stand firmly by NATO and the Western Alliance. We are not a neutralist party and neutralism has no part or place in our policies. We want to see Britain and other European countries make a more effective contribution to NATO.

I know there is nothing more boring in nature than a politician who continually refers to his past speeches, but I find that if I repeat, *ipsissimis verbis*, the speeches I made two or three years ago on this issue, there is a rush to say 'How he's changed since he became Leader of his Party'. In every speech I made as Foreign Affairs spokesman I stressed the central role of NATO in our defence policy and in that wide sector of our foreign policy which relates to defence; and secondly, the paramount need to increase our contribution to the conventional strength of NATO forces. We do not believe this is possible if we pour out our substance on the vain effort to maintain the so-called independent, so-called British, so-called deterrent. Because it isn't independent, it isn't going to be British and its deterrent value in our view adds nothing to the effectiveness of Western deterrent power.

But it does mean such a deployment of our financial and real resources as to limit our ability to make an effective contribution to NATO's ground forces. It does mean a block to our hope of preventing the proliferation of nuclear weapons and it does mean increasing the danger that a conventional outbreak in Europe can quickly escalate into nuclear war.

I believe that our view on this represents the consensus of military opinion in Britain, including many Conservative MPs, and that in this respect Mr Macmillan is inhibited from pursuing the right military policy by the clamant pressure of a small but vociferous band of atavistic back benchers whose intervention was decisive at the time of Nassau.

It is argued that to be realistic and recognise the plain fact that the United States is the custodian of the strategic deterrent on behalf of the Western alliance, that this places us in a position of humiliating dependence on another nation. I do not agree. It is dependence on the United States for the so-called British deterrent which creates the wrong relationship and which means that meetings of Western leaders, instead of being directed to the urgent problems of strengthening the alliance, are dominated by unrewarding, and I would feel humiliating, wrangles about the supply of particular weapons.

Every American pressman I meet asks whether a Labour government would repudiate the Nassau Agreement. I don't like the word 'repudiate' which implies breaking faith with a partner, and I have my doubts about the enthusiasm with which the US Administration approached the Nassau Agreement. My answer is that a Labour government's first task would be to survey the defence position we inherit, to survey the shambles, some say, then to enter into discussions with our American partners about Nassau and about our broader approach to NATO. In view of our policy on deterrents, we should then renegotiate, I have heard the word 'denegotiate', the agreement.

Before I leave defence I should like to say one word about Britain's oversea bases east of Suez. The future of some of them is obscure: one thing we should have learned at heavy cost is that you cannot hold a military base in hostile territory. But in general, though some rundown is possible and desirable to release troops for Germany and for the strategic reserve, I believe it to be a mistake to evacuate key bases where we have the chance to remain. It is a hundred times easier for Britain to remain there, even with a token force, than for us, still less the United States, to seek to enter if trouble breaks out. I believe, therefore, that our maintenance of these bases should be regarded as a specific and invaluable contribution to the alliance.

I have talked today mainly about the relationship of Britain and the United States within the alliance. Frequently I am asked, 'What about the special relationship?' I am never quite sure what this means. I am more interested in a close relationship based on a common purpose, common objectives, and as far as can be achieved community of policy, a relationship based not on condescension or on a backward-looking nostalgia for the past, but on the ability of both parties to put forward their strength and their own unique contribution to our common purpose. Charles Lamb said in one of his essays, 'There is nothing so irrelevant in nature as a poor relation', and if ever our relationship with you were based on that status the sooner it were ended the better: that is why the first priority in British internal policy is to build up our economic strength so that as partners – in the alliance, in Europe, and the Commonwealth – we are relevant and necessary. It is on that, not on any conception of past greatness, that our standing in the world will depend. Our ability to restore the lost dynamic to Britain's economic society, to restore a sense of economic and social and moral purpose, will have far more bearing on our value as an ally and a partner than any vain nuclear posturings. It may not be long before the same truth dawns on President de Gaulle.

Because we reject the notion that Britain is fated by history or some vicious twist of fate or by internal debility to be treated as The Sick Man of Europe. We are not. We have a reservoir of unused and underused talent, of skill and craftsmanship, of inventiveness, and ingenuity, of administrative ability and scientific creativeness which if mobilised will, within a measurable period of time enable us to become – not the workshop of the world; that is no longer our role – but the pilot plant, the toolroom of the world. Our scientists are among the finest in the world. The tragedy is we don't produce enough of them, and those we do produce we do not use intelligently. Some we fail even to hold – and the reason for this is not as one Noble Lord[1] has said: the deficiencies in your educational system – it is deficiencies in our industrial and governmental system, that we do not provide the status and opportunities, above all the key role in our society that the needs of the 1960s demand.

That is why the central thread of Labour policy, the key to our plan to redynamise Britain's economy, is our plan to mobilise the talents of our scientists and technicians, redeployed from missile and warheads, on research and development contracts, civil research and development to produce the new instruments and tools of economic advance both for Britain and for the war on poverty in under-developed areas of the Commonwealth and elsewhere. If we are able to do this, and I have no doubt that we can – we shall be able in a very few years to transform our society and, in the alliance, in our economic relations with the Atlantic Community, and in the wider context of the North-South challenge, to put forward our full and so far unrealised strength, dependent on no one, but ready to play our full role in the inter-dependent community of free nations.

TELEVISION BROADCAST IN MOSCOW, 14TH JUNE, 1963

I WELCOME THE OPPORTUNITY accorded to me through the courtesy of the Soviet authorities, to broadcast to you tonight. Opportunities for our political leaders to speak to the people of the Soviet Union, and for your leaders to speak to the British people, are all too few.

[1] Lord Hailsham.

But, the more we can talk with one another, the better the prospects of understanding, and therefore of peace.

I am not, you will realise, a member of the British Government. I am Leader of the Labour Party, the official Opposition to the Conservative Government in Great Britain. It will be for the British people, in the elections this year or next, to decide whether we, or the Conservatives, are to be the Government of Britain over the next five years.

But, I welcome the chance I have had this week for frank political talks with Chairman Khrushchev, Deputy Prime Ministers Mikoyan and Kosygin, and other Soviet leaders. They have enabled me to hear at first-hand the Soviet Government view on all questions of world affairs and to understand that view more clearly: equally, I hope I have been able to explain the standpoint of the Labour Party on many issues which we have discussed.

All of us recognise that there are great differences between our two countries – in terms of our constitutions and political systems – and of our approach to political and economic affairs. Each of our two nations believes in its own system. Each of us will defend our system and our rights and liberties. And inevitably there are differences between us in our approach to world affairs, differences which in some cases are deep-seated, even fundamental. But, whatever differences there are, we are agreed on one thing above all – differences of political institutions or of foreign policy do not mean that we have to settle these problems by recourse to war. Peace is the highest aim and the condition for the survival of those things in which all of us believe. The choice is not between co-existence and non-co-existence. The choice is between co-existence and co-annihilation.

Wherever we have gone, in every section of the community – offices, coalfields, the man in the street – we have been made acutely aware of the deep desire for peace – not merely the negative absence of war, but a positive and constructive and abiding peace. I can tell you that wherever you go in Britain this same feeling inspires our people. And, as I have recently visited the United States and Canada, I would like you to know from my personal experience that the North American peoples also have this same urgent desire. I was glad to hear Soviet leaders welcome President Kennedy's speech this week in which he said, 'Total war made no sense in the nuclear age, and peace was a necessary rational end of rational men'.

What must we do to make these feelings a reality? We must discuss our problems – frankly, clearly, honestly, as in the important discussion I had with Mr Khrushchev on Monday – and where there are differences then, as Mr Khrushchev has himself said, let them be expressed in the form of a vigorous rivalry in competitive, peaceful co-existence, each striving to outdo the other in economic and social achievement, and in the aid which we advanced countries, whether Western or Communist, can give to raise the living standards of peoples who subsist on the verge of poverty and hunger.

For these frank exchanges to be achieved there must be more frequent exchanges between the leaders of our respective nations. It is only 3½ hours by jet plane to Moscow from London. Yet it is becoming almost as difficult to put two national leaders into the conference room together, as to put two astronauts on the moon. This is why this week we have stressed the need for regular and frequent, almost routine, summit meetings. And to supplement these meetings let there be much greater movement of people from all walks of life, from your country and mine, indeed all members of the United Nations. And I am glad, too, that this week has provided the opportunity for encouraging and constructive discussions aimed at increasing the flow of trade between our two countries. Trade (tergovle) paves the way to peace (mir).

This is not my first visit to Russia. I have now visited your country 11 times over a period of 16 years. Every time I come I notice the great advance in living standards, in housing and construction, and in the expansion of your industry. I have had the chance, by talking to your Ministers and industrial leaders and scientists to hear something of the USSR's massive mobilisation of scientific resources for the purpose of industrial advance. It is our aim also to harness science to industry – to expand our facilities as you have done for educating more scientists and technologists and to give them the chance to produce a new dynamic in our industry. We hope, too, that there will be much greater interchange of scientific knowledge and know-how between our scientists and technologists. Both nations are rightly proud of their scientists and their contribution to scientific advance: inevitably in the modern world specialisation means that our two nations make spectacular advances in different but complementary fields. Both of us, and indeed the world can gain by an exchange and pooling of knowledge.

I have been privileged this week to act as a link – if an unofficial one – between our two peoples. But a visit of this kind should not be an exception. There are vast untapped resources of goodwill, healthy curiosity, and of a friendship which has been tempered in our war-time alliance. In these past years there have been disappointments, divisions even danger.

I ended the broadcast with the following in Russian:

Now, Ministers, traders, scientists, artists, social workers, teachers, workers by hand and brain have their part to play in breaking down the barriers between East and West. For all of us our aim must be that real friendship which leads to peace.

FOREIGN AFFAIRS DEBATE, HOUSE OF COMMONS, 3RD JULY, 1963

I WANT TO CONCENTRATE on the immediate problem that we have been facing in this debate – a nuclear test ban. I do not need to underline the urgency of this – the priority need to avert a fresh round of damaging nuclear tests, the need to prevent a further dangerous impetus to the nuclear arms race, the economic cost to East and West alike, and, perhaps, above all, the need to get one clear and symbolic – indeed, more than symbolic – one positive achievement in the field of co-existence. President Kennedy faces political problems, in any test ban agreement in the Senate. So, in my view, does Mr Khrushchev. I think that Mr Khrushchev has similarly shown great courage in standing by the policy of co-existence in the face, I suspect, of some pressure at home, and, in the context of the Communist world, in the face of almost intolerable pressure within his alliance at a time of great ideological dispute.

We must all face the fact that any failure now in these negotiations, if that failure can be laid at our door, could lead not necessarily immediately – perhaps later rather than sooner – to strengthening the hands of those in the Communist bloc who are only too ready to criticise Mr Khrushchev's co-existence policy. We must remember that Mr Khrushchev has a Senate, too.

The first question that my right hon Friend and I, and my hon Friend the Member for Sedgefield (Mr Slater[1]) who took part in all our talks in Moscow, sought to put was the prospect of a straight, overall test ban covering tests in the atmosphere, in space, under water and underground – the complete test ban. We were particularly at pains to try to dispel the suspicion and mistrust which had arisen between the Soviet Union and the United States from the grave misunderstanding between the two countries' representatives, on the question of inspection. The Soviet representatives, headed by Mr Kuznetzov, had gained the impression that the American negotiators had indicated that if the Russians would agree to at any rate some on-site inspections – two or three – a test ban could be agreed to immediately. The Russians feel that this was the proper interpretation of what was said, and they therefore feel that, having offered three inspections, they were let down when the Americans said that three were not enough.

My right hon Friend[2] and I were completely satisfied, from our talks in Washington, that this was a genuine misunderstanding, that the Americans had acted in complete good faith in this matter, and that they were worried about the fact that the Russians had misunderstood. So we spent some time in Moscow trying to convince Mr Khrushchev and his colleagues of America's good faith in this matter.

But we were left in no doubt that whatever the cause of this misunderstanding the Soviet Government regarded this issue as closed. The offer of two or three on-site inspections was withdrawn. When this statement was made to us we felt that it was too important and too sombre to be left in doubt through any vagaries of interpretation or translation, and we pressed for a repetition. I am sorry to have to repeat to the House that this is quite clear; the offer of three inspections is withdrawn. Unless, therefore, there is a sudden change in the Soviet attitude, between our visit a fortnight ago and the talks when they begin in a few days' time, the possibility of a comprehensive test

[1] My Parliamentary Private Secretary.

[2] Patrick Gordon Walker.

ban – including underground tests – is, we must admit, far from hopeful.

In those circumstances we felt it right to press two alternatives. One of these was the proposal which has been put at different times by the West and by the Soviet Government, but never at the same time, for a ban limited to the so-called three environments – atmosphere, space, and underwater. This is limited. If we had a test ban of this kind it would be limited in its coverage, but I think that the House would agree that it is well worth pressing for.

It would, in any case, outlaw the major tests – the 20, 30 and 50 megaton explosion. It would end the danger of the pollution of the atmosphere. It would limit, though it could not end, the nuclear arms race. But, of course, to have any hope of acceptance in the United States, this would mean that both sides would have to be free to continue underground testing, because a voluntary moratorium in the field of underground testing would simply be to accept the Soviet view on inspection.

Mr Khrushchev, when we pressed him on this, said that the Russians would welcome a three environments ban, leaving the question of underground tests for further negotiation. But, of course, we were not able to get a clear agreement that during those negotiations both sides would be free to continue underground tests. Frankly, we could hardly have hoped to get this. As my right hon Friend said, we were not in a position to negotiate with the Soviet authorities.

What we were engaged in was a reconnaissance in depth which, I think, was of itself quite useful. But I believe that the idea of raising this question, of side-tracking the difficulties away from the somewhat sterile argument about inspection into the more hopeful sphere of a test ban limited to the three areas that I have mentioned, has been useful, and I think that Mr Khrushchev's speech[1] yesterday in East Berlin, the first time for a very long time that he has given this assurance in public, stems from the discussions that we had in Moscow.

At various times East and West have said nearly everything, but they have never said them at the same time. The Soviet Union itself, some three years ago, and indeed longer, pressed for a three-environments test ban but the West did not agree at that time. I do not want

[1] Mr Khrushchev had raised hopes of Test Ban Agreement.

to apportion blame to either side. This is too important an issue to be regarded as a debating point.

What I think is important is to establish, particularly on the eve of these vitally important talks in Moscow[1], what are the areas in which agreement can be reached. Until a month ago – I agree with what the hon and gallant Gentleman has said; we said the same in Moscow – all the emphasis and all the discussions were on the question of inspection. Would they go above three? Would the Americans go below seven? Is there a way round it by suggesting 21 or 22 in three years with a maximum of so many in any one year? I think that the importance of the last few weeks has been to establish that probably the most helpful line lies in both sides reviving at the same time – and saying this at the same time – a proposal for this three-environments test ban. I agree – and I am sure that all of us would agree – that this is not the whole of what we would want, but it is a very valuable step forward.

I feel, therefore, that there is real hope of an agreement if the negotiators will take it up from that point. We did, however, press a further point. It is certainly not an original point, indeed, we have discussed it in this House, namely, a confrontation of Soviet and Western scientists. Soviet scientists claim that every underground test can be monitored from outside, or, at any rate, with the aid of black boxes. Once again, Mr Khrushchev made it clear that the Russians had no objection to a number of black boxes.

It is the Soviet scientists' view that all tests of any significance at all can be monitored from outside. We know that this view is shared also by many distinguished and authoritative Western scientists both in Britain and in the United States, though the view is not shared by the scientists advising Western Governments. So what we suggested to Mr Khrushchev, or, perhaps, we suggested in more detail to Mr Kuznetsov and Mr Gromyko, was this: that either as a means of following up the underground problem once a three-environments test ban had been agreed, or, if we like, more ambitiously, as a means to securing a fully comprehensive test ban, Soviet and Western scientists should meet, and argue the problem out on these lines. (*Interruption*).

I know that the right hon Gentleman[2] has suggested these things

[1] Test Ban Agreement talks, July, 1963.

[2] Harold Macmillan.

many times, but we are trying to make progress now on the eve of these talks. The trouble is that the right hon Gentleman has never suggested it in Moscow, and the important thing here is, if I may suggest it to the right hon Gentleman who, I know, has worked tremendously hard – and we all pay tribute to his patience and initiative – to get some loosening of the Soviet attitude at the top, and that, as I understand it, is what we are hoping to get on 15th July.

It is, therefore, somewhat relevant to the whole House to hear some idea of what the Soviet authorities have had put to them and those points on which they might agree. What we have suggested – the right hon Gentleman and I have often passed this across the floor of the House to one another in debate after debate – was that when the scientists get together the United States should, during a given named period, say, during the next month, or the next fortnight, or whatever it might be, undertake a secret test, at a time and place unspecified, which would be witnessed and certified by United Nations or other agreed neutral observers. If, at the end of the period, the Soviet scientists could say, 'That test took place at 3.35 pm on such and such a date in Nevada' – or somewhere of that kind – then I think that the Soviet scientists would have vindicated their claim of being able to monitor the tests from outside. If they failed to be able to do this, there is, I think, a *prima facie* case for the view that the Western scientists' claim had been vindicated. I hope that we shall see this proposal seriously pressed.

Even if we get the three-environments ban, I think that we are all agreed that it is important to go on and try to achieve the underground tests and an effective test ban as well. The question of a nuclear test ban is so vital to world peace that I hope that the Western negotiators will be prepared to put forward a package plan which is designed to assist a test ban agreement. I think that to confine the negotiations too closely to the test ban may not be as fruitful as if it is backed by other proposals.

I think that there are two proposals which could be of immeasurable help in creating the confidence necessary to get the test ban. First, a proposal involving a measure of disengagement, for example, a willingness to take the Rapacki plan[1] as a basis for negotiation, in the wider context of what is called in the Geneva draft, 'Measures

[1] Polish Foreign Minister's plan for disengagement in Europe.

designed to prevent surprise attack', because, from my discussions in Washington – I do not know whether Ministers will confirm that this is their view; perhaps the Prime Minister will tell us this evening – I formed the view that the United States did not entirely exclude all possible considerations of the Rapacki plan, but felt that it should be put under the general category of 'measures designed to prevent surprise attack'.

It is for this reason that I have been disappointed on a number of occasions, including last week, when we read the text of the debate in another place, that the Foreign Secretary[1] once again pretty brusquely ruled out the idea of considering the Rapacki plan. I will come to the prospects of disengagement later. Secondly, I believe that we should now press and I emphasise, the word 'now', because I think that it should be related to the Moscow talks, with all the vigour at our command, a proposal for an anti-proliferation agreement, a ban on the spread of nuclear weapons beyond the four existing Powers who are, or claim to be, independent nuclear Powers.

This is a proposal which, I think, would not only have an enormous catalytic value in reaching agreement, but it is, of course, intrinsically, in its own right, a highly desirable and essential step. I think that it would help to get a test ban agreement. But, for its own sake, it is something which should proceed any way. I am sure that hon Members on both sides of the House shudder to think of the spread of nuclear weapons to fifth, sixth, seventh, eighth, tenth and twelfth powers especially if those included, as they would, countries such as Egypt, Israel and China.

We had some lengthy discussions on this matter and found that the Soviet Government would welcome such a proposal, a proposal to stop the spread of nuclear weapons; and I think that it could, as I have said, be a great solvent in the forthcoming talks. But the top Soviet leaders insist on one essential interpretation of the anti-proliferation agreement. It is that there must be no spread, direct or indirect, of nuclear weapons.

Frankly, the Russians would regard a multilateral or mixed-manned force as a breach of any such agreement; or, if the multilateral force were in existence before the negotiations, they would regard it as an impediment, indeed, as a fatal bar, to the conclusion

[1] Lord Home.

of such an agreement. What I am trying to suggest to the House is that the Soviet authorities would welcome a proposal for an anti-proliferation agreement. But, at the same time, they would regard this as incompatible with the continued negotiations for a multilateral mixed-manned force.

When the Russians said this they had in mind the Germans. I have said more than once in this House – I think that all of us have said it – and elsewhere, at the NATO Parliamentarians meetings, in Washington and in a number of other places, I have referred to the Russian 'obsession' about German arms. I do not think that that is too strong a word. The point was made last night by the hon Member for Louth (Sir C. Osborne). I do not think that I should ever use the phrase 'love-hate relationship' between the Russians and the Germans. The word 'love' does not quite fit in. But, at any rate, the Russians have a very powerful mixture of respect and hatred for the Germans. After all, going back to Czarist times, almost anything which ran successfully in Russia, from a railway to a cotton mill, was probably controlled or managed by Germans – [HON MEMBERS: 'And Scotsmen']. Yes, and the Scots; I give credit to them. But the Russians have only respect for the Scots; they have no hatred for them.

At all times since, I think, they have a formidable respect for German technological achievements. This, coming on top of, or being followed by, the Second World War, when 20 million Russians died, has created a situation about which I think one is justified in using the word 'obsession'. It is an obsession that we should have had had we suffered at the hands of the Germans in the way in which the Russians suffered.

I have expressed in strong terms my view that any proposal to arm the Germans with nuclear weapons would mean the end of any hope of easing the East-West tension. That has been my opinion. But my words, strong though they may have seemed to me, pale into insignificance when compared with the vehemence with which Mr Khrushchev expressed the same thought when we were in Moscow. I am in no doubt at all that this really would mean the end of any policy of constructive co-existence. It would be as much a turning point in history, and as much a fateful milestone on the road to a third world war as Hitler's march into the Rhineland was towards the last war.

We tried to find out whether the Soviet objection to direct German nuclear armaments extended equally to the multilateral force. Again, we were left in no doubt of the answer. We explained the American position to them and I think that this should be said. The Americans deserve credit for their motives in proposing a multilateral force. Let there be no misunderstanding about this. The Americans are as keen to prevent the Germans from becoming a nuclear power, either directly or through a Franco-German understanding, as anyone in this House. That is the American motive.

They know as well as anyone that from the defence point of view the multilateral force proposal is a nonsense, adding nothing to Western strength. But they are so convinced that, in the absence of proposals of this kind to integrate Germany into an international nuclear force, Germany would become a nuclear power that they are presenting this nonsensical proposal, because it is the only proposal they can offer to stop Germany from becoming a nuclear power.

If we were convinced that this were the only way to stop the German nuclear capability we would reluctantly support the multilateral force proposal. But we are not so convinced. On the contrary, we have feared all along that it would whet the German nuclear appetites, and, in fact, it is doing so, even before we have it. The very mention of it is whetting German appetites.

Herr von Hassel, the German Defence Minister, if he was correctly reported, has said that if there were a MLF – a multilateral force – incorporating an American veto, that veto could not continue for ever. Moreover, when he stated his acceptance, in the statement he made, of the idea of the multilateral force, he said that this proposal did not supersede or replace Germany's request for medium-range ballistic missiles on German soil. We have been warned and the House must be very clear about its answer to this warning.

Further, General Lemnitzer, addressing the Assembly of Western European Union on 7th June, said:

> Our studies at SHAPE indicate that a mixture of configuration – surface ships, submarines and land vehicles – would be the best solution to attaining the military capability which we require.

So there is a very serious development of a 'desire' – if hon Members like – for a spread of nuclear weapons.

I hope that the Prime Minister, President Kennedy, Lord Hailsham[1] – we wish him well despite our doubts about whether he was the right choice – and Mr Harriman[2] will be in no doubt of the importance of this question, that the issue of German rearmament is the key to the whole problem of East-West tension and so to the wider problem of attaining a lasting peace. We must therefore ask the Prime Minister – I hope that he will give us a clear answer – where he stands on this issue. On 31st January, when we debated the Nassau arrangement, I said:

> We have a right to ask where the Government stand on these proposals for a European deterrent, including the nuclear rearmament of Germany. I make perfectly clear now where we stand. We are completely, utterly, and unequivocally opposed, now and in all circumstances, to any suggestion that Germany, West Germany or East Germany, directly or indirectly, should have a finger on the nuclear trigger or any responsibility, direct or indirect, for deciding that nuclear weapons are to be used.

I have used exactly the same words at Washington and in Moscow. This is the policy of our party. When I stated this in January, and I asked the Prime Minister then if he would be equally clear about his own attitude to this question, his answer was equivocal. I hope that he will be clear tonight. It is important, for this reason. Recent reports suggest that the MLF proposal may be shelved, or deferred. Since the Americans put it forward in good faith, as I believe, as the one contribution which they could suggest for preventing Germany from becoming a nuclear power, and since the right hon Gentleman the Prime Minister – whatever equivocations we have had from the Government Front Bench about MLF – is obviously very dubious about it – I think that the whole House is – we have to ask him this question.

Since the Americans say that this is the only way of stopping Germany from becoming a nuclear power and the Government clearly oppose this proposal, what is their alternative? What is the Prime Minister's alternative as a means of stopping the Germans from becoming a nuclear power? Does he agree with the United

[1] On joint Anglo-American Test Ban Mission to Moscow, July, 1963.

[2] American representative on Anglo-American Test Ban agreement mission, July, 1963, Moscow.

States view that Germany either must be included in the MLF, or that Germany will become a nuclear power? I think that the House and the country would be greatly reassured if the Prime Minister would express himself on this question as clearly as we have from this side of the House.

If the right hon Gentleman does not, we want to know what is the alternative. It is no secret, I think, that last year, at the time of Mr McNamara's Ann Arbor[1] speech, which many of us welcomed as aimed at confining nuclear capabilities to the two real nuclear powers, the Prime Minister was encouraging and supporting General de Gaulle's nuclear ambitions in his rather pathetic attempt to win French support for Britain's entry into the Common Market.

Is it now the fact that whereas Mr Khrushchev, President Kennedy and, at any rate, this side of the House, and, I think, many hon Gentlemen opposite – in fact, practically all of them – are all strongly opposed to German nuclear arms, the Prime Minister and the Government are, perhaps, prepared to see a situation developing in which Germany could become a nuclear power on the ground that it would make his own so-called independent nuclear deterrent a little more respectable than it is? I hope that the right hon Gentleman will now make his position clear on this tonight, more so than he did in January. If that were his attitude I think he should not be in any doubt that he would be gambling with peace for reasons of election calculations. Let us hope that we get a clear answer to this tonight.

I want to put another point to the right hon Gentleman, and I hope that he put this point to the President of the United States last weekend, because it was one of the central issues included in a summary of impressions that we made available to the Government of our talks in Moscow. This is the issue of China. We were left in no doubt that the question of nuclear arms for Germany is tied up in the Russian mind with that of nuclear arms for China. I have little fear of the Soviet Union, in present conditions, wanting to give nuclear weapons to China – far from it – but my colleagues and I were told that it will be immeasurably harder to justify refusing them to the Chinese if Germany is brought, whether directly or indirectly, into the nuclear picture, and it will be immeasurably easier to refuse them nuclear arms if the Soviet Government can point to an effective anti-

[1] McNamara speaking at Conference, Ann Arbor, Michigan, June, 1962.

proliferation agreement covering both direct and indirect nuclear capability. Thus, the effect of an anti-proliferation agreement goes far beyond even the hopes that some of us have placed on it.

Before I sit down, I want to refer to two questions which I mentioned briefly in passing. One is the German question, on which the Russians feel and express themselves so strongly. It is very important to get away from jargon and slogans. There is not one German question – there are at least three – and it is important to disentangle them. I shall not disguise from the House the fact that when Mr Khrushchev spoke on this question – he made a very long statement about Germany – he emphasised his points with such vehemence that the table between us shook, and I think that my colleagues will confirm that I replied with equal frankness about our attitude to this.

Sir Kenneth Pickthorne (Carlton): And I suppose Khrushchev shook.

Mr H. Wilson: I think that the issues we are trying to debate are a little beyond the comprehension of a pedantic grammarian. We are all extremely fond of the hon Gentleman, and enjoy his interruptions, but I sometimes think that if the world were ever practically destroyed by a nuclear explosion, the hon Gentleman would creep out of his shell next morning, if, happily, he were preserved, and complain that somebody had split an infinitive.

The position is that while I think that there is a great deal of common ground on the question of German nuclear arms, certainly between us and the Soviet Union, and, I think, between many hon Gentlemen opposite and the Soviet Union, there is no common ground as yet on the question of West Berlin or of the proposed German peace treaty. On this subject we used the same words as we have used in this House in past debates, for example, on 5th July, last. I suggest to right hon Gentlemen opposite that when they discuss this question with the Russians they should insist that there is not one, single, homogeneous German question, as the Russians always insist, but that there are at least three, the three I have just mentioned – Berlin, the peace treaty and nuclear arms.

The so-called urgency of a peace treaty on Russian lines exists as a matter of urgency only in the Soviet mind. It is not acceptable, and it is certainly not urgent. There is no need for one, and on Berlin I think that we must continue to point out that the geographical accident, or the historical accident, that West Berlin is an enclave within an area coloured red, or green, or whatever it is, on maps has no bearing on the future of two million citizens of West Berlin. They tend to say that this is geographically part of East Germany and that, therefore, certain events must follow from that.

We insist, as the House does, that the two million citizens of West Berlin must be free to make their own decision about the kind of society and the kind of political system in which they live. I remember telling Mr Gomulka, who had been very passionate on this subject, and had made a long reference, when dealing with something else, to the problem of slavery, that his proposals for Berlin would mean the creation of two million slaves who today are free men and women. I think that this should be clearly stated.

Let us try to disentangle the nuclear arms question, on which I think the Russians have every right to speak as they do, from these other issues, because we are playing their game, we are endangering peace if we talk as Dr Adenauer does, or as Mr Khrushchev does, of the German question. There is not one, but, as the Lord Privy Seal knows, there are many.

The other point is disengagement. I have said that this could be a great solvent both to the Berlin question and to the problem of nuclear tests. The Rapacki plan has been repeatedly turned down by Her Majesty's Government, and sharply at that, but there are some attractive things about it. It involves inspection on a substantial scale. It could lead to useful experience being gained and useful confidence being created to see how East and West can get together in a scheme that involves so much inspection. It contains built-in provisions against surprise attack. We emphasised in our discussions that we are not committed to every detail of the Rapacki plan, far from it, though we feel that it could be accepted as a basis for discussion. It should be tabled and discussed.

We emphasised, both in our talks with Soviet leaders, and with Mr Rapacki himself, whom we met in Warsaw – and I think that this must be emphasised – that it should not be put forward or used in any sense which would mean altering the balance of forces or the military dispositions between East and West. Once the Rapacki plan is looked at in such a way to destroy the balance of forces, then any value it has disappears as a basis for negotiation. I therefore strongly urge the Government to be more forthcoming on the question of the Rapacki plan and to make this clear at the Moscow talks.

The principle of nuclear-free zones and areas of controlled conventional disarmament should be pressed for other parts of the world as well as central Europe. It may be that we could make progress more quickly in the establishment of such zones in other parts of the world. Why cannot we agree, as we pressed in Moscow, that the whole Continent of Africa should be declared a nuclear-free zone and guaranteed as such with adequate inspection by all the major Powers through the United Nations?

It is clear that we would have to exclude Egypt in the early stages – she is now being armed with German rockets – until we could get a similar nuclear-free zone established for the Middle East, and, as we urged on Mr Khrushchev, a ban on arms shipments to the Middle East, which we know the Government would wish to support. But why should not we have one for Africa, and one for Latin America? Let us at least make a start with this even if we are not yet ready – and I hope that we would be – to make a success of a nuclear-free zone for central Europe.

These are concrete proposals on which we would welcome Government support tonight. I have tried to indicate some of the ways in which international negotiations, beginning with the vital conference in Moscow on 15th July, could lead the world in the direction of peace. The ideas put forward by my right hon Friends yesterday are not academic exercises. They have been to a large extent tested in the Kremlin, and I urge again the need for talks at the Summit.

Whatever our hopes for a conference this month, the Soviet system is such that it is only at the top that we have real prospects of the flexibility needed to break down the rigidities of Soviet policy – only at the top can we really get the flexibility that is necessary for negotiation and a successful agreement. That is why we stressed the need to a Summit conference.

The world has not had a happy experience of Summits. I hope that I am not unduly cynical, but their timing appears to have been too much related to electoral considerations in this country. In 1955, for example, the Earl of Avon – then Sir Anthony Eden – persuaded a very reluctant President Eisenhower to authorise him to announce, in time for the election of that year, that there would be a Summit after the election. After the election, we had the Summit – it failed.

In 1959, the right hon Gentleman the Prime Minister, with the good will of the whole House, put on his white fur hat and visited

Moscow. He was working for a Summit, and he was right to do so, and he eased the path to the Summit, I believe, by indicating to Mr Khrushchev – I use the word 'indicating'; I do not say that he said it in so many words as a binding commitment – that he was inclined towards a measure of disengagement in Europe. Mr Khrushchev certainly got that impression.

That led to agreement about a Summit, and the General Election in that year was fought partly on Summit hopes and Summit promises. There was a great deal of discussion about the date to be fixed for the Summit. This argument ran right through the election. But the Summit was doomed, even before the U2 flight, by the fact that any ideas the Prime Minister had about disengagement – and I believe that they were sincere in his mind – were firmly vetoed by Dr Adenauer on the Prime Minister's pressing the matter further in the pre-Summit preparations. So the Summit failed.

Since then, there has been no progress. But now, with the same predictable regularity that we welcome the quadrennial spasms in industrial production, there is talk of a Summit again – and we welcome it, however mixed the Prime Minister's motives may be in this matter. We have talk of a Summit once in four years. Is it not fantastic? Moscow is only 3½ hours by jet from London, and we are getting to the point where it is easier for two cosmonauts to rendezvous in space than for a Soviet and a British Prime Minister to rendezvous in the same conference room.

I said last week – if a British business man runs into a problem – with a contract, or deliveries, a specification or after-sales service – at the drop of a hat he will fly half way round the world to solve it. But when we face these vital, challenging, dangerous problems, affecting world peace, we rely on this stately quadrille of Notes, of diplomatic representations, démarchés and détentes, instead of the plain, honest-to-goodness, commonsense proceeding of putting national leaders in a room together to settle the issue.

I think that one reason – and I do not underrate it – is the fear of failure, the fear of the shiver of disappointment that would go through the world if heads of Government met, and failed to reach agreement. This is understandable, and I think that it leads to the sterile insistence that everything must be cleared in advance and, as far as possible, agreed in advance, before heads of Government meet. But it cannot be agreed in advance, because, in the Soviet system, the authority to agree rests only at the top, so the leaders do not meet or, if by chance they do, the very fear of failure tends to produce a sort of anxiety neurosis which makes failure well-nigh inevitable.

This is why we have put forward the idea – and it was warmly welcomed in Moscow – of regular, routine Summits to be held at a fixed date whether there had been prior argeement or not. That would have less fear of failure and, for that very reason, more hope of success. We suggested that the Prime Minister of the USSR and the Prime Minister of Britain, whoever he may be – and, perhaps, when he decides to return to the comity of nations, the President of France – should go to New York, each to lead his country's delegation to the General Assembly each October and, while there, – they could take the opportunity to make important speeches in the General Assembly if they so wished – meet the President of the United States – preferably, I think, under the aegis of the United Nations – for Summit talks.

None of us underrates the formidable problems that are confronting the worlds' peacemakers, of whatever party he may be or of what country, during the next few years. We believe that this limited, but, I hope, constructive proposal for regular – perhaps annual – Summits, taken with the other proposals we have put forward in this debate, although none of them is very dramatic or spectacular, could be the first steps towards an enduring peace.

SECTION VI

What is British Socialism?

The speeches and articles in this concluding section deal with different aspects of the approach to Socialism.

The New Statesman *article was written during the 1959 General Election campaign and deals, in the form of a reply to a challenge by Dr Peter Townsend, with my conception of social priorities.*

The Party Political Television broadcast of 8th May, 1963, was a transcript of a television talk devoted to three matters of direct concern to every family in Britain, housing, local rates and education.

The 'Future of British Transport' was a speech made in the House of Commons, on 30th April, 1963, the second day of the debate on Dr Beeching's rail closure proposals. This debate gave me an opportunity to outline Labour's general policy on inland transport.

Finally, the article for the New York Times *was an attempt to summarise, for an overseas readership, the present position and Socialist outlook of the British Labour Party.*

CHAPTER NINE

*

The War on Poverty[1]

IN LAST WEEK'S *New Statesman,* Peter Townsend[2] ended his challenging article with these questions:

> Can it (the next Labour Government) stomach the thought that the social legislation of its 1945–51 predecessor can be bettered and, what is more, should now be critically reviewed? Can it make sure that the evidence necessary to formulate policy on such subjects of national importance as poverty and living standards is being collected, either by a better financed research and information department of its own, or preferably by some independent body? Can it disengage itself from the cloying attentions of those who think it better to invest in machinery than people?

The answer is an unequivocal 'Yes'. The surprise is that Peter Townsend, who has himself done so much back-room work for the Labour Party on the problem of pensions and superannuation, should find it necessary to put these questions. Much of the argument about Labour's policy for *Security and Old Age*[3] has inevitably been on the expert and technical level, it is true. But the readiness with which the party leadership endorsed the present proposals when they were first produced, and the warmth with which they have been received by local parties, bear witness to the burning desire among Labour Party members at all levels to end poverty and to advance far beyond the 1945–51 reforms to a much more real equality. It is possible in any case to draw too sharp a distinction between the objectives of greater

[1] This article appeared in the *New Statesman,* October 1959.

[2] Sociologist, now Professor of Sociology, University of Essex.

[3] Labour Party policy statement on Pensions and Security in Old Age, 1957.

equality and economic expansion. After all they are not incompatible. We need both: the theme of all the campaign speeches I have heard has been not just 'expansion' or 'redistribution', but 'fairer shares in expanding prosperity'.

Where I think I take issue most with Peter Townsend is his identification of the Labour Party with the purely Tory view that an increase in national production automatically raises the poorest section of the community to a more tolerable position. What Labour leader has ever said this? Or even thought it? After the war we did two things – first, in 1946, we raised the least privileged, absolutely and relatively; and for the next five years raised the national income to pay for it. What is our policy today? First, and immediately, to raise retirement pensions and other social benefits, bodily lifting the least privileged group of our people on to a higher standard of living, before doing anything for the rest of the community. At the same time as we do that we shall embark on the necessary measures to raise production.

Indeed, I see that the main Tory counter-attack is that we propose to carry out our social reforms before we have the money to pay for them. Given a Labour victory, the test is this: will there be, 12 months from now, a narrowing of the gap between rich and poor, quite apart from any general upward movement there may be as the result of increased national production? The answer is, quite simply, that there will. This has been the central theme of both our election speeches and the party's television programmes.

Labour would be wrong to deny that there is increased prosperity in the country; and we do not seek to do so. The question is not are we better off than just after the war? But how much better off could we be today if we had had a government dedicated to industrial expansion instead of one which, for three years out of the past four, has held down industrial production? We should be equally wrong to allow the recognition of this prosperity to disguise the fact that so many of our people face real, bitter poverty, even if so much of it is hidden away in our back streets. I remember the first time I spoke on this subject in the House of Commons, on the occasion of the Government's 2s 6d increase in National Assistance scales in December, 1954. We did not then have available to us the result of Peter Townsend's painstaking research on the facts of poverty today. I based myself on the valuable survey of social conditions in St Helens which Norman MacKenzie had contributed to the *New Statesman*, and I concluded:

> This survey showed that about one-tenth of the people are living in the poverty zone; that is, either on or just below the poverty line.
>
> These people are the new submerged tenth of the population that the government have done so much to ignore.
>
> Perhaps the tragedy of these lives is that they go on to a very large extent in secrecy, in privacy, almost concealed behind lace curtains in back streets.

Labour's attack on poverty is on a broad front. There is a common tendency to think of social advance purely in terms of cash pensions, or at best cash pensions plus tobacco coupons. This approach ignores a whole range of social policy. It is true that Labour's great post-war reform, the National Health Service, has helped middle-class families; but it has also enormously narrowed the gap between classes. Regular dental service, working-class women able to go to the doctor when they need (and how many failed to do so before the war), above all the extension to the whole of the nation of specialist hospital services, which previously so many of our people could not afford – here was a silent revolution where universality meant lifting up the greater part of the nation.

The same argument applies to what Labour intends to do now. A higher priority for the Health Service – more hospitals, shorter waiting lists, an occupational health service, a chiropody service, the abolition of the prescriptions charges and other imposts on the service; these are just as relevant to the drive for greater equality as the pensions scheme itself.

Then housing: the repeal of the Rent Act and the restoration of rent control are themselves a reversal of Tory class policies. A Labour Chancellor who raises the revenue to restore the housing subsidies – or, what is the same thing, holds back a tax remission to the Surtax class which a Tory Chancellor would have made – is redistributing income. A Labour Chancellor who makes available capital to local authorities for housing purposes, at low rates of interest, is redistributing income. The restoration of the housing subsidies and a return to 1951 interest rates for the Public Works Loan Board would mean a reduction of £1 a week on the rent of a newly-completed 1959 house. In fact, of course, we should not over the five-year period of the

Labour government need increased taxation – the cost would be met out of the social dividend of our increased national production. To distribute that social dividend with a marked bias in favour of those who need help most – rather than, as the Tories have done, to those who need help least – is just as much a contribution to equality as the straightforward Robin Hood approach to fiscal affairs.

But apart from rents, housing standards are equally part of the social revolution. We shall build more houses to let. They will be far better than the homes of recent new tenants. In many respects – because they are more modern – they will be a great deal better than most owner-occupier houses built before the war. A New Town in place of a slum is redistributory in more than the demographical sense. The same argument applies in terms of working conditions. Not only does full employment strengthen the hands of trade unions in demanding better wages and conditions, our proposed legislation on the occupational health service, and our pledge to implement the Gowers Report on working conditions – these, too, are narrowing the economic gap, even if they cannot be measured in purely cash terms.

Or, again, education: the four new schools in the Kirkby overspill area in my own constituency[1] are a great improvement on the Liverpool schools the Kirkby boys and girls have left behind. In terms of buildings and amenities they are an improvement, I should imagine, on any public school; but the fact that they are – all four of them – fully comprehensive represents a gain in terms of equality beyond the capacity of the statistician to measure. Once again, the Labour Chancellor who stamps out tax-dodging and applies the yield (or, by selective decision, the yield of an increased social dividend) to such purposes is making our society more egalitarian.

Or, to take a subject which has not featured much in press discussions of the election – our proposals for the arts and for sport. To spend Treasury money on establishing – or saving – a municipal orchestra or repertory theatre in Coketown is another deliberate decision not measurable in cash. Our proposed Sports Council was directly inspired by J. P. W. Mallalieu's[2] supplement in the *New Statesman* last autumn. His analysis of the sports facilities of this

[1] The Huyton Constituency near Liverpool.

[2] Labour MP for Huddersfield East.

country, and, in particular, of the privileges in this field attaching to boys in the upper-income strata, especially those at public schools, shows that our £5 million a year will be one more step towards levelling up.

Some may call this piecemeal, it has even been called a rag-bag: but human beings, and their wants and needs, are complex. Whether it is a question of ending acute poverty, or of raising the standard of living of those who, though not in poverty, are relatively under-privileged, the answer must be a variety of measures. Piecemeal, if you like, but I would regard it as the outcome of a group of Socialists bringing to their study of eight or ten or a dozen different social problems the unifying and transforming influence of a Socialist approach.

The Conservative counter-attack on our programme is simply the defeatist one that the country cannot afford it. We are, they say, unprecedently prosperous – and yet we cannot afford a basic pension of £3 a week. Mr Butler tells us that, if the old age pensioners are given more purchasing power, prices will rise in the shops. Lord Hailsham says that our programme will mean inflation, higher taxes and a balance of payments crisis.

We reject this approach. There can be no argument that if production rises, not as much as under the post-war Labour government, but, say, at the same rate as in other European countries in the past few years, the national income will be £3,500 millions a year higher by 1964. On the same argument the Exchequer revenue will rise automatically, without any increase in taxation, by £1,000 millions, considerably more than the cost of our programme. The Conservatives are, in fact, saying either that we cannot hope to progress at the same rate as elsewhere in western Europe; or, if we do, that more favoured sections of the population must reap the benefits.

We reject that, not only on economic, but on social and moral grounds. It is because we believe that all men were created equal that we reject the condescending, Edwardian 'masters and men' approach of Mr Macmillan. We were not brought up on this doctrine of first and second-class citizens. In the part of the world I come from, men are very ruggedly equal. The Yorkshire Socialist revolts from poverty, not so much because it is a product of inefficiency and a badly-run social system, but because it is a crime against God and man. Our

Socialism does not come from the London School of Economics or any other seat of learning. It comes from revolt, revolt against the inequality that is endemic in Tory freedom.

It is the same with unemployment. It would be easy – and here academic training can help – to find a hundred reasons, economic and social, why unemployment is wrong, a hundred factors which can affect it. But the Socialist approach starts earlier than that. I suppose I was 14 when I had my first lesson in economics. A friend of ours in the wool industry, like many others, was unemployed. He could not afford to buy the coal he needed. Fifteen miles away an unemployed miner could not afford to buy the cloth those idle Huddersfield mills could have woven. No one could explain this thing to me. And they still can't.

That is just the approach of one Socialist, but every one of us in the Labour leadership could give a similar explanation of our approach to these questions. As the so-called 'Shadow Chancellor', I have had to deal with four Conservative Chancellors and five Budgets. What has been really irksome, as the figures and the policies unfold, is to hear what the Chancellor has had at his disposal and to see year after year the utterly wrong sense of priorities which has dictated his decisions. Recent Budget debates have sharpened controversy and provided what seems to be the acid test of distinction between the Tory and the Socialist. The Tory says that all income belongs to its recipient; that all state levies upon it are at best a regrettable necessity; that it is wrong to refer to a Chancellor's decisions as 'largesse', 'tax hand-outs', or to suggest that the Chancellor is in any way giving anything away: what he is doing is refraining from withholding so much. Our approach is different: we say that all wealth is derived from the community; that the Budget is an instrument not for perpetuating the unequal distribution of income and wealth, but for correcting it. We say, therefore, that a Chancellor in the happy position of being able to reduce taxation must apply the welfare test – where can I do most good, add most to the total happiness? By relieving tax here, or there, or by increasing help in some other direction? This April, the Tory reduced income tax proportionately to income: the Socialist would have used the surplus first to relieve hardship, and only then have considered tax relief. To the Conservative a system of progressive taxation is a distortion of the economic laws of capitalist society; to us the co-existence of conspicuous wealth and avoidable poverty is a distortion of the moral laws of civilised society.

The same basic party conflict exists on take-over bids. Mr Macmillan belatedly orders an inquiry, not because he is opposed to take-over bids, but because a particular one has gone wrong. It is not wrong to make millions out of the Rent Act: it *is* wrong to make a bid for which you can't find the cash. It is not the crime they oppose, it is being found out. We for our part oppose a system under which rich men can make millions – tax free – for rendering no useful service to the community, while those who really do the work are insufficiently rewarded. When Mr Macmillan was defending the Trinidad oil deal[1] three years ago, we attacked a state of affairs in which one shareholder holding £1,000 of Trinidad stock could make £6,000 tax free in ten minutes: it would take a coal-face worker in one of our most productive coalfields 10 years to earn that amount after tax.

That is why this election campaign cannot be judged purely in terms of our programme. The work of government involves year to year and day to day decisions which may not feature in election programmes. Perhaps four out of five of the big governmental issues which dominate the headlines in the next four years will be on issues which no one today can forecast. That is why I emphasise the importance in the fight against poverty – at home and abroad – not only of measures, but of men – of men who will face the decisions and assess the priorities in the light of their Socialist faith and their burning intolerance of man-made inequality.

[1] The sale of British owned Trinidad oil interests to an American company

CHAPTER TEN

*

Party Political Television Broadcast on Housing, Rates and Education: 8th May, 1963

I WANT TO EXPLAIN TO YOU TONIGHT how we propose to overcome three problems, each of them seriously affecting the welfare and happiness of millions of families. These problems are homes, rates and education.

Why in 1963 have we thousands actually homeless, millions more living in intolerably over-crowded conditions, millions more in houses which lack modern amenities?

I know from my post-bag and from my constituency work of many tragic cases of broken homes resulting from bad housing conditions. I had a shocking case of overcrowding recently and when I took it up with the local authority, I was told, well this family has only been on the list since 1954. Years go by and that family is growing up without ever really knowing what a home is.

Why are there three-quarters of a million officially scheduled slums in Britain today? In Liverpool itself there are 79,000 slum dwellings, and on top of this a waiting list of 46,000 families. At the present rate of building these slums won't be cleared in this century.

The immediate answer is because we are not building anything like enough houses. And of those that we do build, far too few are being built to rent to families who cannot afford to buy, and far too few are being built for young couples setting up home for the first time.

What do we propose to do? First, the next Labour Government will step up the numbers built by local councils at reasonable rents. The number of council houses built last year was 124,000 (compared with 190,000 in 1948 only three years after the war). It's no good blaming the local authorities in every case. Some, of course, are simply falling down on the job. But those that *are* trying find themselves hamstrung by Government policy.

Take interest rates. They have doubled under this Government. A house built in 1951, when we had a Labour Government, costing, say £1,400 was financed at 3% interest. Spread over 60 years this made a total cost of £3,000. Today this £3,000 has gone up to £7,150. And of this increase £3,500 is due to interest charges. £3,500 out of your pocket simply because of Government financial policy.

And take land. Why every day are we hearing of housing land multiplying four or five times in value in a matter of three or four years? Here are just two cases, one in South London last year: land for housing at £26,810 per acre, £970 for each unit for land alone. The other, West London: two acres at £32,500 per acre, that is £1,600 for every flat or house built on that site, for land alone. This is the direct result of what the Conservatives call a free market in land – freedom for speculators and property racketeers to buy up building land and make fortunes by exploiting scarcity and people's desperate need for homes. A Conservative Government is too closely linked to the speculators and property interests ever to be able to deal with this racket.

So we will appoint a Crown Land Commission to buy for the community – at a fair price – the freehold of land on which building or rebuilding is about to take place. For the Labour Party, it is a cardinal principle that property values, which are created by the action of society as a whole, should accrue to the community, not to property speculators.

Why should young couples who are trying to build a home of their own face these excessive interest rates on their mortgage and pay intolerable prices for their land?

Like many of you, I know what these mortgage rates mean. My wife and I are buying our house on a 90% mortgage – it will be ours in another 15 years. Mortgage rates in the past five years have been around 6–6½%, compared with 4% in 1951, another reflection of the Government's bankrupt monetary policies. Of course they've just dropped a half per cent. They did just before the 1959 election too – and went up again soon afterwards.

Labour's plan is to push interest rates down for housing, and to provide up to 100% mortgages. That's exactly what the Labour Party have done on the London County Council. We shall also encourage popular schemes such as that in Birmingham, where the Labour Council are building houses for sale, and are giving 100% mortgages with low interest rates.

Our proposals for land will be of direct help to families building their own houses. Instead of being priced out of the market, as so many are today, they will be able to get their land at a price related to its real value. Of course this will not affect land belonging to owner-occupiers.

Then there are the tenants of privately owned flats or houses. They face these problems – rents, security against eviction, and for many millions of houses the problem of bringing them up to date.

In every part of the country we hear of exorbitant increases in rents, sometimes to four or five times the previous figure, and we hear of countless stories of real individual hardship. Thousands have been evicted. Every year 200,000 more houses come within the threat of eviction. All this is due to the Conservative Rent Act of 1957, the Landlords' Charter. The Rent Act has made the housing position worse, not better.

We shall repeal the Rent Act, in order to stop all further decontrol of rented houses. The tenants of houses that have already been decontrolled will be given security of tenure. Decontrol through change of tenancy will cease and so will evictions. To protect tenants against unreasonable rents we intend to set up Rent Tribunals to fix rents at fair levels – properly related to housing conditions – when appealed to by either the tenant or the landlord.

Now what of the older houses. Why in 1963 are 15 million people in this country living in houses without fixed bath and hot water systems, three million in houses with no internal toilet?

We will require landlords to bring their houses up to a decent modern standard, which will include the provision of fixed bath, piped hot water and an inside lavatory. If they refuse to do so, the local councils will be required to purchase the houses and carry out the necessary improvements.

Next the leasehold problem which threatens so many families in areas such as London and the Midlands and South Wales. We shall introduce legislation to allow leaseholders to buy the freehold of their homes.

Now I want to talk about rates.

People are worried about this year's increased rate demands, which have sharply underlined the problem of local rating.

But, the main reason for increased rates is rising local spending, on education – including technical education, and also in health, roads, housing, lighting and other essential services. Since we regard adequate expenditure on these things as an expression of what a civilised community means, we are certainly not going to attack these services.

What is wrong is that the weight now placed on the local rating system is too great for that system to bear. Local rating is basically an unfair system of taxation; it doesn't take account of income, of ability to pay, or family commitments. When too heavy a load is placed on it, the whole system is in danger of breaking down.

We take the view, we've pressed it again and again, that the entire system of local rating and finances should be surveyed by an independent and authoritative commission appointed by the Government. We shall do this. Meanwhile, urgent action will have to be taken and a Labour Government will take that action. I will mention just three points:

First, we shall replace the crude block grant system by a progressive return to the system of specific grants for individual services, particularly in education. These grants will involve a higher percentage of central government assistance, particularly for such priority items as teachers' salaries.

Second, we shall end the present government's doctrinaire policy of penally high interest rates, which place a crippling burden on local council finances, and we shall restore the local authorities' right to borrow on reasonable terms through the Public Works Loan Board, instead of being forced to borrow on exorbitant terms through the City of London.

Thirdly, by our plans to end the profiteering in urban land, we shall greatly reduce the cost a council faces when it sets out to build houses and schools. At the same time, public ownership of building land will mean that the ratepayers will be able to reap the benefit of profitable town centre development, which at present goes in the main to Mr Cotton, Mr Clore, and the like.

Now, education. In my last broadcast, I said we cannot afford to neglect the educational development of a single boy or girl.

Today, we are just not facing up to this problem. There are far more children of school age; more of them want to stay on at school and their parents want them to. More of them seek entrance to college and university. It's the government's job to see that they can.

One boy and girl in every five is in a class of over 40 in our primary schools. More than half of those in secondary schools are taught in classes which, by present official standards, are too large. How, even with the most gifted and dedicated teachers, can we possibly pretend that these children are getting a proper education. We want local authorities to employ more teachers and get the size of classes down; this won't be done by the present government's policy, and it certainly won't be achieved by extending to education the Enoch Powell[1] philosophy of imposing charges to pay for an expanding service.

In University education we are lagging far behind other countries. The Russians are training many times as many highly qualified technologists as we are, so are the United States.

Last autumn, 5,000 young people with the right passes at A level were denied University education solely because there was no room. As more students reach university age this will get worse. We have called for an emergency programme for more building, for better use of present buildings, and after that for systematic expansion by building new universities.

In the modern world we cannot go on with only one in 20 of our young people receiving higher education. We must get rid, too, of the traditional snobbery which still hampers technical education; the Colleges of Advanced Technology, and the whole of this vital field of technological education must be given their rightful place in the university world.

For all this expansion we need, above all, more teachers – as, indeed, we need more doctors, scientists, more trained people of all kinds. Why then, do we waste talent by the old '11-plus' procedure? Why do we decide a child's whole educational future when he is still 10 years old, why do we reject seven in every 10 for further education?

The government have been there 12 years, why haven't they done something about it? Labour will get rid of segregation at 11, and keep the door of opportunity open to all children.

Tonight I have been talking about problems which face every

[1] Then Minister of Health.

family in the country. Why is so little being done about these problems? Partly because we have a Government which is too tired, too complacent, which has lost confidence in itself, and is out of touch with ordinary people, and ordinary families' problems.

Britain faces tremendous challenges, in our view, exciting challenges, if only we will mobilise the full resources of our nation.

This is the time for change, dynamic, exciting, thrilling change. And the first decision we must take is to change the top direction of our national life.

CHAPTER ELEVEN

*

Debate on the Beeching Railway Report, House of Commons, 30th April, 1963

BEFORE I EXAMINE the Government's case, I should like to reply directly to Mr Marples's challenge about the possible strike.

I regard the battle on the future of the British transport system as political. It should take place in the House and ultimately at the polling booths. Of course, there are questions, such as compensation and the protection of union members, which are matters for collective bargaining and for whatever industrial action is thought appropriate, but the Government's proposals for railway closures are a political matter.

We certainly do not want a strike. The NUR does not want a strike. I am not quite so sure about some hon Members opposite. I acquit the Minister. I am sure that he does not want a strike, although I am bound to tell him on what I have heard that his inept and flat-footed handling of the meeting with the unions made a strike more and not less likely. If there is a strike – and I profoundly hope that there will not be – the responsibility for it will lie clearly on the Government, who, for 10 years, have systematically destroyed the integrated transport system which we had and who have undermined the whole financial structure of the railways. It does not lie in the mouths of the Government to talk about unconstitutional action when it was they who set aside the whole machinery of railway conciliation and arbitration 18 months ago and imposed a wages *Diktat* on the industry.

Having said that, the first thing that I want to say on the main issues that we are debating is that we are not attacking Dr Beeching or the Beeching Report.

Within the narrow contents of his appointment Dr Beeching has produced a Report which makes a valuable contribution to the basic information needed for the formulation of a national transport policy. Certainly, within the terms of reference that he was given, Dr Beeching has done a competent and efficient job.

Dr Beeching was given a job of surgery to do, and he has done it, deep, incisive, antiseptic; but he was told to apply surgery in a situation where surgery was not the main or relevant answer, and, as was made clear from the Minister's speech yesterday, the surgery has preceded the diagnosis.

The fault lies not in Dr Beeching, but in the Minister, in the Cabinet and in the Prime Minister who, in his new vantage point from the 1970s, looks like succeeding in producing a situation in which the speed of travel is reduced to the speed of the stage coach.

I want to put this plain challenge to Mr Marples; suppose the Minister had given Dr Beeching these terms of reference, namely, to survey the whole of inland transport, having regard to alternative services, to economic development, to social needs, to distribution of industry policy and to real cost, as opposed to narrow book-keeping considerations. Does he think that we would have had the same Report? Of course we should not, or the same proposals for closures.

This is not to say that some closures will not be necessary. We have never claimed otherwise. We said this last year during the debates on the Transport Bill. Every union, including the NUR, has said it, too. No one wants to perpetuate the railway map of the 1860s, a map which shows the results of Tory private enterprise run mad. Because they were afraid of monopoly they built competing lines, and this fallacy of thinking that one has competition in rail transport is a fallacy in which Ministers themselves believed until Dr Beeching came along this year.

Some of the railways of the nineteenth century were built by avaricious company promoters for their nuisance value in the hope of being bribed not to build by existing railway operators, or, if they did have to build, of being able to sell at a profit. Again, the fantastic land costs and the parliamentary costs of building these railways saddled the railway system with a capital burden which has lasted up to our times. We hold no brief for the mistakes of Victorian entrepreneurs.

Some cuts are necessary. The question is which, and how to assess them. I think that many businessmen, including, I suspect, some Conservatives, approach this problem on the basis of a false analogy with manufacturing industry. Consider any representative manufacturing industry. Consider the soap industry. If there are 12 soap factories producing below capacity, one might decide to close two and concentrate production on the rest. One will probably choose the two least efficient to close, and closing them has no effect on the efficiency of the other 10, nor is the consumer affected. He still gets all the soap he wants.

But this does not apply with transport. To close one sector of the railway system affects all the others, because traffic arising in one area affects the profitability of the rest of the system. All parts of the transport system are members one of another, so when one closes part of this it is not an ordinary business decision. It is more in the nature of an amputation. Moreover, to close one sector means denying to transport users in that area transport facilities which they otherwise would have had.

This Report is based on narrow book-keeping considerations. It bears no relation to wider economic considerations affecting the national interest as a whole, still less to the social considerations.

What would be the position if we were to apply the Beeching technique elsewhere? The Board of Trade runs a useful service for exporters, obviously at a loss. Because it makes a book-keeping loss, should it be closed? It would save several thousands of pounds if it were, but it would lose millions of pounds of export trade. I tremble to think of the Beeching technique being applied to another service, the Post Office. Should we close those post offices and those delivery systems which work at a loss, and keep only those that work at a profit? We apply the opposite approach in the case of rural electricity. The whole basis of rural electricity policy under successive Governments has been to extend rural services at a loss and to recoup them with the profits made on easier parts of the system.

So with the railways. We may close a railway losing £8,000 a year, but suppose this means spending £250,000 on improving the roads, on providing alternative services, or subsidising bus services in those areas. Suppose we save £8,000, and then add immeasurably more in social costs through increased road congestion? The Minister's advisers have calculated that congestion on the roads is losing

£500 million a year through wear and tear and through loss of working time, to say nothing of the cost in human lives.

Mr Marples said that he will be the judge in every case, and he repeated the procedure that he is required by Statute – his Statute – to follow. In every case the decision will be taken, we were told, only after an impartial, cool, judicial appraisal by this the most judicial of Ministers. He went on, repeatedly, to refer to the intention to close one-third of the railways. Indeed at one point he said that when he had disposed of that he would have a look at the next third, which he regarded as somewhat more marginal.

This is the judicial procedure made familiar in Alice in Wonderland – sentence first, verdict afterwards.

I want to ask Mr Marples, first, what consideration he has given to the economic consequences of his policy. Let us look at capital investment. We are spending £70 million a year on railway modernisation and, on the basis of Government figures, about £500 million on investment in road transport, including lorries. We are to save, we are told – although there is some doubt about it – between £30 million and £40 million a year gross by the closure policy, although part of it will be achieved by transferring the burden from the railways to the National Coal Board and to coal, gas and electricity consumers. It is not a net saving from the national point of view.

How much more capital expenditure will this mean on roads, road haulage goods vehicles, and buses, and how much additional current expenditure will be needed to subsidise bus companies and for additional road maintenance? I would regard it as inconceivable that this decision should have been taken without the fullest costings.

Secondly, I want to ask what thought Mr Marples has given to the problem of road congestion. What estimates has he made? Has he had surveys made, and estimates of the new building that will need to be done? In 1957, his advisers calculated that 62% of our Class 1 roads were already, by that time, used beyond the Ministry of Transport design capacity. Thirteen per cent of the trunk road and Class 1 road mileage was then being used at more than double the Ministry of Transport design capacity. That was in 1957, and we all know how much road congestion has increased since that date.

What will he do to solve this problem when he has closed one-third of our railways? Will he build more motorways? At what cost does he think this programme will be reasonable? How does he think that he will solve the transport problem? I cannot remember who said, recently, that the motorway is the shortest distance between two traffic jams. Perhaps he will tell us what will be the additional cost in road congestion, or what road expenditure will be required to avoid additional road congestion.

Thirdly, what consideration has been given to development district policy? Here we have the Government plan. Over 30 Ministers go to Chequers to look at Britain in the 1970s[1], but their plan for 1963 apparently – this is their idea of planning – is to spend millions in order to persuade industry to go to the development districts, while, at the same time, a different Department is closing many of the railways which are serving those areas. Is this planning?

We have read a statement by the railway authorities that the railway serving the Wiggins Teape[2] area was likely to be closed, but is being kept open for the Wiggins Teape development.

Let us suppose that the railways close down and that someone then wants to bring new industrial development into the area, next year or the year after. Let us suppose that the line to Fort William had been closed and there had not been a Wiggins Teape, but that a future Wiggins Teape came along. What would have been the position? The firm would not have been located there, because there would have been no railway. It is impossible to pursue a realistic development planning policy with the approach of the Minister of Transport.

My fourth point concerns rural development. We all heard last night, or have read, the speech of Mr T. W. Jones[3]. A Welsh Planning Bureau, or whatever it is called, is being set up, and the event is being celebrated by the closing down of most of the lines serving rural Wales! Has the Welsh Planning Bureau been consulted about these proposals? Yesterday, the Scottish Tourist Board issued a statement saying that it feared:

> that the proposed railway amputations would mean the withering away of whole Highland communities.

Fifthly I want to ask Mr Marples about national economic development. Was the NEDC[4] consulted before he came to the

[1] Tory Ministers' Conference at Chequers called by Mr Macmillan in 1963.
[2] A proposed new pulp and paper mill development near Fort William.
[3] MP for Merioneth.
[4] National Economic Development Council: 'Neddy'.

decision that he put forward yesterday? Has anyone worked out what the transport needs of the country will be, or even what the potential railway revenues will be in the 1970s and 1980s, based on the NEDC plan of a 4% increase in production year in, year out, for the next 20 years? Or is the NEDC target meant to last just from now until the next General Election?

The Government believe in planning for this year, anyway, but on this major issue the Minister is allowed to close one third of the nation's railways without even inviting the views of the NEDC. There has been no such instance of administrative frivolity since the same Government decided to enter the Common Market without asking their economic advisers what the economic consequences would be.

Sixthly, I turn to the question of the docks. We are glad that having taken this decision, Mr Marples is setting up a joint committee to evaluate the effect of what he has decided upon the implementation of the Rochdale Report[1]. But why did he not take into account the full implications of the Rochdale Report before he came to his conclusions on railway policy? Is he satisfied that cutting the railways out will solve British Railways' financial problem?

Over the last 10 years, 3,600 miles of track have been closed. That is 19% of the mileage previously in operation. Presumably this 19% – roughly one-fifth of our track mileage – must have been the least remunerative of the lot. Presumably that is why it was first selected for closure. Yet its closure saved only 7% of the working deficit of British Railways in 1960, and this takes no account of the additional cost to the nation of the closures, or the loss of main-line traffic caused by the closures of feeder services. Will Mr Marples explain his calculations?

If the closing of one fifth of the track mileage makes so little difference to the operating deficit of British Railways, what will the next one third do? Why should Mr Marples think that there will be any difference? Or does he agree with the Annual Report of the Central Transport Consultative Committee, which said:

> the negative policy of closing down uneconomic facilities, while contributing a small financial saving, is not the panacea it is sometimes made out to be.

I now come to the broader issue. The problem that British Railways

[1] Rochdale Report on Docks, 1963.

face is one that is found in almost every country in the world. There is hardly a country where the railways pay their way. The problem is created, first, by the growth of private motoring – the avalanche that Mr Marples said would hit us in the near future – and, secondly, by the creaming off of the more profitable parts of freight traffic by road haulage. Those are the reasons for the world-wide railway crisis, and the only way to solve it, as we have said repeatedly, is by an integrated transport policy which does two things: first, ensures that the profits creamed off from rail to road are brought into the transport pool, where they belong, and are not siphoned off by the owners; and, secondly, ensures an economic division of traffic between road and rail. These are the two essential items of an integrated transport policy.

That is what the Labour Government set out to do in the 1947 Act. I do not claim that we made no mistakes; of course we did. I will mention one. By fixing the value of compensation, the total monetary volume of transport stock, at the end of 1947, when low interest rates were ruling, and then appending an interest rate to that stock in 1949, based on higher long-term rates, we saddled the railways with an uneconomic interest burden, and made it a fixed charge on railway earnings.

But basically, whatever mistakes we made, we achieved viability for the transport system, a viability which continued until the wreckers got at it after 1951. Of course, British Railways were still paying their way until 1953. This was remarkable – it really was – because of the growth of road competition on a scale far exceeding pre-war, especially with C licences[1], because the House will recall that the privately owned railway system was already facing financial disaster before the war.

We all remember the brave efforts of the Prime Minister, when a railway director, to work up the Great Western Railway into a profitable proposition. The year that he was appointed a director it paid £7 10s % on ordinary stock. In 1931, it paid £5 10s % on ordinary stock and in that year the GWR asked the National Wages Board to reduce wages. In 1932, it was £3 % on ordinary stock and again in 1933 it was £3 % on ordinary stock. In November, 1932, the GWR

[1] Road goods haulage licences granted to industrial concerns for carriage of their own goods only.

asked for a 10% cut in the wages of railway staff. Then it started paying dividends out of reserves.

Then, in 1935, the GWR paid £3% on ordinary stock by dipping into reserves. In 1936, it paid £3% on ordinary stock for the previous year, on earnings only slightly over 1%. In 1938, it paid £4% on ordinary stock. This was possible only by deferring urgently needed capital expenditure.

We are now having to meet that expenditure. The plan for Euston Station was prepared years ago, but the private companies would not touch it. Now it is having to be done at much increased cost. By 1939, when the dividend was only 10s % on ordinary stock, we were told that the company distributed for the purpose of dividends £8,210,000 when it was not being earned. After nine years of Mr Macmillan, the Great Western Railway lost its trustee status.

The reason why I am mentioning this illustration – and I could say that compared with this the LNER was really a hair-raising story – is that already, in 1938, the railways were bankrupt. In 1938, they were plastering the bill boards with the demand 'The Railways Demand a Square Deal Now', and by 'Square Deal' they meant some kind of protection against the depredations of road haulage. Yet at the time there were only 513,000 lorries on the road. By 1952 there were 1,046,000, and yet British Railways were still paying their way, a remarkable achievement.

The reason why publicly owned transport was still breaking even, even with all this increase in road haulage, was that of the lorries on the road 96,000 were publicly owned and their profits contributing to the national pool. It was the 1953 Act which destroyed the ability of British transport to pay its way. It was the action of a Tory Government, not their first or their last, looting national assets to provide nice pickings for their friends.

The railway crisis began from the moment that a doctrinaire Government scrapped the idea of a national integrated transport policy, and the Beeching Report is the consummation of that policy. These closures, with all that they mean, are the direct consequence of political vandalism, made worse by repeated political interference to stop British Railways charging economic rates, and, of course, by the continued and unregulated growth of private road haulage competition. As a result of ten years of this policy we now get the panic measures of the Beeching Report, at the very moment when the Americans are building new passenger lines for commuter services in their big conurbations.

Let me mention the position in France, where war damage destroyed 75% of the rolling stock and most of the marshalling yards. But as a result of a vigorous policy of public enterprise, modernisation, high investment in new rolling stock and electrification, and although France has a bigger mileage of track than we have and with only half our numbers of locomotives, passenger coaches and wagons, their average load per wagon of 17 tons is about double what ours is. Their loss is minimal compared with ours. One reason why France has had this success is partly because its railways have tackled the problem of co-ordinating road and rail.

France has weighted taxes to induce road hauliers to concentrate on routes insufficiently served by the railways and it has higher taxes on road haulage where it is in competition with the railways and where the roads are congested. France has a system of fixing road and rail charges on the basis of the real cost of operation. We could do the same and win through, but the Government will not try it. In place of integration, which the French are trying, we have disintegration. We are even subsidising road haulage. It has been estimated – I know that there are many different methods of making the computation – that the 20-ton lorry is subsidised to the tune of £20 a week.

Now I turn to what in our view we should do. First, on the Beeching closures. No decision, no major decision, on closures should be made until there has been a comparable and equally ruthless survey of transport as a whole. In every case, in every area, there must be a costing not just of railway profit and loss but of the real economic cost of providing alternative transport.

Secondly, the plan as a whole should be referred for a full-scale study of the national economic consequences. The NEDC should make estimates of the effect on the Beeching calculations of the NEDC Report. That Report involved an increase in the national production of 4% per annum. An increase of 4% per annum for 20 years gives about 100%. Has anyone thought of calculating what this means in terms of railway traffic and revenue, or do the Government believe that we are not going to have a 4% increase per annum for 20 years?

But even more important than the effect of the NEDC plan on the

Beeching plan is the effect of the Beeching Report on the NEDC plan. So I ask Mr Marples either to announce that he will have second thoughts, and make this reference to the NEDC, and take no action in the implementation of the Report until the NEDC has been consulted, or admit that in this vital area of planning the Government refuse to plan.

Thirdly, the Government should make an estimate of future developments in the transport field. They are not looking ahead. They talk about being modern. The truth is that they are facing the problems of the 1960s with the restrictionist philosophies of the 1930s. This is the philosophy which inspired Shipbuilders Security Ltd, Jarrow, or the 1959 decision of the Government to consign the Lancashire cotton industry to the knackers' yard.

I therefore ask the Government to look to the future. What place has been given to the monorail in future transport planning in connection with urban transport? Can we really decide what we are to do about London transport, and the closure of commuter lines, until a decision has been taken about that? In connection with some of the more remote systems of transport, have they overlooked the possible future of the Hovercraft – itself, if I may so, a triumphant product of public enterprise?

Fourthly, I ask Mr Marples to begin again and to see what would be the future of British Railways as part of an integrated transport system. What thought has been given to the possible role of British Road Services as providing a modern and effective feeder service to British Railways, both of them under the same ownership, and not disintegrated as in the 1962 Transport Act?

Fifthly, having made this survey, let us have a national plan; a plan directed to national economic development; a plan integrated with, and not destructive of, sound regional and development area planning. I say seriously that this plan cannot work, nor can transport become a viable public service, except on the basis of the two principles which I have laid down: first, that the profits of all sections of transport, the more profitable and the less profitable, are more closely integrated; and, secondly, that there are effective means of securing a right division between road and rail traffics.

On the first of these, in 'Signposts for the Sixties' we have said that an essential step must be to expand the public sector of road goods haulage, not only as a feeder service, but as a natural road service, by taking the artificial ceiling off the expansion of BRS wherever it is economic and profitable for BRS to expand. Equally, the plan must provide for the right distribution of traffic between road and rail. One essential part will be to make whatever changes are needed in A and B licensing regulations, including distance limits. Here we have the Government, after 12 years in office, and after deciding their rail transport policy, setting up an inquiry to look at a 30-year-old licensing system. Having done nothing about it for 12 years, now they are to look at it, having decided on their rail policy.

Let us be frank. The problem cannot be solved without tackling the problem of the C licences and a national transport plan will have to provide for this. The number of C licences has risen from 365,000 in 1938 to 834,000 in 1952 and to 1,254,000 in 1961. It is impossible – the House must face this – to have an effective or viable transport system, or to avoid a degree of road congestion which will mean a total seize-up on Britain's roads before very long if the number of C licences is to continue to expand indefinitely.

Various suggestions have been made for dealing with this problem. One school of thought suggests much tighter licensing, the refusal of a licence except on the basis of proof of need and the absence of alternative transport facilities.

Some existing C licence holders may be as uneconomic from the point of view of the nation as new applicants. Transport managers, like the rest of us, have an innate tendency to empire-building.

With road economics as they are at present, they are often able to persuade their board's finance directors to agree to a C licence fleet – even to operate at a loss sometimes – because of the value of filling the roads with moving bill-boards advertising the firm's products on the roads and in the traffic jams. That is why some students of road-rail co-ordination consider that the problem can best be solved by stiffer charges for C licences, which would measure their contribution to the road traffic problems and which would make not only new applicants, but some existing licence holders, stop to count the cost. These are the sort of questions that a national transport survey and a national transport plan would have to solve.

Equally, there must be a more direct attack on urban road congestion. I ask Mr Marples why should not the drivers of heavy lorries be forbidden to use city and town centres except on proof of need? I invite any MP to stand for half an hour in Parliament

Square. Or, if he has not the time to do that, to keep his eyes open during one of the frequent traffic jams in Parliament Square, and to ask himself how many of the lorries which we see there really need to go through such crowded central areas? There are sand and gravel lorries, and all sorts of lorries with heavy loads of steel, using the centre of London as a mere convenience for driving from one part to another. One or two may be being used on important work delivering to building sites, but I very much doubt that. If access to urban centres were made more difficult, how many of them would use the ring roads, which is what we want them to do?

Finally, there is the broader problem of urban renewal, the reconstruction of our cities, the broader aspect of town and country planning. London's transport problem has been made infinitely more intractable by ministerial cowardice in refusing to tackle the problem of office building in Central London which, every year, adds tens of thousands of additional office workers to the numbers of our peak hour traffic. I think that I am right in saying that 40,000 new jobs a year have been created since the middle 1950s in the London conurbation, most of them in office employment in Central London. Obviously, this adds to the problem of urban congestion.

Yesterday, we had Mr Marples' hints, that his proposals are intended simply as a stopgap until we can replace our cities. For fifteen years, or whatever is the period, Mr Marples says that he will build roads in all possible directions, making us a nation of concrete. And then, suddenly, with a stroke of his ministerial Biro, he is to rebuild all the cities. How in heaven's name does Mr Marples think that this is to be done? The Minister of Housing and Local Government cannot hope to remove all the slums in Liverpool by the year 2000 at the present rate of progress. Of course he cannot – and he knows it.

How are we to get this major reconstruction? The road programme has been made excessively costly by private landlordism. I should like to ask what were the land costs of the Cromwell Road extension, or the Hammersmith flyover, or some of the other urban developments. I will tell Mr Marples that there is no hope of any rebuilding of our cities, on the lines which he held out yesterday, on the basis of private ownership and private speculation in urban development land.

Our policy on urban land would have to be followed before there could be any hope of rebuilding cities on the lines which Mr Marples put forward yesterday. Because, of course, transport is not a single problem capable of being treated in isolation. It is part of the wider planning problem – economic planning, social planning, town planning – and this problem can be solved only by a Socialist approach. The Government cannot begin to solve problems such as this. That is why they have taken refuge in restrictionism and panic cuts.

I think, too, that there is a political motive in all this. They have deluded themselves, and I think that they hope to delude the country into thinking that a savage closure policy can be represented somehow as modern, as tough – even as honest. They think that the electorate yearns for a policy of strength through suffering. Having won the last election on materialism, they hope to win the next on masochism. Of course, they will fail.

What is even more relevant to Britain's future is that the measures which they are now setting in hand, and which the Minister announced – or adumbrated, or whatever it was he did with his speech yesterday – will retard our economic development and that only by a broad, comprehensive and forward-looking national transport plan, which is part of a national economic plan, can we in this country face the challenge of the future.

CHAPTER TWELVE

*

Wilson Defines British Socialism[1]

WITH PUBLIC OPINION POLLS, by-election results and the expectations of political commentators pointing firmly toward a Labour victory at the next General Election, I am frequently asked, 'What *is* British Socialism today?'

The answer is that British Socialism is democratic Socialism. While we have clear ideas of what the organisation of Britain's economy must be in the context of a Labour Government, we insist that any changes must be achieved by the constitutional, democratic processes of our country. We have always rejected the revolutionary approach. Equally we oppose the use of industrial action – strikes or similar trade union pressures – for the achievement of political objectives. Labour leaders have taken firm action to discourage such activity.

We seek to persuade a majority of our fellow electors in a democratic, parliamentary election to vote a majority Labour Government into power, in support of the programme which we shall have put to the electorate. Once elected, the legislative changes we shall propose will be carried through in accordance with our parliamentary traditions. Equally, all the executive acts of the Government will be subject to the scrutiny and control of the elected legislature.

What, then, is the basis of the Socialism which this now strong and confident alternative Government presents to the country?

I can set it out best by reference to the declaration adopted by the Party in 1960. After the 1959 election, there was deep and searching controversy about the Party's long-term ideals and aims – particularly about the famous Clause IV in the Party's constitution which set out our objective in these words:

[1] This article was written for the *New York Times*, September 15, 1963.

> To secure for the workers by hand or by brain the full fruits of their industry and the most equitable distribution thereof that may be possible, upon the basis of the common ownership of the means of production, distribution and exchange and the best alternative system of popular administration and control of each industry or service.

After considerable argument, much of it in public, the Party's national executive committee almost unanimously agreed on a new declaration, which was later accepted by an overwhelming majority at Labour's annual conference. Setting out the Party's beliefs on racial discrimination, world relationships, the war on world poverty, social justice, industrial democracy and the freedom of the individual against the glorification of the state, it summarises Labour's view of social and economic needs in the sixties:

> It (the Party) is convinced that (its) objectives can be achieved only through an expansion of common ownership substantial enough to give the community power over the commanding heights of the economy. Common ownership takes varying forms, including state-owned industries and firms, producer and consumer co-operation, municipal ownership and public participation in private concerns. Recognising that both public and private enterprise have a place in the economy, it believes that further extension of common ownership should be decided from time to time in the light of these objectives and according to circumstances, with due regard for the views of the workers and consumers concerned.

Since the adoption of this declaration, the Party has concentrated on the preparation of more detailed statements on the main issues facing the nation. The principal manifesto, adopted in 1961, is 'Signposts for the Sixties', which describes the main lines of Socialist policy in the modern context and which, together with a series of statements on such issues as pensions and social security, housing policy and transportation, will form the basis of our election programme and the work of the next Labour Government.

The fundamental inspiration of 'Signposts for the Sixties', and the statements which followed, is the need to make Britain up-to-date, dynamic, vigorous and capable of playing her full part in world affairs. The policy breathes the ideals which have animated the

Labour movement throughout its history but it is modern, relevant and directed to problems which call urgently for vigorous and radical solutions. It is an attack on the complacency, on the stagnation, on the Edwardian nostalgia which seem to underlie the attitudes and postures of the Macmillan Government.

We begin from the need to strengthen Britain's economy, to secure a steady and purposive expansion in industrial production. For the past 12 years, we have lagged behind the rest of Europe – behind almost all our trading rivals – in both production and exports. Britain's economic record under the Conservatives has followed a cyclical pattern of three years of stagnation, with industrial production static or even failing, followed by a feverish and fitful economic boom – the 'quadrennial spasm' in each four-yearly, pre-election period.

The main reasons for our economic failure have been threefold:

First, we have had the sacrifice of economic expansion to an outdated system of economic regulation based on monetary policy and excessive interest rates. Each election boom has been followed within months by a balance-of-payments crisis, which has led in each case to high interest rates (7% in 1957 and 1961) and other measures designed to bring expansion to a standstill and hold production down. The Conservative economic philosophy that exports can be encouraged and costs held down only by making British industry operate markedly below capacity has now been so discredited that even the most conservative journals – from *The Economist* to *The Financial Times*, from *The Times* to *The Daily Telegraph* – have rejected it in favour of sustained economic expansion.

Second, British industry – with honourable exceptions – has been too hidebound, backward-looking and restrictionist; too ready to believe, in a setting where ancestor worship and hereditary succession are still prevalent, that 'what was good enough in father's (or grandfather's) day is good enough for me'.

Third, we have failed to develop a sufficient dynamism in our attack on export markets. This is partly due to an introverted preoccupation with a fairly profitable home market. The pre-election boom has usually been directed to a sudden and carefully contrived expansion in home-market consumption, by both tax concessions and sudden expansions in hire-purchase (instalment credit) trading.

The creation of a 'candyfloss' boom leads inevitably to increased imports and a diminished drive for exports. Too many of our manufacturers fail to condition themselves to export needs, or to go out and seek challenging new markets. The Government has published figures showing that a mere 40 British firms account for half our total exports. Even in the preferentially protected Commonwealth markets, we have lost ground year after year to our competitors from the United States, Japan and Germany. In world trade generally, Britain accounts for only 15% of exports of manufactured goods, compared with 22% a few years ago.

It is against this background that the Labour Party has put forward its plans for sustained and purposive economic expansion. For years we have called for an economic plan for Britain, based on a steady annual expansion, and on the capital-investment and modernisation programmes necessary to achieve it. Now even the Conservatives have accepted the principle of economic planning.

Two years ago, faced with the worst of the long series of post-war economic crises, a Conservative Chancellor of the Exchequer announced the establishment of the National Economic Development Council, directed to produce a plan for a steady 4% annual increase in industrial production with correlated increases in exports, capital investment and the capacity of the principal utility industries.

The council's 'Socialist' programme has been greeted uneasily by Conservative MPs, to whom 'planning' was, until two years ago, a dirty word. Government leaders who fought previous elections on the slogan 'Conservative Freedom Works' are now said to be toying with a new phrase: 'Conservative Planning Works'.

Labour, of course, welcomes this deathbed conversion. We do not underrate the importance of economic 'targeting' – it is useful that privately owned steel and publicly owned electricity should now agree to work to the same target for expansion. Moreover, a widespread acceptance of the view that next year's national production will be 4% higher and that of 1965, 8% higher, could have a useful cumulative effect on boardroom investment decisions. But few people think that the Conservatives' conversion to expansion will long outlive the election period – any more than it did in 1959.

Labour, therefore, proposes a much more dynamic approach. NEDC will continue, but we shall also need more specific measures to turn its targets into reality. Industry must be awakened to the need for purposive capital investment, for modernisation of industrial techniques and for a more energetic export drive.

We hope to achieve this by a comprehensive series of measures. We shall modernise and streamline our tax system to encourage enterprising and expanding firms and to penalise the hidebound and lazy. There will be more emphasis on encouraging those who earn money by their contribution to production and exports, as against those who make money by industrial take-overs and speculative property deals. We shall introduce an effective capital-gains tax.

The tax burden will also be more fairly shared by a drive against tax avoidance, which has reached a high and costly degree of technical proficiency in Britain. (I once said that if one tenth of the effort which now goes into tax avoidance were redeployed on our export drive Britain's balance-of-payments problem would be solved.)

A special drive will be needed to stimulate exports, so that industrial expansion does not continue to lead to a foreign-trade crisis. Besides tax incentives, there will be special measures to encourage investment in exporting and import-saving industries. But to achieve a steady increase in production and a more than proportionate increase in exports will mean the creation of new industrial capacity, with a heavy bias in favour of new industries. Recent studies have shown that Britain, despite the lead she enjoyed only a few years ago in electronics and other products which set the pattern of export demand, has recorded a smaller increase in these new industries than her principal industrial rivals.

For this reason, the central feature of Labour's economic policy is the creation of such new industries. Britain's scientists are among the best in the world. Our failure is that we do not produce enough of them and do not make adequate use of those we have. Lord Hailsham has called attention to the loss of scientists to the United States and attributed it to deficiencies in the American educational system. He was wrong. The deficiencies lie in Britain's industries which, by and large, fail to make sufficient use of them or to grant them the status and influence to which they are entitled.

Priority will be given, therefore, to training more scientists and technologists – which will require sweeping and radical changes in our educational system – and to Government help and sponsorship in encouraging scientific research and the development of new industries based on its findings. We shall not be dogmatic or doctrinaire about the ownership of these new industries. Some will be privately owned, some publicly owned – the important thing is to get them established.

Let me give an example: fifteen years ago the post-war Labour Government established the publicly owned National Research Development Corporation to take over inventions and discoveries made in such British research institutions as the universities and Government laboratories, to give them patent protection and to develop them through the costly pilot-plant stage to the point where they could be exploited industrially. The NRDC was given an endowment of £5 million ($14 million), and of the inventions it has succeeded in developing, I will name only two.

One was an electronic brain, developed at Manchester University, which led to the creation of a flourishing British digital-computer industry and which was an ancestor of the 'Atlas' computer now being exported to the United States, whose highly computerised industry has not produced its like. The second is the Hovercraft, which represents one of the major revolutions in modern transport. Both were produced on a partnership basis between the state-owned NRDC and private industry.

We intend to extend this kind of public enterprise much farther. More will be spent on research and development. Our aircraft and missile-defence programmes have familiarised us with the techniques of Government research-and-development contracts and we shall extend them to civil industry – indeed, we shall need to do so if measures of world disarmament or even less far-reaching changes in defence production, are not to produce widespread redundancy among scientists and technical workers.

The research units of private firms, Government research establishments, university research teams – even groups of scientists teaming up on a 'guild' basis – will be offered the chance to prepare feasibility studies leading to R and D contracts aimed at producing break-throughs in industrial technology. The new industries which result, many of which will be publicly sponsored (as was the research which will have led to them), could in a short time re-establish Britain's leading position in the industrial world.

These proposals, a central priority of Labour policy, enable us to set in its true context the argument, misrepresented with such devoted care by our opponents, about public ownership and nationalisation. If by nationalisation is meant the transfer to public ownership of assets at present held privately, the main proposal for nationalisation in our policy is the re-transfer to public ownership of the steel industry – or, rather, of that part of it (by no means the whole) which was denationalised by the Conservatives. Some measure of nationalisation in this sense will also be involved in our proposals for the creation of a national 'grid' water-supply system, but this is hardly controversial.

In transportation, where British Railways have been brought to a condition of virtual bankruptcy by a combination of neglect in the pre-public-ownership era and the formidable depredations of road competition, we shall restore an integrated system. This will be done more by expanding the existing, highly profitable, publicly owned sector of the road haulage industry than by transferring additional trucking firms from private to public ownership.

For the rest, our plans to extend the public sector – to occupy the 'commanding heights' – consist mainly in the creation of new industries along the lines I have mentioned. But we shall also remove the present restriction on the ability of existing publicly owned industry to manufacture equipment for its own use or for export. The National Coal Board, for example, will be allowed to manufacture its own mining machinery. And in cases where an undertaking's profits are wholly or mainly dependent on Government orders, as in parts of our aircraft industry and the pharmaceuticals industry, whose profits at the expense of the National Health Service are a public scandal, we reserve the right to share in those profits by a share in the equity.

Again, the present Government is too prone to pour out the taxpayers' money into the begging bowls of so-called private enterprise. A Labour Government will be more austere in its stewardship of public moneys, but where industrial subsidies are justified, we reserve the right, as any prudent private investor would, to match our investment with a corresponding share in the profits and the control.

There is one final sphere where we insist on the right of society to intervene. In recent years, British industry has been overrun by the take-over bidder, frequently operating for the sake of quick financial gains rather than for increased industrial efficiency. Where a proposed take-over or merger looks like affecting a vital industrial interest, we reserve the right to intervene, to hold an inquiry and then, as appropriate, either to veto the proposed bid or to permit it – with safeguards for the consumer or other vital interests. In appropriate cases, where the needs of industrial efficiency dictate a monopoly, we would reserve the right to ensure that such a monopoly should be subject to public control.

In this article I have confined myself to an exposition of modern British Socialism in the economic and industrial sphere. I have not dealt in detail with our plans for education – the counterpart, in the sphere of human investment, to our plans for capital investment in the sphere of plant and machinery. Nor have I dealt with our plans for social security and the welfare of the old and underprivileged, or with housing – where, on the Government's clear admission recently, private landlordism has failed. Here, too, as in industry, excessive interest rates have penalised building by and for owner occupiers.

In this connection, there is another problem with which we have to deal. Private speculation in building land, resulting in rocketing prices, is setting a sharp limit to new house building, whether by public-housing agencies or by owner occupiers. It is imposing penal burdens on tenants and householders alike. It is frustrating long-overdue plans for urban renewal and urban redevelopment in dingy town and city centres. For this reason, we propose to take into public ownership all land in respect of which planning permission has been given – either for new building on virgin land or for re-development of old property.

I have tried, within the limits of this article, to set out the Labour Party's conception of Socialism against the background of the 1960s and within the context of the British political scene. It is essentially a pragmatic conception, related to the needs of the age and the world in which we live. And, because we are democratic Socialists, its implementation in terms of legislative and executive action depends entirely on the consent of the British people.